THE TORAH ROAD TRIP

THE TORAH ROAD TRIP

ABRAHAM RIDES SHOTGUN

BRUCE LEVIN

MICHIGAN
Toronto
Chicago
Toledo
INDIANA
OHIO
Cincinnati
WEST
VIRGINIA
KENTUCKY
VIR

My Route Transporting the Torah from New Britain, Connecticut to Chicago

979-8-9904810-0-8 Paperback
979-8-9904810-1-5 E-book
979-8-9904810-2-2 Hardcover

Library of Congress Control Number: *to come*

Book design by Glen Edelstein, Hudson Valley Book Design

First printing edition 2024.

RapSessions Publishing
1558 Country Lane
Deerfield, Illinois 60015

To Mr. What-you-macall-it…Al,
Al Pal, Al-truistic, Senex, The Socks Guy,
Alouisius, Al Levine the Putting Machine,
to Abraham,
to who else but my father

Then Isaac said to his father "My father"
And Abraham said "Here am I, my son"
(Genesis 22:7)

CONTENTS

Chapter 1
HIYA TIGER!

Usually, it would just be me out there. I actually kind of liked it that way. Everybody else, including my mother, were in their cars, making it always kind of hard to tell just how many folks were waiting. Not me. It didn't really matter … frigid temperatures, rain, snow, whatever, I was always out there on the platform. For the Berlin, Connecticut, railroad station, just outside of my hometown of New Britain, was one of my favorite places to be.

Many times it would be completely dark out there. Except for the few rusted, dimly lit overhead lights, the buzzing neon sign from the Berlin Plumbing Supply Company across the way was about the only other source of light. Sometimes some of its letters would be flickering or out altogether. I remember this one time, the "E," the "I," and the "N" in "BERLIN" were burnt out, spelling out my initials "BRL" (for Bruce Robert Levin). That sign made it seem as though I owned the place. Perhaps it was a symbol of recognition, a tribute to me for always being out there.

Even though my mother and I both expected the five o'clock, six o'clock, or seven o'clock train whichever it may be, from New York would be late, we always got to the station early at my insistence. Part of the reason was because of my love for trains, as I didn't want to miss seeing it come in. And so most of the time I'd be waiting out there for a while in the silence of the evening, except of course for the incessant buzzing of that Berlin Plumbing Supply Company neon sign across the way.

Then from a ways off, a light would suddenly come out of the darkness, shining in my direction like a gigantic flashlight looking for something or somebody, maybe me. I'd pick up the beam, just as it came around the bend that must have been almost a mile away, continuing to light up the sky as it began to creep closer. I would turn around for a moment to raise my hand and give a quick, pendulum-like signal to my mother, much like a train conductor does when he gives the all-clear sign to the engineer, and then it was back to staring down the shining Cyclops as it ever so slowly glided toward me.

The black and reddish-orange striped New Haven FL-7 diesel with its contrasting large white block letters, N over H on both sides of the engine, along with an inverted color scheme of white with a reddish-orange, N over H block letters on the front, just like the Lionel engine I had at home gifted to me by my parents on my fifth birthday, seemed to be hardly moving as it made its way into the station as I waited in anticipation. But as it got closer and I began to start to wave to the engineer to get him to blow the whistle or at least wave back, its light would become bigger and it seemed to gather speed, and before I could see if the engineer waved back, the monstrous diesel with all its roaring and dinging was upon me and then suddenly past me, and I could feel its force almost pushing me back.

I would look for him in the windows of the passing Pullman cars, but I could never seem to spot him. They were still moving much too fast. As the train shrieked to a halt and everybody started piling out, I would continue to intently look for him, wondering from which car he would emerge. But it was he who always seemed to find me first. I would hear the whistle, his whistle…"Whill, Whill … Whill, Whill," a catchy whip-poor-will-like chirp to which I had become lovingly accustomed, which he claimed his father, my Zeyda, had used with him when he was little and which I presumed his father's father had used with his father, and that I imagined I would find myself using with my children to keep the family tradition going. Then there he was.

The New Haven train from New York pulling into the Berlin Station

Like a genie, from out of the steam of the air brakes of one of the Pullmans, he would appear. The guy whom I looked up to. The guy who pretty much granted my every wish, who would take care of everything for me. My dad, who was always there for me. Coming over to me, he would extend his hand for a shake, always a firm handshake, and greet me with a "Hiya, Tiger!" letting me carry his briefcase as we walked to the car together.

In the summer, when it wasn't dark so early in the evening, as soon as we got home from the station, I'd hit him up for some pop-ups. The poor guy, he barely got in the door before I had my glove on my left hand and the bat and ball in the right, ready to go.

"Just a few, ok Dad?" I'd ask. But it always turned out to be more than a few, sometimes right up to the time when the dusk was turning to darkness and I couldn't see the ball anymore. I wanted the practice, but I think it might have been more about me intent on showing him my stuff.

Chapter 2

MY FAVORITE PASTIME

FOR ME GROWING UP, life was all about baseball. I inhaled it whenever I could, and I spent practically all of my free time in the spring, summer, and even fall playing it, watching it, or listening to it. Baseball was in my blood, part of my DNA.

Our backyard was home base, the diamond in the rough, which became the neighborhood go-to for sandlot baseball. Just about every night in the summer, guys from all over the neighborhood would show up for a pick-up game. Sometimes there would be as many as 10 kids or more.

The backyard gang would include my next-door neighbor, blood brother and best friend, David Goldstein. Dave and I were pretty much inseparable. Occasionally we found ourselves slipping into the land of boredom with nothing to do and resorting to the buddy phenomenon of "What do you want to do?" "I don't know ... what do you want to do?", but most of the time there was never a lack of things to do.

During the spring, summer, and fall, we were outside practically all the time. In addition to baseball, there was fishing, bike riding, croquet, basketball, football, and golf. In the winter, most of our time was spent working on and playing with my electric trains, for which I had quite the set-up. Beginning with my fifth birthday when I received my Lionel O Gauge starter set that included the replica of that same New Haven F7engine that would be pulling my father's train to and from New York every week, I would get something related to my electric trains for practically every gift-giving occasion, be it my birthday or Hanukkah. For Hanukkah, that would mean a total of eight train-related presents, a different train car or accessory on each of the eight nights. On birthdays, it would be an engine or a bunch of train cars and accessories. And so, I was able to amass a layout that spanned across two 4-by-8 plywood boards built up on wooden tables four feet off the ground that featured about a half dozen engines; a myriad of boxcars, coal cars, flatbeds, oil tankers, and cabooses; miniature toy trucks and cars; as well as all kinds of plastic model structures, most of which had to be assembled and glued together, including railroad depots, water towers, factories, gas stations, and other commercial buildings. Originally housed in our basement, the train layout became so expansive and such a major hobby of mine that it warranted a move into its own separate room off the garage, which previously was called the "Storage Room" but then became my beloved "Train Room."

Not to brag, but I had the biggest transformer you could get back in those days, allowing the engineer at the controls to run four trains all at once. Sometimes Dave and I would get carried away and run the trains so fast that they would jump off the tracks. On the outside track, this would invariably result in the engine, and sometimes some of the cars attached to it, falling down to the floor and consequently breaking or affecting something in the engine that would require a repair. One week it would be the light blue Boston & Maine engine, another week it would be my Pennsylvania steam locomotive that puffed out smoke as it went along the track, or the Rock Island. But never the New Haven. That was my pride and joy. It was my first and favorite one. It was much too valuable to run on the outside track. Then, each time, after bringing one of my dinged-up engines into the hobby shop for repair, I would promise my mother that we wouldn't run the train that fast anymore, but of course in no time we would be back at the controls running the speeding train off the track.

Like so many other kids born in that era, we also spent quite a bit of our time in front of the television, watching shows like the "Three Stooges," "MASH," "Hogan's Heroes," and obviously baseball, Major League games as well as Home Run Derby. Whenever we were watching TV, Dave would always have a pad of paper and pencil in hand, drawing layouts of various houses and buildings he envisioned creating, displaying his innate architectural talents and laying the groundwork to become the professional architect he would later take on as his career. So naturally, when it came to model train layouts, Dave brought a lot to the table.

But back to backyard baseball. In addition to Dave, the rest of the players included my next-door neighbors on the other side, the four Slater boys: Greg Jr., Peter, Tim, and John-John; other guys in the neighborhood, Mikey Ford and the Wise brothers, Raymond and Phillip; as well as some guys who were friends of theirs and sometimes even friends of their friends. Just about every evening in the summer, we would get together and shoot up to pick sides, and then play until we couldn't see anymore. Some guys would bring their own bats although I had plenty on hand, and for bases we used white rubber mats bolstered by rocks.

With the amount of play and all the running that went on, much to my parents' dismay the grass between the bases was pretty well flattened or matted down, to the extent that you could make out some well-defined base paths. But it wasn't the ideal field by any means, in that our yard had a little upslope to it around second base and there really wasn't that much room in the outfield to speak of. Plus, there were a few trees on the edge of the outfield that we had to contend with but still, we made do.

We had set our own rules. Anything hit into the woods on the fly in center field or into the Slaters' yard in right was considered a home run. And anything hit over the 10-foot or so evergreen bushes on the left side separating our yard from the Goldsteins' constituted a dinger as well. Our yard wasn't all that big, so it was relatively easy to hit one out. But still it required a pretty good poke. And anything that rolled into the Slaters' yard or the woods in center field or hit directly into the evergreens was a ground rule double.

There must have been the equivalent of buckets full of baseballs hit into the woods and bushes, many of which we could never seem to find. It was as though they just disappeared. Or sometimes we could see them, but they were out of our reach or stuck in a cluster of surrounding branches and were just too tough to get at with all the prickly evergreen needles in the way. I suspect some of those lost or entangled baseballs must still be there today, vestiges of all those good memories on the field.

Even if it was just Dave and me out there, be it during the day or evening, we played our own two-man version of the game. We called it "MLB Ball." One of us would pitch and the other would hit for a three-out half inning, with each of us representing a different Major League team. During each at-bat we pretended we were a different player on the respective Major League team that we represented. And we would rely on imaginary players, or utility players, as we sometimes called them, to help us on the base paths and out in the field. They were all pretend players. These were our virtual guys behind the scenes, the guys who were always there for us, the guys we could always rely on to occupy bases, to field pop-ups and grounders, and to be part of the team. Without them, we couldn't have had a game. So, if I was up and hit a routine fly ball to left, it would be an automatic out as we figured that the virtual position player would have been out there to catch it. But if I hit a ground ball between short and third or a solid line drive to left field that we figured would have fallen in for a base hit, well then it would be a single and I would yell out "man on first." Then if I got another single it would be men on first and second. Then let's say I hit a ball in the evergreens, it would be a ground rule double and accordingly, a run would have come in and there would be men on second and third, and so on, until there were three outs and the inning was over. It got a little bit sticky and argumentative at times as to what constituted a hit or an out. Or if there was a grounder to short with a man on first, whether it was a double play or just a single out, which depended upon how hard the ball was hit. It would be a judgement call. But all in all, the system worked out pretty well, and we were able to pitch, hit, and have a game.

Sometimes Dave and I would change it up a little bit and play Home Run Derby, just like the show we watched on TV, with two of the top hitters in the Major Leagues going up against each other in a nine-inning competition to best the other in home runs. Again, one of us would pitch and the other would hit. Like regular baseball, the hitter would have three outs an inning. If the hitter swung and missed for a strike or made any kind of contact other than hitting it a home run, be it a foul ball, ground ball, pop-up, direct shot into the bushes, or any kind of hit anywhere in the field, it was an automatic out. And we would just keep track of how many homers we would hit. Like a regular game of baseball, if we were tied at the end of nine innings, we went into extras. Sometimes the tally of home runs would get pretty high, as it wasn't unusual for each of us to put up a number of over 20.

Occasionally, a home run would sail over the evergreens and go smack into one of the Goldsteins' two basement storm windows, breaking the small rectangular window into smithereens and sending shards of glass all over their basement and lawn. Dave's mom would bolt out of their house with hands on her hips, yelling for him to clean up the mess. But in the scheme of things, breaking a storm window wasn't so bad. It didn't ever affect the field of play, as both sets of parents tolerated this relatively minor cost of playing. It would have been ok if those were the only broken windows. It got much worse.

One summer, while Dave and I were careful not to jeopardize or interfere at all with the contour of our sacred and beloved baseball field so that we would be able to maintain our ritual of baseball just about every night as usual, we transformed my backyard into a nine-hole par three golf course as well. On one side of our house, at the juncture where our back yard came together with our front yard, we became landscapers for the day and created a putting green. We just took the Goldsteins' powerless hand mower and kept going round-and-round and over-and-over the same carved-out circular patch of grass until it was cut down to just the stub, as though the grass had gotten a crew cut. As such, it took on the appearance of an almost authentic putting green. We then designated nine different spots spread throughout the backyard to serve as tee-boxes, marking them off with little square wooden posts that we had bought at the hardware store, each with an index card taped to it designating the number of the respective hole and the approximate yardage involved.

While the idea of constructing a putting green and converting our yard into a golf course wasn't an easy sell by any means, my parents begrudgingly agreed to go along with it. No doubt, they probably figured the grass was already being significantly compromised with the worn-down base paths and the general wear and tear of the yard from all the baseball activities taking place on it, that really how much worse could the grass get. Besides, I think my father, being the avid golfer that he was, kind of liked the idea of being able to come home and practice his short game.

Originally, we had set up the course for our own pleasure. But after a few rounds of playing, we got the enterprising idea to charge a fee for our friends and others to play, with the exception of my father, of course, who we felt it might be best to just grant him carte blanche usage. Not too much, just a nominal fee to make the course official. I believe we charged something like 35 cents a round. In our entrepreneurial spirit, we even put a sign up in the front of our house, advertising the nine-hole course to the neighborhood.

Yep, the Levin backyard had turned into quite the sports complex. This might have been the world's first attempt to combine baseball and golf all into one field of play. And we were able to pull it off. The golf never got in the way of our baseball games or visa-versa, since our so-called putting green was on the side of the house and accordingly was separated from the baseball field. And when we played baseball, we would merely just take the wooden posts out of the ground. It all coexisted pretty well. Dave and I got to play some golf, add a little money to our pockets, and still use the field for baseball. We were even thinking of expanding the course to 18 holes. That is until one of my drives went through my parents' bedroom window.

This wasn't like taking out one of the Goldsteins' little storm windows. With the breakage of this bedroom window, we had crossed the line of no return and consequently no golf. My parents immediately put the kibosh on any future backyard golf, and we had to hang up our golf sticks as well as take the course-marking sticks out of the ground. Like my parents' bedroom window, our dream of having a unique combination baseball-golf sports complex was shattered, and we were relegated back to just baseball.

But the most memorable broken window was yet to come. It happened on a typical summer night when my family and I were sitting around the dining room table having dinner. Suddenly from out of nowhere a baseball comes crashing through the big front bay window in our living room, which was adjacent to the dining room. Dave had been outside in the front yard with a bat and ball in hand kind of warming up, waiting for me to finish dinner so we could hit the field in the back yard. Not sure why he was in the front yard and not the back, but he certainly made his presence known. I have to say this little surprise made my night. While my parents, especially my mother, were noticeably upset (although I imagine not as upset as they would have been if I was the culprit), I couldn't help but laugh and was actually beaming at the time, basically because it wasn't me who did it.

Again, this was a far cry from a storm window, even more dramatic than a bedroom window. Needless to say, any house-adjacent baseball was halted, certainly in the front but also in the back. But fortunately, this moratorium was short-lived. After a week or so of our parents observing us just sitting around moping and doing nothing, saying "What do you want to do? ... "I don't know, what do you want to do?", we were given a reprieve and were back on the field, promising them that we would be sure to confine all baseball activities to the back yard.

Although Dave was out on the field with me most of the time, when he wasn't, I was often out there playing baseball by myself. I would act out my own version of Major League games, although I kept this whole imaginary world to myself. I pretended I was various Major League players, either pitching (in which I would simulate a full over-the-head wind-up and pretend to let it go), or hitting (in which I would toss the ball straight up and hit it mid-air someplace), or fielding (in which I would merely underhandedly throw the ball straight up high in the air and catch it as though it was a pop fly). With all of the time I put into baseball, especially my self-simulation of constantly throwing and catching those pop flies, our neighbor Dr. Slater, Greg Sr. told my parents that he was convinced I was destined to be a Major Leaguer. Oh, how I hoped he would be right.

If I wasn't playing baseball, I was watching it on TV or listening to it on the radio. Living in Connecticut, midway between Boston and New York, I logically should have been either a Red Sox, Yankee, or possibly a Mets fan. Yet, my favorite team in those days was the Braves. First it was the Milwaukee Braves and then in 1966 they moved and became the Atlanta Braves. To this day, I'm not sure exactly why I started out as a Milwaukee Braves fan—maybe because they were on TV so much in the late '50s when they won back-to-back National League championships and had star players such as Warren Spahn, Lew Burdette, Eddie Mathews, and my favorite player Hank Aaron. Hank, or Henry, Aaron was also known as "the Hammer" or "Hammerin' Hank." He played right field and always batted either third or clean-up in the order.

Henry Louis Aaron was born and raised in Mobile, Alabama. He had seven siblings, and one of his brothers, Tommie, also played in the Major Leagues on the Braves. The Aaron boys are one of the 100 or so sets of brothers who have played in the Major Leagues together. With the family being poor and not able to afford baseball equipment, when growing up, instead of using baseballs and bats, Hank and his younger brother Tommie practiced by hitting bottle caps with sticks.

In 1952, the same year I was born, a scout for the then Boston Braves discovered and signed Hank while he was playing on a team called the Indianapolis Clowns of the Negro American League. At the time, he went by the nickname "Pork Chop," supposedly because that was the only thing he would ever order in a restaurant. According to one of his teammates, he would have pork chops three meals a day, starting with breakfast when he would eat two.

After stints with the Eau Claire Bears (the Braves' Northern League Class-C farm team) in 1952 and then the Jacksonville Braves (the Braves' Class A minor league team in the Southern Atlantic League) during the 1953 season, the newly named Milwaukee Braves, which had recently moved from Boston at the beginning of the 1953 season, brought up Hank at the start of the 1954 season when one of their starting outfielders, Bobby Thomson, suffered an injury. Hammerin' Hank never looked back, as it didn't take him long to make his presence known and quickly establish himself as one of the premier Major League ballplayers of all time. In 1956, in only his third season in the majors, he captured the National League batting title, hitting .328. And then in 1957, he was the National League's Most Valuable Player and helped the Braves clinch the National League pennant and then lead their comeback from a three-game deficit to beat the Yankees in the World Series.

He went on to play a total of 21 years for the Braves, 12 of which were in Milwaukee and 9 in Atlanta. At Atlanta Fulton County Stadium in April 1974, despite racial threats on his life, he hit his 715th career homer, breaking Babe Ruth's record of most home runs ever hit in the majors.

Just after the 1974 season was over, Hank returned to Milwaukee, the city where he started his career, to play with the Brewers, formerly the Seattle Pilots, for another two years before retiring. He finished with a whopping 755 home runs, a record that to date has only been broken by Barry Bonds' controversial steroid-tainted record of 762 homers.

While he's probably best known for his home run prowess, Hank, who was inducted into the Baseball Hall of Fame in 1982, also holds the all-time records for the most career RBIs (runs batted in) with 2,297, the most extra base hits with 1,477, and the most total bases with 6,856. Plus, he is third in total career base hits with 3,771, fifth in total runs scored with 2,174, and on defense has three gold gloves to his name. And he is among the Major League players with the most All-Star appearances, having been selected every year from 1955-1975.

But at the time in the late '50s and '60s, way before he would reach these impressive milestones, I was a big fan of this up-and-comer. Maybe it was the way he carried himself, the way he went about his business on and off the field that impressed me the most— his quiet, unassuming manner, and his smooth, effortless swing. It was said that he had such a calming demeanor at the plate that it looked like he fell sleep between pitches. But Hammerin' Hank had such quick, strong wrists that allowed him to catch up to and get through the ball, unlike few others could. I believe it was Curt Simmons, a famous National League pitcher, who said that "throwing a fastball by Hank Aaron is like trying to sneak the sunrise past a rooster."

Naturally, Hank was the guy I modeled my swing after, with my bat high off my shoulder and cocked way above my head, shaking and twitching as I waited for the pitch; the guy whose number 44 I went with on the back of my baseball jersey on school teams; and the guy who I zealously rooted for every time he came up to bat.

Over the years, I've collected some valuable Hank Aaron memorabilia, including a signed Atlanta Braves jersey of his, and an autographed bat and ball. But the most noteworthy item in my collection is the personal letter I received from him. In February 1962, when I was 9 years old, in the fifth grade, out of nowhere I got a letter in the mail in a standard white nondescript envelope with the words "Major League Baseball Players Association" in the upper left corner. I couldn't imagine what it could be. At first, I laughed to myself that maybe Dr. Slater's prediction was going to come true, and I was being scouted to try out for the Majors. With my heart beating a mile a minute, I ripped it open to find the same words "Major League Baseball Players Association" on the letterhead, along with a two-paragraph typed letter from none other than Hammerin' Hank himself, talking about the upcoming season and extending me his best wishes with his actual signature at the end. I wondered how on earth he knew about me, how he knew I was such a big fan, how he got my address. Needless to say, this was quite the "Show and Tell" item at school.

When I showed the letter to my parents, a big smile came over my dad's face, implying that somehow, he was behind this. As it turned out, my father had set the whole thing up. Being in the men's and boys' discount clothing business, he was able to pull some strings. As it happened one of his wholesale sock vendors, Mobil Socks, also sold socks to some of the baseball teams, one of which was, believe or not, the Milwaukee Braves. My father had talked to his sales rep at Mobil, who in turn talked to his coworker who handled its baseball accounts, a guy named Stanley Kreenick. And somehow, Mr. Kreenick was able to arrange for Hank Aaron to send me a letter. Even though the spelling was a little different, I guess it was only appropriate that the name of the company was Mobil Socks, being that Hank originally hailed from Mobile, Alabama.

MAJOR LEAGUE BASEBALL PLAYERS ASSOCIATION

TN 7-0688

THE BILTMORE
NEW YORK 17, N. Y.

February 17, 1962

Mr. Bruce Levin
31 Windsor Road
New Britain, Conn.

Dear Bruce:

I have heard from my good friend Stanley Kroinick that you have been a fan of mine for some time. I am always pleased to hear that I have friends all over the United States.

I am down in Spring Training now getting in shape for the coming season. I am pretty sure that it will be a great season for the Braves and we will go all out to bring the Pennant to Milwaukee.

Thank you for thinking of me.

My best personal regards.

Sincerely,

HANK AARON

The letter I received from Hank Aaron in 1962

Every time the Braves were on TV on NBC's Saturday game of the week, which was fairly often given they were one of the best teams in the Majors at the time, I was plopped down sitting on the floor right in front of the TV taking in every pitch. My mom would make me hot dogs and always had peanuts on hand for me to make me feel as though I was actually at the game. She would tell you that I was an emotional wreck when I watched these games, as my mood would swing with every swing of the bat. I would always be yelling at the TV, often questioning the manager's decision to leave a pitcher in or take one out, or to bunt or not to bunt, or whatever. There was no let-up on my part. Even if the Braves were way ahead, no lead was safe for me as I hung onto every pitch. It wasn't until they finally retired the side of their opponent in the ninth inning that I was able to let out a big sigh of relief.

Naturally, I was all smiles when they won. But if they lost, it wasn't a pretty picture. I would get so mad and upset that I couldn't hold back the tears. My mother, of course, would say it was just a game and that they would get 'em tomorrow, but it would take me the rest of the day to get out of my funk.

Still, win or lose, I looked forward so much to watching those games. So much so that if they were supposed to be on TV and were rained out, I would be so disappointed that I would experience my own water works. Yep, I even cried when they were rained out… a true fan. Who says there's no crying in baseball?

Then of course there were the games on the radio. Every so often, I would catch a Braves game that would be nationally broadcasted via network programming. Other times, if they were playing at night against the Mets or the Pirates, I would try to get the game on the radio. I would be better able to pick up stations from afar late at night.

Searching for radio stations at night was another pastime of mine. Part of it was the hunt, as I wanted to see how many stations and how far of a distance away I could pick up. The later the time at night, the farther the stations I would be able to pull in and the clearer they would be. I remember one of the farthest I was able to pick up was WOWO in Fort Wayne, Indiana. On occasion, I could also pick up WWVA in Wheeling, West Virginia, and WJR in Detroit, where I would be able to listen to a Tigers game.

The radio dial provided me with a whole world of discovery. There was something about lying down in bed before going to sleep, with the lights out, going on an expedition or adventure of sorts to different places. It was fascinating to be able to pull in all sorts of different types of programming. Besides baseball games, I came across various talk shows where people would call in with their problems, news shows, sports commentaries, and sitcoms. One time I even picked up some type of Southern revival ceremony being broadcasted on WWVA. Radio was my gateway to the world in those days.

In terms of finding ball games on the radio, New York would be no problem given its proximity to my home in Connecticut, but

Pittsburgh was more of a challenge. Depending on the weather and conditions of the airwaves, I would usually be able to pick up late innings of Pirates games on its flagship station KDKA, and amidst the constant static I could make out the raspy voice of Bob Prince, the long-time Pirates announcer, doing the play-by-play.

When my mother or father would come into my room to say good night, their question was always the same: "How can you hear anything with all that static?" To them, it must have been really annoying to listen to, but to a die-hard baseball fan like myself who was intent on following every pitch, it was just background noise that you learned to put up with. After a while, you didn't really hear it—it just blended in with the game.

Chapter 3
AL LEVIN TALKING

Never the customary "Hello" or any other salutation, but just "Al Levin talking." That's how my dad always answered the phone.

Everybody called him Al, even though his formal, biblical name was Abraham. Only his brother and my dentist "Uncle Doc," whose real name was Harry but who everybody called Doc, referred to him as Abe, sometimes. No one really knew him as Abraham. He was always Al.

Over the years, as a loving son, I had come up with my own nicknames for him, some of which were a derivation of the name Al like "Al Pal." Then during my middle school days I plucked the term "Senex" from the Latin vocabulary, meaning old man, and went through a phase calling him that. And then later on, with the expansion of my vocabulary in high school, I came up with the name "Al-truistic," which I thought was particularly fitting given that he was always true to his word and always showed devotion for others.

Of course, taking on a pseudonym wasn't all that unusual for our family. Besides Al, alias Abraham, there was my mother who started out her life as Bernice, but took on the nickname of Nikki when she was a teenager. In the fifth grade, my sister Deborah changed her name to Lexye, supposedly short for "sexy Levin." And, in the back of our station wagon, on one of our many family car trips from Connecticut to Pennsylvania to visit my mother's brother's family, the newly crowned Lexye and I decided that we would give our grandmother, whose first name was Helen, the affectionate nickname of "Spice," because she always added that little something extra to everything. I seem to be the only guy in my immediate family who still goes by his original name.

Even my next-door neighbor, blood brother, best friend, fellow backyard baseball player, and later on best man at my wedding David Goldstein ended up getting on the name changing train when he adopted the last name of Johannas, taking on one of his ancestral names from his family tree.

Believe it or not, according to the Bible, even the original Abraham went through a name makeover. He started out as Abram. But when Abram was 99 years old, God appeared before him to announce a name modification. As it is written…

"Neither shall thy name any more be called Abram, but thy name shall be Abraham; for the father of multitude of nations have I made thee."

(Genesis 17:5)

Actually, in the Bible, there's quite a bit of precedent for changing names among our ancestors. Upon Abraham getting his new name, his wife, Sarai, not to be outdone, also received a slight name alteration. As it is written…

And God said unto Abraham…
"As for Sarai thy wife, thou shall not call her name Sarai, but Sarah shall her name be."

(Genesis 17:15)

And as such, Sarah, meaning "princess," was recognized as the "mother of nations."

Then there was Jacob, son of Isaac, son of Abraham. Supposedly,

Jacob got his original name (Ya-akov) by grabbing at the heel (eikev) of his slightly older, firstborn twin brother Esau as they came out of their mother Rebekah's womb. As such, Jacob was associated with the term "the Tripper" (derived from heel-tripper), which turned out to be an appropriate pseudonym for him, as he was known for always playing tricks on others to make them stumble.

Jacob was said to have tricked his twin brother Esau into turning over his birthright, entitling Jacob to assume the traditional firstborn son's responsibility of being the patriarch in the family, which was a big advantage in those days. As the story goes, as a man of the field who liked to hunt, Esau was coming back home from a hard day out in the field and met up with Jacob who had just made up some red pottage or lentil stew. Esau was so faint and famished that he agreed to hand over his birthright to his younger brother Jason in exchange for the pottage. As it is written…

And Esau said to Jacob: "Let me swallow, I pray thee, some of this red, red, pottage; for I am faint."
And Jacob said: "Sell me first thy birthright."
And Esau said: "Behold I am at the point to die:
and what profit shall the birthright do to me."
And Jacob said: "Swear to me first" and he swore unto him; and he sold his birthright unto Jacob.
And Jacob gave Esau bread and pottage of lentils;
and he did eat and drink, and rose up, and went his way.
(Genesis 25:31-34)

There was also the time Jacob posed as Esau to trick his father, Isaac, into thinking he was the older brother, so he could receive Isaac's blessing as the older brother. Later on, upon trying to meet up and make amends with Esau for all his trickery, Jacob encountered and found himself wrestling with a being he believed to be an angel, perhaps Esau's guardian angel or some type of messenger of God. The story goes that after fighting this being to a stalemate that lasted until dawn, before they finally parted, Jacob asked for a blessing. As part of this blessing, the angel upon asking for and learning Jacob's name, decreed "Your name shall no longer be called Jacob, but Israel" (made up of the terms "ysr" meaning to wrestle and "el" meaning God); **"for thou has striven with God and with men, and has prevailed" (Genesis 32:29).** And so it came to pass that Israel became Jacob's new name.

God made the name change official when he later appeared before Jacob and blessed him, and with Jacob's new name of Israel proclaimed him the leader of the Jewish people. As it is written…

> **And God said unto him:**
> **"I am God Almighty.**
> **be fruitful and multiply;**
> **a nation and a company of nations shall be thee,**
> **and kings shall come out of thy loins;**
> **and the land which I gave unto Abraham and Isaac,**
> **to thee I will give it, and to thy seed after thee**
> **will I give the land."**
>
> **(Genesis 35:11-12)**

But if there was ever a guy who fit the profile of Abraham, formerly Abram, it was my father. For in addition to being the father of the Levin clan, he could have easily been the father of many nations.

Born in Khatrinislov Gubernia, in Russia in 1908, he was the son of Chaim and Manya Bellanov Levin. His brother Lou was several years older, then came his sister Rose, then him, and then Harry, alias Doc. Dad spent his early formative years in Russia, until he was about 4 years old when the family took the big boat over to the United States.

But while in Russia, rumor has it in our family that when young Abraham was about 3 or so, maybe 2, he was abducted by the Cossacks. I don't have a lot of details on this, only that he was somehow snatched up and taken for the night. Supposedly, one early evening he was outside on the family's farm in the backyard playing with his brother Lou, and this pack of Cossacks on horses, probably somewhat drunk, suddenly came galloping in and one of them swooped him up off the ground onto his horse and then rode off with him into the Russian sunset.

What happened that night with the Cossacks, no one knows for sure. Perhaps he went through some kind of ritual, a bonding ceremony, or special teaching, through which he was able to learn some valuable ways of the world. Or perhaps he imbibed a little bit of their magic moonshine. Whatever it was, it just might have been that one mysterious night with the Cossacks, away from his family, that helped give him that spirit of adventure, that worldly confidence and wherewithal to take anything on, that diplomatic ability to get along with others, and that special savoir faire… that certain "secret sauce" that would prepare him for things to come.

The Levin family circa 1911 or 1912, just before they left Russia.
That's Al, right in the middle in the first row.

How my grandparents survived the hours that Abraham was gone is hard to imagine. But sure enough, he was returned to Chaim and

Manya the next morning. I suppose it could have been a situation like in one of O'Henry's stories, "The Ransom of Red Chief," in which the abducted child protagonist was such a nuisance and a terror that the kidnappers ended up paying the kid's parents to take him back. But rather, knowing my father, I can only imagine that he must have somehow reasoned or negotiated with the Cossacks to take him back home. Even at that early age, he had probably already developed that special knack about him to talk his way into or out of anything.

This knack carried forth into whatever his endeavors were, whether it was in school, on the playground, later in business, or his personal life. He seemed to always be able to work his way into and out of things, even for something minor like when he and my mother would be invited to another couple's house for a dinner party on a Sunday evening, when that's the last thing he'd want to do with his precious weekend time.

When it came to Saturday and Sunday, Dad had a routine. If it was in the spring, summer, or fall, he would spend the day at our country club, Cliffside, playing golf in the morning, having lunch, and then playing gin in the afternoon. But he would always be sure to make it home by late afternoon around 4:00 to take in the weekly PGA golf tournament on TV. He went from playing gin to drinking gin, always having at least one gin and tonic but never more than two, while he watched his favorite pastime. For him, this routine was clearly like heaven. And if it was in the winter, even though he couldn't play golf, he would still maintain the tradition of playing gin, drinking gin, and watching golf, as a golf tournament was on TV almost every weekend.

On some Sundays, though, the golf match wasn't always quite over by 6:00 pm, especially if the tournament was emanating from the West Coast and/or it went into sudden death. And so there were times when my father had to leave his cozy den to go to a social engagement my mom had arranged on their behalf. Clearly something he didn't seek out, but being the good sport that he was, he always went along with the plan. But still he wasn't to be denied.

Somehow, whether it was his determined and assuming way or just innocent charm, he was able to pull off the unthinkable for most guests: he'd turn on the host's TV, sit down and watch the end of the match, much to the mortification of my mother. He sometimes even got the host to delay serving dinner until the match was over.

Dad also had a knack for talking his way out of things. Again, maybe it was that experience with the Cossacks that prepared him so well, not that he didn't have quite a bit of luck at times. But then again, he seemed to be the type of guy who brought on his own luck. Like the time when he was pulled over by police one day on the highway. This must have been back when he was in his 30's or maybe even in his 20's. The story goes that upon stopping him, the officer of course started out by asking for his license and registration. When my father handed over his license, the officer looks at it and said, "Hey buddy, this license isn't signed." Without even a flinch, as though there was perfectly nothing wrong with having an unsigned license, my father abruptly but rather nonchalantly replies, "Officer, do you have a pen?" Giving my dad a pen and watching him sign his license in front of him, the caught-off-guard cop then proceeds to tick off a list of offenses my father was apparently guilty of committing on the road.

"Well Abraham, you were speeding, tailgating the guy in front, going in and out of lanes without using a blinker, and overall driving recklessly," said the officer.

Now my dad, who could always maintain a keen sense of humor, gives him what I imagined was a look of consternation and said to him in response: "Gee officer, you might as well throw in a charge of murder."

Well, wouldn't you know it, Dad probably got the one and only officer who thought his comment was funny, as the cop gave out a half-hearted laugh and one of those "get the hell out of here" retorts, and let him go without a ticket or even a warning. If that was me and I had committed those offenses, I would not have had the nerve to come back with a quip like that. But if I did, I'm certain I would have gotten a ticket and maybe even a night in the slammer. My dad was law-abiding to be sure, but he had this self-assuredness that allowed him to get away with stuff.

Plus, he was the kind of guy who always seemed to know where he was going and if he didn't, he'd figure out a way to get there. And he was determined to get there as timely as possible. Never leaving anything to chance, Dad was always stopping to get directions. When it came to this habit, you could say that he went a little bit overboard. We'd be driving together somewhere we'd never been before, and as we got closer, he would continue to pull people over left and right, whoever happened to be around, to get an update and some reassurance that we were going in the right direction. It was as though the person he asked last, who in theory was closer to the destination, would have some better, more accurate information to go on.

And he could never leave early enough. Wherever he was going, he would always leave earlier that he had to. Then, as soon as he got there, he was already thinking about coming back, figuring when he would leave and what the best way would be to go back. Truly, he was always ahead of himself. Everything seemed to be precalculated, well thought out. He was a man with a plan, a man on a mission.

It also seemed everything always came so easy for him. Maybe that was because I was looking at it from a son's perspective, but he seemed to have it all figured out. I was just hoping that when I grew up, I would figure it all out, too.

Chapter 4

GO TO THE LAND THAT I SHALL SHOW THEE

MY FATHER GREW UP FAST, and I mean really fast. He sure had a lot of jobs along the way, and experienced a lot of stuff. All these experiences paved the way for some great stories. He had a repository full of them. I never got tired of listening to them, as from time to time he would tell the same stories and even though I knew all of them practically by heart, I would enjoy them just as much each time. They never got old.

Dad had a knack for telling stories, pulling you in and making it seem like you were there with him. I have to admit, I was a little envious of all his escapades and experiences. There was a rousing spirit of adventure about them, the type of adventures I would have liked to share with him, but instead ones I had to live vicariously through. Indeed, many of these stories have been included in this book.

One has to wonder how many untold stories there are about my dad. I suspect, and I can only imagine, there must have been a lot of stories he didn't care to share. Stories he thought he was better off not telling, for whatever reason.

Whenever he did embark on relating one of his life's stories, he often used the expression "back in those days" to set the tone. And if he thought something was funny, he often started out with his own distinctive "heh…heh" kind of laugh. I'm the same way when I tell a story… it must be hereditary. And if he couldn't recall something, he would resort to the term "what-you-macall-it," which while one might have been left up in the air as to exactly what he was describing, I could usually still follow and make out what he was talking about. I like to think I knew all his "what-you-macall-its."

Upon coming over from Russia in 1912, the Levin clan settled in Waterbury, Connecticut, first on a farm and then in a flat on the outskirts of the city. At a very early age, even before he learned how to speak English, my dad was out there on the streets, hawking newspapers along with his brother Lou. If he brought home 15 cents or a quarter, it was a good day's work and a welcome addition to the Levin family coffers. However, during his foray into the world of street gambling to try to stretch his dollars, he would often play marbles and sometimes lose it.

Dad tells the story of how he and his brother Lou were out there on the street one day selling papers and Lou put a cigarette in his mouth, which unbeknownst to his parents, was something Lou had an occasional tendency to do. So much so he even rolled his own cigarettes. But not having a match to light it, he tapped a guy on the back that he was approaching and asked, "Hey mister, do you happen to have a light?" Well, it turned out that guy was none other than their father, who, needless to say, was not too pleased with Lou's request. No doubt when the perpetrator got home that night, it was lights out for Lou.

While at Wilby High School in Waterbury, Dad worked in the men's and boys' clothing section at a department store called Brown Brothers in the north part of town, earning about $20 a week. To supplement his income, he played pool and a lot of cards. One of his high school friends had a brother who worked at an office downtown, and every Thursday night there was a card game there. So, after Dad got through with work at Brown Brothers at 9:00 pm, he hopped a trolley car to join the game and didn't get home until midnight. Little did he know at the time that men's and boys' clothing would be a business he would someday return to and eventually settle into for a career. But in between, there would be a lot of different types of jobs he would take on.

Around that time, word had spread that there was a land boom going on in Florida. Opportunity was knocking. Evidently, just as the original Abraham was spurred on by a message from God, **"Get thee out of thy country, and from thy kindred, and from thy father's house, unto the land that I will show thee" (Genesis 12:1)**, the Abraham from Waterbury felt a similar beckoning. He had heard his calling. And so it came to pass, in July 1925, shortly after graduation from high school, with only 17 years of life under his belt and no prospect of a job, he decided to pick up and go down to the Sunshine State, to what he hoped would be the "Land of Milk and Honey," to seek his fortune.

Dad went down to Florida with a friend of Lou's named Leo Blumen, who was four years older than him. Plus, he knew some guys from Waterbury who had gone down there earlier, as well as a distant cousin of his who was down there selling real estate. But still, for a young guy who had never been outside the confines of Waterbury since his original journey over from Russia, it had to take a lot of courage to leave home and go so far away.

Lou gave them a ride to New York, where they took a boat down to Miami. Once there, until they could get situated, they stayed in a big rooming house with the guys they knew from Waterbury, while they went out in search of job opportunities. At first, they floundered a bit. But upon connecting with the cousin in real estate, they learned of a little grocery store up for a sale in the Hialeah area, just outside Miami, with a small bedroom, bathroom, and kitchen in the back that sounded intriguing. Everything rolled into one.

So Dad and Leo, neither of whom knew anything about running a grocery store, bought the place and went into the grocery business. As the story goes, they did pretty well, especially considering their inexperience. But after about a year or so, Leo's brother-in-law passed away, and upon his sister's request, Leo went back to Waterbury to run his brother-in-law's retail business, leaving Dad to run the store by himself, which he did for a while.

Now, as the sole proprietor of the grocery story, he found it difficult to stay open until late at night, when most of his business occurred. So, in his desire for more reasonable hours, Dad switched gears to the dry-cleaning business where he could close up by 6:00 pm.. He had a customer who owned a dry-cleaning store in Hialeah, only about a mile away from the grocery store, and they worked out a deal to just trade stores, even-steven. Dad got the dry-cleaning store, and the other guy got the grocery store. There was no doubt that from the outset, Dad was going to be a man of action and a dealmaker.

So just like that, Dad was now in the dry-cleaning business, again a business he knew nothing about and would have to learn as he went along. He found it advantageous to hire a couple of guys to do alterations and pressing, while he spent a lot of his time picking up and delivering all of the dry cleaning. He ended up being fairly successful in the business as well, not quite as good as he did with his grocery enterprise, but enough to scratch out a decent living and still send a little something back to the family in Waterbury. And indeed his hours of work were much more reasonable.

It's hard to imagine an 18-year-old being that industrious, but it seems there was very little time for sun 'n' fun back then for young men like my dad trying to make their way in the world. He worked hard, not thinking beyond tallying each day's sales receipts. But unfortunately on September 18, 1926, just after Rosh Hashanah and on the cusp of Yom Kippur, a catastrophic hurricane put a permanent stain on his dry-cleaning business. With winds up to 150 miles an hour when its eye hit, this fierce storm, which would become known as "The Big Blow" or just simply "The Hurricane," was described by the U.S. Weather Bureau in Miami as probably the most destructive hurricane to have ever struck the United States. Due to this storm, hundreds of people lost their lives and property damage was beyond com-prehension. In terms of Dad's dry-cleaning store, the property damage was so extensive that it ripped off the roof. So much for his dry-cleaning business.

Yet as the saying goes, when one door closes, another opens. As part of his dry-cleaning customer base, one of the places Dad had frequently picked up from and delivered to was the Hialeah racetrack. Accordingly, he became indoctrinated into the world of horse racing, and established a rapport with some of the trainers and other guys working at the track. As such, he was able to line up an opportunity at the track, chauffeuring one of the prominent trainers there. His job was to pick up the guy in North Miami at 5:00 am and drive him to the racetrack in Hialeah, do some odd jobs here and there at the track, and then take him home after the races were over at around 5:00 pm.

One of Dad's odd jobs was sending telegrams to the trainer's father and brothers whenever there was a so-called "sure thing" in a race. The trainer operated out of one of the biggest stables at the track, owned by a wealthy guy named McClean who also owned the Washington Post at the time. McClean's stable included some of the fastest horses at the track, who frequently were winners in their respective races. As such, they were often deemed a "sure thing," even though on average the favorite horse ended up winning only about a third of the time. Still ended up being a good bet.

No stranger to the betting scene, Dad must have no doubt harkened back to his formative years of marbles and cards and put a few bets down for himself occasionally. Also, as part of his job, he placed bets on behalf of his boss, the trainer. I remember this one horse-betting story my dad told that he claimed nearly cost him his life…

One day, the trainer calls me into his office and gives me $400 and says, "Al, I want you to go out and place this money on Saturday's race." This was a Thursday. In those days, there were a lot of bookies, every bar had a bookie, every hotel had a bookie. Instead of betting at the track and bringing down the odds on the horses, you bet with a bookie.

So I went out to the bars and told the bookies there, "I want you to bet on Black Hawk for me in the sixth race, to win."

Black Hawk was a horse owned by the son of the president of Cuba. The horse was running in the sixth race because that race had the slowest horses… horses that had never won, never did anything. I found this out later.

I placed bets, $20, $30, about a dozen of them. I gave the trainer the slips for the bets. Then I realized from a stable hand that this horse had run seven times in the 45 days he had been at Hialeah. He had always run last. Every time, the trainer's order to the jockey was "You gotta run last." So, I knew there was something going on.

Then later I found out two things. They weren't sure the horse was going to win, so they gave him a little shot of something. Also, they could not put a good jockey on him – couldn't put a decent jockey on a horse that had run last in seven races, so they had to put a what-you-macall-it… an apprentice jockey on him.

So the horse ends up going off 110 to 1. There's no way this horse can win, so everyone assumes. Always runs last, what chance does it have to win. Nobody in the track bet on the horse.

In those days, they did not have the starting gate like they have now. Now the horses are pushed into the little cubicles before they spring them. Back in those days, all they had was just the wire, and the stable hands would try to get these horses up to the wire, and when the starter saw that they were practically all set, he would spring the barrier and off they would go.

So they start to get lined up, and this horse is acting a little frisky and the jockey is having a hard time holding him. Heh…heh, you don't have to believe what I'm going to tell you, but this is the truth.

As the starter threw up the barrier, this horse rears and turns around and is facing in the wrong direction. The other horses start off and before the jockey can turn him around and get him straightened out, the other horses were 400 or 500 yards out. Now this horse, once turned around the right way, begins to run and boy does he run, and sure enough gains on all the other horses. But when the race is over this Black Hawk horse loses by a neck… comes in second.

Now, can you just imagine if this horse had won, and not come in second, and if I had gone to try to collect all those winning bets at the bars. I wouldn't be here today to tell you about that particular incident. I would have been killed; somebody would have killed me.

Chapter 5
AN AL OF ALL TRADES

DAD STAYED IN FLORIDA FOR A WHILE working at the racetrack. But it came to pass that sometime in early 1927, coming up on the budding age of 19, after soaking up its rays, its hurricane rains, and job experiences, he decided to head back to Waterbury, Connecticut. Florida, the land of sun and potential prosperity, was no longer the bed of opportunity it had been just a few years back. What with everyone and their brother going down there to buy up land and seek fortune, the economics of it all caught up with investor speculation and the bubble burst. Plus, the horrific storm of September '26 had taken its toll and was a big factor in further contributing to its downward economy. Many folks, including those guys from Waterbury whose rooming house Dad and Leo first stayed at when they came down to Florida and who had opened up stores there, ended up never making it.

And while one could say that Dad had achieved a fair amount of success down there in the land of opportunity and had made quite a bit of money, unfortunately by the time he left Florida in 1927 he didn't have a lot to show for it. To use his exact words, "I managed to come home broke." Of course, the devastating effect of the hurricane had a lot to do with it, but I suspect more than that in the end it was playing the horses that did him in.

Yet there was still some hope that his time there would end up leaving him with some monetary gain down the road. Going back to when he owned the grocery store, the enterprising Al on a whim actually purchased some land down in Florida, 50 acres to be exact, for a total of $1,200. At the time, things were booming so much down there that he thought it would be a worthwhile investment. He had always been a guy with some vision. While he wasn't sure exactly where this piece of land was, somewhere in Miami Beach, he had a bona fide deed to show for it.

On his trip back home up North, Dad stuck the promising deed in his suitcase with the rest of his stuff. He took a ride with a friend to Philadelphia, and then from there got on a train to New York and then another train onto Waterbury. But instead of going right home, first he went to the Thom McAn's shoe store right near the train station, where both his brothers Lou and Harry were working at the time, along with some other guys he knew. He couldn't wait to see the boys. From there, they all ended up piling into Lou's car to go home, prompting Dad to put his suitcase in the wheel well between the fender and the running board.

Well, when they got to the house, there was no suitcase to be had. Apparently, during the ride home, it had fallen out from the wheel well. They went back to retrace their ride, but the suitcase was never to be found. Dad lost everything he had in there—his clothes, other personal things, his presents that he had brought back for everybody in the family, and of course the deed. Who knows what those 50 acres would have been worth today?

Dad went back to living with his family, who now lived on the second floor of a three-family dwelling in the Waterbury area. I never got too much information on what he did over the next several years as I'm not sure where he worked or even if he did work, only that he played a lot of cards at a fraternal organization called the Knights of Pythias. Whether that lack of information was attributed to the fact that he just couldn't remember or was just a function of him just not wanting to account for what he was doing at the time, I couldn't say.

In 1929 or 1930, amid the onset of the Great Depression, Dad went back into the dry-cleaning business, first for Harold Shalette Dry Cleaning and then Hart's Dry Cleaners, both in Waterbury. Hart's was more of a high-end dry cleaner, catering to the wealthy people in the area.

Meanwhile, Dad had become friendly with the manager of the Sears, Roebuck & Co. store in Waterbury, who lived on the top floor of the building he and his family lived in. This fellow took a liking to Dad and extended an ongoing, standing offer to work for him. So when Dad decided to hang up his dry-cleaning occupation for yet one more time, he took his neighbor up on the offer and went to work for him.

And so it came to pass that sometime in 1932, still in throes of the Depression, Dad started working in the paint department of Sears for $20 a week. After only a few weeks, the manager gave him a 10% raise to $22 per week, not bad for someone just starting out on the job. But then a week later, Dad was a victim of a companywide 10% salary cut, taking his pay down to $19.80 per week. About a month later the same kind of monetary phenomenon happened. Realizing what was about to take place, his manager gave him another $2.00 raise. But then, only a week later, a notice came down from headquarters that there was going to be yet another 10% cut in salary for everybody, leaving Dad with an ongoing math problem and an overall dwindling salary of $19.60. Not keen on the sense that he was making less money than when he started despite his two pay raises and that his salary was clearly moving in the wrong direction, Dad said goodbye to Sears and the paint business in search of another opportunity.

His old friend Leo Blumen, with whom he went to Florida and bought the grocery store, had gone to work for a convenience or sundry-type store called Allen's Cut-Rate. Making around $70 per week managing a store in nearby Bristol, Connecticut, which was pretty good money in those days, Leo suggested to him that he contact Allen Johnson, the owner of the chain, to see if there was a management opportunity at any of his other stores. Dad followed Leo's advice, and sure enough. Johnson hired him to start in 2 weeks.

Meanwhile, Dad's brother Lou had quit his job at Thom McAn's and was now selling insurance. It was a new, special kind of insurance called Investors Syndicate, which offered a savings plan as part of the policy. So, over the two weeks prior to starting at the Allen's Cut-Rate job, Dad figured he might as well try his hand at selling some insurance policies as well. In that two-week span, he tapped into some of his friends and ended up selling a bunch of policies, netting him a commission of $300 or so. Enticed by this insurance opportunity potential, he called Johnson to tell him that he wasn't going to take the job after all.

Well, as he put it himself, after another week or two of selling insurance, Dad ran out of friends and even acquaintances, and realized that this gig might not be the opportunity that it was cracked up to be. With his charm and flare for selling, he no doubt would have been very successful in pursuing this as a career. He just didn't see himself taking the cold-call route, going out and soliciting.

Bravely, Dad went back to Johnson and told the chain owner that he would like to reconsider and take the job after all. Johnson was not too pleased, telling him that he ought to throw him out of his office, but nevertheless Johnson agreed. Yet another example of how Dad had a knack for talking his way into things.

He started as assistant manager at Allen's Cut-Rate store in New Haven, Connecticut, about 45 minutes away from Waterbury. And as he tells it, he had quite a first day.

> I reported to work in the New Haven store on a
> Monday morning at 8:00 or 8:30 when the store opened
> up. And my first transaction for the company was a
> real beauty.
>
> Allen Johnson used to live in New Haven, but his
> office was in Waterbury. On Saturdays, he would first
> go to his office in Waterbury and then make the rounds

to all of his stores to pick up the money they had taken in that week. He had about six or seven stores at the time.

Since he lived in New Haven, on Monday morning early, he would come to the New Haven store before the banks opened and leave the money to be deposited in the New Haven bank so he could cover the checks he was going to send out the following week. He would have the manager go over to the bank around the corner to deposit it.

Johnson came in and chatted with me and Joe Goldstein, the manager, and then left for his office in Waterbury. So Joe says, "You might as well be useful. Take this over to the bank (which was about a block away) and make the deposit."

So I took the bag of money and went over to the bank and made the deposit. I noticed there was a lot of activity toward the back of the bank, quite a few people there, but I didn't pay any attention to it at the time and walked back.

But, after this precarious situation continued to weigh on me, about 11 o'clock, I said, "Joe, I don't know, I made that deposit, but there were a lot of people in the bank." He says, "Holy mackerel!" and ran right over there, but the bank was already shut down. It turned out all the banks were closing.

So my first official task at Allen's Cut-Rate was to make a deposit that they never got back, heh…heh. They lost all that money.

The good news is that Dad's days at Allen's Cut-Rate got better. Despite getting off on the wrong foot with Johnson and starting out with a rocky first day, things worked out pretty well there. After working in the New Haven store for six months, he was transferred to a store in Boston.

When he first got to Boston, Dad moved into a rooming house with some of his fellow managers working at other Allen's Cut-Rate stores. But then when his brother Harry came up to Boston to go to Tufts Dental School, Dad ended up sharing an apartment with Harry and two other fellows.

Soon after, Dad was promoted to manager of yet another store in Boston, the one on Beacon Street. He described the Beacon Street store as being very small, with not enough room for storage of any surplus inventory. Consequently, all inventory storage was downstairs, that could only be accessed through a trap door right near the front of the store. Dad recalled that this made life at the store very difficult. Once a week, merchandise in wooden boxes would be delivered by truck at night, sometimes as many as 30 or 40 boxes. And then the next morning, starting at 7:00 am before the store opened, all this merchandise had to be carried downstairs, which was a big job in itself, especially going down the shaky, thin staircase with a box or two in hand. Then, throughout the day, they would bring up boxes when needed. And every time they brought up a box, because the trap door was right in the front of the store right near the general entranceway, they needed to close the store temporarily. First somebody needed to lock the front door, then open up the trap door, then bring up the box, then restock the merchandise, then close the trap door, and then re-open the store. Dad had to put up with this arduous process for over a year, until the summer of 1935 when he was transferred back to manage the New Haven store where he originally started.

Once back in New Haven, Dad rented a house nearby in the resort town of Woodmont and brought his mother and father down to stay with him for the summer. "Al-truistic" to the core, he took his family's welfare to heart as he always did and made sure they were cared for. A true mensch and loving son, through and through.

Shortly after he started back working at the Allen Cut-Rate store in New Haven, Dad became very suspicious of something going on in the store. As he tells it…

I was there only one week, and I sensed something was wrong in this store. I couldn't put my finger on it, but it bothered me. I could not fathom what was wrong in that store, what was going on.

There were two girls working in there, not youngsters. One was single, an Italian girl, engaged to my former immediate boss Joe Goldstein, who had been managing the store whom I replaced. He was the same guy who on my first day at Allen Cut-Rate asked me to make a deposit at the bank, which the company never got back because the bank was in the process of going under. Anyway, he was transferred to the warehouse in Hamden, Connecticut, from which they used to ship all the merchandise out to the stores. He was going to become an executive of the company. The other gal was a nice Irish married woman.

During the time I was with Allen, in those three years, we caught a lot of girls stealing… stealing this, stealing that. But these two gals had been at the store since it first opened and seemed to be good, reliable, long-term employees.

Well, one Sunday afternoon, I happened to be walking in Woodmont and bumped into Allen Johnson. We sat down for a soda. He says, "How do you like it down there?" I said that I liked it very much, but I said, "You know, Mr. Johnson, there's something going on in this store. There's something wrong, I just can't put my finger on it. I don't know if the girls there are stealing, but there is something wrong in the store."

He said, "Those girls have been with me for 10, 12 years. I'll stake my life on the honesty of those two girls. That's the first store I opened. You won't find anything awry with those girls."

About a month later, I hit on what it was. We used to sell perfume in bulk. We had big fancy bottles in a beautiful display… Christmas Eve, Chanel No. 5, and what-you-macall-it, Evening in Paris, all the big names. All different kinds, a beautiful display. Customers would come in and ask for an ounce of whatever brand they preferred, and the salesgirls would pour out the perfumes into tiny, little bottles of that size and give them to the customers. I want to say it was $1.59 or $1.69 an ounce or something like that.

Every Monday, the usual procedure was to take an inventory of the entire store with lists we had and order merchandise that had been sold or that needed replacing. We would order only what we needed. So visibly if you saw an empty space, you knew that item had been sold out and needed to be replenished. Or if you saw only one item there and knew you had to have four, you ordered three. But the bulk perfume was an exception. We would reorder the perfume in bulk for the display bottles, but only if it went down to a certain level. You would order four ounces of this, that, etc.

But then one morning, taking orders, I came to the perfume and I noticed something. The girls used to get a commission on a lot of the products that had big profit margins on them, one of which was the perfume. There was a 10% commission on all bulk perfume. How they kept track of it was if the manager was in the store, she would write out Evening in Paris, $1.59, or Chanel No. 5, $1.69, and the manager would sign the slip. If neither the manager nor assistant manager were in, the other girl would sign the slip.

Every Monday, I went downstairs and made up the payroll, and the girls gave me all their commission tickets. Each commissionable item in the store had a little sticker on it with "A, B, C, D, E, F, G," such as lipstick, perfume, etc., and each one denoted a different amount... 5 cents, 8 cents commission. The amount could be 1%, 3%, etc. And so the girls would tear off the tab from the sticker and give them to me at the end of the week so I would tabulate their commission and make that part of their salary.

So one day, while taking inventory on the perfume, it hit me heh…heh, what was wrong with the store. I would look at the bottles, and if they were half full, I wouldn't order any. If they were down to 4 ounces of it, I would order 4 ounces of what perfume was missing. So, while inventorying these perfumes, it hit me like a ton of bricks. Here I am looking at bulk perfume sales every week... $30, $40, $50, $100 worth of perfume sold for each girl, and I'm not reordering perfume or anywhere near the amount that these slips designate is being sold! Lo and behold, I realized I was not signing off on that amount, and that sure enough most of the slips had been signed by the other girl. They were taking these slips and writing out sales for perfumes that were never sold, and I would automatically – like Joe used to do – take them in and give them the commission on that.

So I got on the phone to Allen Johnson and told him we had a problem and he better come over right away. He came to the store and brought Joe with him. I took Allen downstairs to my accounting area and showed him exactly what the situation was. I showed him the figures and the slips and told him I hadn't ordered any bulk perfume in weeks. He double-checked his records on how much perfume he had ordered over the past year, compared to his inventory to what had supposedly been sold and of course he realized what had been going on. So he realized these girls were stealing.

In the meantime, he had left Joe Goldstein upstairs with the girls. When it was closing time, Allen Johnson went upstairs and said, "Girls, I want to see you both first thing in the morning. We have to discuss something." Of course, the girls never came back.

Joe remained with the company and eventually married the girl anyway heh…heh, but I don't know what happened afterwards.

But I was sorry that it had occurred, 'cause I had to hire and break in two new girls, and that was quite a job. Then a couple of months later, we rented a larger store across the street – I had four or five girls working for me, and we were doing a big job at that time.

Meanwhile, Dad became friendly with another store manager at Allen's Cut-Rate named Theodore or Teddy Schwartz, who he knew from Boston and who was also transferred down to New Haven to manage another store that Allen's Cut-Rate had opened there. The two hung out together a lot when they weren't working and ended up sharing an apartment. And as both their business and personal relationship progressed, sure enough in 1936, learning about a vacant store with a good location in nearby downtown New Britain, the two of them decided to leave Allen's Cut-Rate to go into business together and open up their own sundry-type store there. They called it Bond Cut-Rate.

While Johnson had a reputation for being a tough cookie and leaned hard on all his managers, he was always nice to Dad. For Dad had built up a good rapport with Johnson over the three years or so he worked for him and indeed had earned his trust, especially since he solved the mysterious internal stealing ring perpetrated by Allen Cut-Rate's two long-time female employees, no doubt saving a lot of money for the appreciative owner.

But despite all that Dad did for him and the strong rapport they had together, when Johnson found out that Dad and Teddy were breaking away to open up their own store, any fondness he might have had for Dad went out the window as Johnson turned into a ruthless competitor. At the time, there was already an Allen's Cut-Rate store in New Britain located on the other side of town. But with the opening of Bond Cut-Rate, the cut-throat Johnson got so mad that he ended up renting out space across the street from Bond Cut-Rate and opening up another store there in New Britain for the sole purpose to drive Bond out of business. As Dad explained it, it was best described as a "spite store." Every time Bond Cut-Rate advertised a special, Allen's Cut-Rate undercut the price.

The two Cut-Rate stores ended up fighting quite a battle, and Allen's Cut-Rate almost prevailed. But thanks to an insurance windfall on a fire at the Bond Cut-Rate store that didn't really cause any damage, but that Dad and Teddy were somehow able to legally finagle and collect on from the insurance company for about $20,000, the two entrepreneurs were able to flourish. With these extra funds, the so-called "David" of Cut-Rate stores was able to bring in more unique merchandise than Allen's was able to offer, such as billfolds and flashlights, and thus attract enough business to be competitive with their counterpart "Goliath" across the street and stay afloat.

What's funny is that over 30 years later, while at the celebration of my college graduation, Dad and the father of one of my close college buddies Don Miller recognized one another and discovered that they had actually worked across the street from each other in New Britain at the two competitive Cut-Rate stores. Don's father, Irving, started working at Allen Cut-Rate shortly after my dad left there. What a small world.

Come spring 1939, after three years of running Bond Cut-Rate and making some inroads but not setting the world on fire, Dad realized that while the sundry business may provide enough earnings to make a decent living, it had its limitations. It was never going to be the ticket to success he wanted for himself. So instead, with an eye toward opening up a haberdashery store in a vacant space across the street next to Allen Cut-Rate, he convinced his partner Teddy to agree to buy out his share of Bond Cut-Rate. Even though, as was the case with most of the other businesses he had previously ventured into, he didn't really know the first thing about the haberdashery business, on a whim but with a vision, he thought such a type of store just might be something that would be a unique, welcome addition to the growing, bustling town of New Britain.

Chapter 6
THE GRAND OPENING

AND SO IT CAME TO PASS IN THE FALL OF 1939, Dad opened a haberdashery in downtown New Britain. He called it Regal Men's Shop. He came up with the name Regal because he felt it conveyed a premium image. Evidently, he wanted to imply the notion that it was the type of store that sold clothes fit for a king. This was to be his first foray into the world of retail men's clothing, around which he would start to build a budding organization and hopefully pave the way for a flourishing business. It all started out with this one store in New Britain, Connecticut.

While today New Britain, or to use the local pronunciation "New Brit-ANN," much like other towns in Connecticut such as Waterbury, Wallingford, Meriden, and Bridgeport, is considered one of those industrial cities of yesteryear, at the time it was a bustling place. Home for Stanley Tools, Fafnir Bearings, and a plethora of other tool-related factories, New Britain became known as the "Hardware City of the World," famous for its screws, nuts, and bolts. And because of its extensive industry and growing population, back then the town for its size had a busy downtown area with a lot of retail commerce to show for it. But other than the local department store Raphael's, there weren't all that many retail options for men's clothing. So, Dad's hope was that Regal Men's Shop would establish a strong presence in town and prove to be a successful venture.

My father was working late into the night ahead of his grand opening set for 9:00 the next morning. He was giving his attention to every detail and putting the finishing touches on his store window displays. Like any haberdasher worth his clothes will tell you, what's on display in the store window front is an important part of merchandising and the design of it is an art unto itself. It's all about the presentation. And while he had hired a design consultant out of New York to help him with the basic layout of the windows and give him some pointers, he continued to adjust here and there in the quest to come up with just the right combination and allure of garments and mannequins to catch and engage the eye of a potential customer.

Around 2:00 am or so, just as Dad was about to call it a night, seemingly out of nowhere, this well-dressed fellow in a suit and tie emerged out of the foggy Connecticut night and proceeded to kind of stumble his way up to the window, giving off the impression that he had had a few too many, as Dad explained it. At first, the guy approaching didn't say anything, but nonchalantly just stood there kind of frozen, as though he was imitating one of the mannequins in the window, and just gazed up at my father for a few seconds in bewilderment. But after taking a few moments to size up the situation and continue to stumble around a little bit, with determined conviction he abruptly shouted out, "Hey mister, I want to be your first customer!"

True to his word, even though the store hadn't officially opened and before my father could even jump down from the window and invite him in, the guy went into the store and made a beeline for the ties, where he promptly picked one out to go along with his suit and said, "What do I owe ya?" And so, Regal's first purchase was in the books.

What's more, not only was this guy Dad's first customer, but he ended up becoming his best friend. That initial transaction kicked off an instant alliance. They were roughly the same age and seemed to be cut from the same cloth. Right off the bat, the two hit it off and became very close. His name was Yale Sabel, a lawyer by trade. The way my father described him, he had a tremendous personality and the gift of gab. Always the life of the party, he was the type of guy who would take on the role of emcee at a gathering, a guy who would always leaving you laughing.

From what I understand, even though I never really got any of the juicy details, Dad and Yale were quite the dynamic duo. They formed a solid alliance, gallivanting around town, playing cards all night or hitting the clubs and wooing the ladies. They often took trips to the Berkshires, a resort in the mountainous area of western Massachusetts encompassing the towns of Lenox, Stockbridge, Pittsfield, Sheffield, and Great Barrington, where they would play golf and otherwise entertain themselves. If only I had more tales to tell about these two guys... but I figure those must be among the many untold stories Dad couldn't share. I can only imagine the fun the two must have had together.

So things were pretty good for Dad in those days of the early 1940s. With that first purchase Yale made, Regal Men's Shop got off to a burgeoning start and ended up doing pretty well. Good enough for Dad to open up a couple of additional Regal Men's Shops shortly thereafter in the nearby Connecticut towns of Middletown and Manchester, which he was able to do through the ongoing credit extended to him through his bank. He had established a good relationship with the bank's lending officer. And because he would make it a priority to always pay back his loans on time, he was able to continue to go back to the well for more and more credit, paving the way for his expansion. He would always tell me that if I ever took out a loan from a bank, always make sure to pay it back on time. That was the key to establishing a good precedent and solid relationship with the bank.

But Dad would soon hit somewhat of a sophomore slump. While the Middletown store got off to a good start, business was very slow in the Manchester store and sadly he ended up selling it only three months after he opened it. Apparently, the town of Manchester wasn't the type of location he thought it would be. But just the same, he had two stores that were making hay, and he was on the map.

Meanwhile, the dynamic duo of Al and Yale continued their adventures together, both single and carefree, enjoying the highs of their good life. Yet as time went on, Yale was unfortunately stricken with some kind of rare, mysterious skin disease that caused him a lot of suffering. From time to time, he would break out with rashes all over his body. In fact, his condition, which was never officially diagnosed and for which they could never seem to find a cure, was so serious and distressing that it was referred to as the "Oy-oy-oy disease." But despite his physical ailments, Yale didn't let it hold him back from cavorting around with my father and thriving in their social circle. The two were still always out on the town, living it up and going strong.

Chapter 7

YOU'RE IN THE ARMY NOW

WHY DAD NEVER TRIED TO GET OUT of going into the Army was something he claimed he could never understand about himself. Especially for a wheeler-dealer guy who was so adept at talking his way into and out of everything, it was an inconsistency with his modus operandi that he couldn't explain. To use his own words, "I think in my entire life, it was the most questionable thing I had ever done. Whether I had just not given it enough thought, or it didn't even dawn on me to try and be exempt. I don't know. I had so many, many reasons not to go into the Army and many ways of staying out of the Army."

One of those reasons was that Dad had his parents living with him, and his father was practically blind, which in the eyes of the Army would have been considered a significant hardship case. Another reason was that he himself struggled with on-and-off leg pain, which if he had it checked out would probably have booted him off the draft list.

What's more, his friend Yale had connections. Yale's brother-in-law Marty Horwitz, who was in the insurance business and carried Dad's personal and business insurance, was chairman of the Draft Appeal Board of the State of Connecticut. Before taking in his parents, Dad would have meals at the Horwitz house three or four times a week along with Yale. In essence, being so close to Marty, Dad basically had a built-in insurance policy of another sort, of being able to avoid the draft. No doubt Marty would have taken care of it if Dad had broached the subject.

Nevertheless, there must have been some type of inner force, his subconscious, or something deep down inside of him that inspired and drove Dad in the direction of the armed forces and kept him from focusing on how to beat the system. Perhaps it was the Abraham inside of him, the Father of All Nations, who was subconsciously seeking to lead his people to a peaceful Promised Land. Or it was his patriotic spirit that spoke to him, his loyal sense of responsibility, or feeling of obligation to serve his country. Or perhaps it was the whole anticipated experience of it all, the spirit of adventure, to go to new places and see other parts of the world that was the inertia behind it all. Similar to the journey he took in Florida, here was yet another opportunity to go out and experience the world and drink up what life's cup had to offer.

But whatever it was, Dad never said anything to Marty, never put any wheels in motion to figure a way out of it, or never even seemed to think about avoiding it. And so, as it happened, in the spring of 1943, having just turned 35, just one year shy of the cutoff age for the armed forces, Dad was drafted into the U.S. Army.

The reality of what lay ahead for him quickly set in. It was as though there was a sudden realization that indeed he was in the army now, a looming plight he had got himself into, so he focused his negotiating efforts on getting an extension and trying to put off the inevitable. By leveraging his hardship situation with his parents, Dad was able to put off reporting for duty for four months until August.

During that time, Dad had to make sure to put steps in place to keep his Regal Men's Shops afloat and plan for a smooth transition for someone else to manage the stores while he was away. So, in his "Al-truistic" way, always doing what he could for his family, he brought in his brother Lou, who was still in the insurance business at the time and lived in Middletown, to manage the new Middletown store. And he brought in his brother-in-law Harry Steinman, his sister Rose's husband, to manage the original New Britain store. Harry and Rose had fallen on some hard times, having owned a sundry store in Waterbury that had gone bankrupt and then having opened up a men's clothing store in nearby Torrington, Connecticut that Dad had helped them with but didn't quite make it. And so that summer of 1943, he spent a considerable amount of time getting the new familial managers settled and prepped in their respective stores.

The extension also allowed him to spend more time at one of his favorite haunts, The Berkshire Hills Country Club in western Massachusetts, with his buddy Yale. From Memorial Day on throughout the summer, the dynamic duo would make the Berkshires their home base and pretty much just play golf, play cards, and socialize there. They liked the country club life. But every Monday morning they would make the two-hour drive back to New Britain together. While Yale, as a lawyer, would attend to his respective affairs, Dad would make the rounds to the New Britain and Middletown stores, talking to Lou and Harry and doing what needed to be done to take care of business. And then the two would stay over in Connecticut that Monday night and put in a full day on Tuesday, but come Tuesday night they hopped back in the car and made their way back to the Berkshires, staying there until the next Monday. Basically, they only worked two days a week. Not a bad routine.

While Dad was supposed to report to the army in August, somehow in his masterful way he was able to get a further extension for a few more months. But as it came to pass, come November, he was called up and left New Britain with a group of 35 other draftees bound for Fort Devens in Massachusetts.

What happens to him in the Army is best told by my father himself, as it's another one of my favorite stories of his. As he put it, "It was a once-in-a-lifetime story."

I got there on a Friday, got my uniform, went through orientation, and was assigned along with the other 35 fellow draftees from New Britain to a large barracks that held about 100 guys.

It was only two days later on Sunday morning around 11 o'clock as I was just sitting around in the barracks continuing to lament with the other guys about our situation, when a soldier comes in and shouts if there's an Abraham Levin in the house, that there's a phone call for him. As you'd expect, they called you by your formal name in the Army. The call was from this guy Davey Melnick, whom I had met briefly about 10 years ago in 1933 when I was in Boston working for Allen Cut-Rate. I had become pretty friendly with Melnick's brother over the years, but hadn't spoken to Davey since 1936 when I left Boston and went back to Connecticut. It was kind of mysterious that all of a sudden out of the blue here was this guy Melnick calling me, and even how Melnick knew I was there at Fort Devens.

Anyway, Melnick, who was still working out of Boston, explained to me over the phone that he had somehow gotten word through his brother that I was at Fort Devens and was calling to invite me out for dinner, for some Chinese food. That in itself was enough to draw my attention and accept his offer, as I loved Chinese, it was my favorite. Melnick must have remembered.

Apparently, Melnick had some friends who were officers at Fort Devens and was able to arrange a pass for me. So I took a train to Boston that night and met him for dinner. We got caught up with each other over dinner, and then after dinner went to Melnick's office nearby where we discussed my situation and what Melnick could possibly do to help me, given his connections at the base. Melnick asks me, "So Al what do you want to do?" At which I responded, "What do you mean what do I want to do? What can I do?" So then, right in front of me, Melnick picks up the phone and calls a friend of his at Fort Devens to see what he can work out, and while on the phone to his friend at the base does a sidebar with me and asks, "So Al is it all right if they send you to New London for basic training and then bring you back here for the rest of your duty, probably some type of administrative job, and you won't be shipped out?" Seeming too good to be true, naturally I gave him a confirming nod. Being in the army for only two days, this was an incredible proposition.

So I don't have to tell you, I go back to the barracks in pretty good spirits. And I wait and I wait. Just about every night, about 2:00 am, a soldier storms into the barracks and wakes everybody up and says "Shipping Orders," and then calls various names, where you're going, and what time you leave. Well, almost a month goes by and my name isn't called. I'm practically the only one left in the barracks from the original New Britain troops who I came in there with. But finally, one night, my name is called but no destination is mentioned. My name is the only one called, so I figure of course it must be my special assignment and that I must be going to New London.

Well, guess what? I find myself being grouped together with about 300 other guys from different barracks, and it turned out we weren't going to New London. Rather, we boarded a train going to Fort McClellan in Anniston, Alabama, for infantry training, which was the on-deck circle for being shipped out into battle.

Heh…heh! So much for my friend Davey Melnick's influence. I was going back down South, an area of the country I hadn't been since leaving Florida in 1927.

Shortly after I get down to Fort McClellan, the occasional reoccurring pain in my leg kicks up. That same pain that I should have checked out beforehand and possibly could have used to help me get out of being drafted in the first place had come back. I reported to sick hall, but the doctor or whatever so-called medical professional on duty there didn't give me the time of day and dismissed the pain as nothing. But my leg kept bothering me, and finally after several weeks of talking to this guy and that guy and working the system, I was able to get an appointment slip to the main office of the medical building.

The morning that I had the appointment to go to the medical building for my "what-you-macall-it," I got up, went to the PX bright and early at 6:00 am, had breakfast, then bought a newspaper and went over to the medical building. It was a great big room, with a banister along the walls and offices all around. I checked in at the reception desk and then sat down and started reading my paper. A lot of other soldiers started coming in, all waiting to be examined. About 8:00, this very dignified soldier walks in, he was a colonel, white hair and distinguished, and goes into his office. Apparently, he was the head physician there. The next thing I know, a couple of minutes later the colonel comes back out and yells "Where's my newspaper?" None of the company clerks had it nor did they know where it was, as apparently the colonel's paper never got delivered that day. Overhearing all this, I stood up and offered him mine. Before I knew it, one of the clerks came running over to me, snatched the newspaper out of my hands and handed it to over to the colonel, who gave me an appreciative nod of sorts and then went back into his office.

I kept waiting and waiting for my appointment. I must have been waiting out there for more than an hour. Upon following up with the soldier at the reception desk that I checked in with, I was told that the doctor I was scheduled to see was way behind and that I would need to be patient. Meanwhile, a little while later, the colonel comes out of his office again and sees me still waiting out there and after going up and conversing with the soldier at the reception desk, the next thing I know I'm being escorted into the colonel's office for my appointment. As I walked into the examination room, having noticed that I wasn't 21 or 22 like most of the other soldiers, he says to me "So soldier, I see you're quite a bit older, what's your story?"

We start talking, and somehow, I end up telling him about how I was in the men's clothing business in Connecticut, but was drafted when I was 35. Upon the mention of men's clothing, his eyes seemed to light up and he says, "Geez, I've been looking for some decent gloves to wear as it can get kind of cold down here during the winter, but they're hard to find around here. You wouldn't know where I could get some would ya?"

I said sure if the colonel would like, I'd be happy to send you a couple of pairs. "Is there anything else you would like?" I asked.

"Do you sell men's shorts, I mean like briefs?"

I said "Sure, you got it!"

Then he said to me, "Let's look at that leg of yours. We'll want to get some X-rays today, and then when you come back we'll see what's going on."

Well believe me, as soon as I got out of there, I couldn't get to a phone fast enough. I called my brother Lou and told him to send me down a shipment of the stuff right away—the gloves, the briefs, plus a couple of other accessories for good measure like some undershirts and handkerchiefs.

To cut the story short, I was seeing him every couple of weeks, just about each time bringing him a new shipment of clothes—ties, belts, socks, jeans, more briefs, more what-you-macall-its, you name it. By the end of my 17-week stint of infantry training, I must have outfitted the guy with a complete wardrobe and then some. For his wife, I even threw in some beautiful umbrellas, which I got from some friends of mine in New York.

Meanwhile, the X-rays of my leg turned out negative. And the colonel could never find anything really wrong with it. I guess it was one of those types of pains that just comes up from time to time that you can't explain. But fortunately it did subside and get better over time.

At the end of my training, I got a pass to go home for 12 days, but then I was to report to Fort Dix in New Jersey, from where it seemed inevitable that I was to be shipped overseas. I was pretty upset.

But just before I left, I received one more package of clothes from up north, so I went to the colonel's office to drop it off. He couldn't get over all the packages I was bringing him, and always joked with me that this has got to stop.

"Well," I said, "this is it. I'm leaving." And I proceeded to tell him of the orders I had just received.

He looks at me for a bit, and then picks up the phone and speaks to some party on the other end, not sure who it was, and says, "I got a man here who is 35 years old and the condition he's in with his leg and all, and well I don't think we can conceivably ship him out."

As I listened to him on the phone, I recalled a similar attempt by my so-called friend Davey Melnick that didn't quite come to fruition, but rather might have been the reason I was down here in the first place. So, I wasn't getting my hopes up.

But the next thing I know, the colonel hangs up the phone and tells me "You're Class D now soldier, you can never be shipped out of the country." And in the same breath asks me, "Why don't you stay here and be my clerk?" It was unbelievable!

And so it came to pass that Dad never saw battle. After going home for his 12-day leave, he came back to Fort McClellan down in Alabama to work as an assistant company clerk for the colonel doing odd jobs and administrative stuff. After a couple weeks, he had his sister Rose and a friend of hers drive his car down from Connecticut. And in no time at all, he had embraced and learned the ins-and-outs of his new assignment and as such, especially having a car down there, pretty much had his own lay-of-the-land at the base.

**Abraham Levin serving as a company clerk
in the Army at Fort McClellan in Alabama**

Dad ended up spending the remainder of his time in the army in Alabama, far away from any battlefield or any type of danger, but rather doing menial administrative tasks and playing cards at night at the Officers Club. But all the time, realizing how fortunate he had been. Fortunate that he had bought a newspaper that morning and brought it with him to his medical appointment; that the colonel never received his regular newspaper that day; that the army physician whom he was supposed to see was running behind schedule and as such he was instead seen by the colonel, perhaps because of the fact he had given the colonel his newspaper; that the colonel needed some gloves; that he had gone into the menswear business prior to his stint in the army; and that he had that one last package of clothes to give to the colonel before he was supposed to be shipped out to Fort Dix.

Yet again, Dad had worked his way out of a tenuous situation. In this case, it was lifesaving. For just about everybody who had been shipped out from Fort Dix, including practically all those fellow New Britain guys he had originally been drafted with and went to Fort Devens with, ended up being wiped out in battle.

Chapter 8

THE OY-OY-OY DISEASE TAKES ITS TOLL

SOMETIME IN THE FALL OF 1945 after the war ended, after he had served in the armed forces for just about two years, Dad came back to Connecticut and resumed the same type of life he had when he first left for the army. He took back the reins at Regal, overseeing both the New Britain and Middletown stores, with his brother-in-law Harry and his brother Lou continuing to manage those stores respectively. The two stores continued to do pretty well, and he had eyes toward possible further expansion.

Dad continued to pal around with his buddy Yale, who unfortunately was still suffering from his case of the "Oy-oy-oy disease." Over the years, it had gotten worse, with still no cure in sight. It got so bad that periodically he had to spend a week or two at a time in the hospital. But their friendship endured, including continuing on occasion to go up to the Berkshires together, their home away from home. I can only imagine the times they had, all the ladies they must have met.

My old man must have been quite the chick magnet! Even though Dad was getting on in years and saw himself as a confirmed bachelor, no doubt he was seen as the ideal eligible candidate for matrimony. A good-looking fellow who had never been married, owned his own business, and was a former soldier, he must have been considered quite the catch.

While up at a Berkshires resort on July 4th weekend in 1948, the stars were aligned for Dad to meet Nikki (alias Bernice) Schenck from Great Neck, New York. She wasn't going to go at first, thinking she wouldn't know anybody. But her friend kept nagging her, and finally at the last minute she agreed to go and arrived on Friday of that weekend.

They didn't discover each other until that Saturday evening at a big shindig that the resort threw for its guests. Even though Dad was quite a bit older—she knew he was older but didn't really have a feel for how much older—the two hit it off immediately and were together that whole evening until the party broke up. They continued to get to know each other for the whole next day on Sunday up until the holiday weekend was over.

From then on, they would see each other in New York City, where Nikki worked in the entertainment business and where he would sometimes go for business to meet with his clothing vendors. So, whenever Dad went to the city, which was suddenly becoming much more often, he would call her and ask her to meet him. They often went out for Chinese at this place called Lum Fungs.

Nikki came up with a nickname for him, Aloysius, meaning famous warrior, but spelled it "Alouisius," incorporating not only Al's name but his brother Lou's as well. The names of two Levin Bros combined in one.

And so, as it came to pass, at the ripe-old age of 41, after holding out for many years as a bona fide bachelor, Dad finally took the plunge and asked Nikki to marry him. She was only 25, 16 years his junior. So, while in those days a woman who was 25 was considered as bordering on becoming an "old maid," others teased that Dad "robbed the cradle" because of their age difference. Regardless of all the ribbing, they knew they were meant to be together and were married on May 29, 1949, at the Warwick Hotel in New York.

**Al and Nikki are married at the Warwick Hotel
in New York City on May 29, 1949**

With Dad being on in years and the biological clock ticking away for the so-called old maid Nikki, the two set out to work on having kids right away, as my sister Deborah was born in June of 1950, and yours truly came along two years later in May of '52.

In the case of both of our births, when it was time, Dad just dropped my mother off at the hospital to "do her thing." Then he went to work, and came back once we were born. That's the way it was done in those days. Unlike today, men didn't typically come into the hospital and accompany women during the birth of their child. If they did come in, it wasn't as though they would be with her in the delivery room, but rather they would likely just pace around anxiously in the waiting room.

As a married man and new father, one would think life would have been quite a bit different for Dad. For not only did he have the increasing demands of his growing business, but also now he had the responsibilities that came along with being a husband and father. Yet, while he embraced and assumed these new added responsibilities and seemed to be able to deliver on them when he had to, he didn't have to stray too far from his previous carefree, independent lifestyle that he was so accustomed to and treasured. He had a knack for balancing his husband and fatherly duties with everything else, always coming out looking good, at least in the eyes of his adoring wife. He was kind of lucky in that sense, in that my mother still let my father continue being Al. That is, he still found time to get out to play golf and cards, still took his yearly golf excursions with the boys to Bermuda, and still saw Yale frequently.

While Dad and Yale weren't really out cavorting around anymore, the two remained close. They would still play a lot of golf together. And Yale would frequently come over for dinner. But as time passed, sometime in the mid-to-late fifties, the mysterious "Oy-oy-oy disease" eventually took its toll. Yale's condition got worse, as he was spending most of his time in the hospital, and he eventually passed away. No doubt his good buddy Al was at his bedside. While I never thought of my father has an overly emotional guy per se, I imagine he was pretty crushed at the loss of his good friend Yale, especially since he was taken so young.

To show his love and dedication for his friend, even though neither one of them was particularly religious, Dad got some support and financial backing from some of the other members of our local temple in New Britain, Temple B'nai Israel, and somehow arranged for a Sephardic Torah to be composed and shipped over from Israel and donated to the temple in Yale's name. How this all came about, how he thought of a Torah in the first place to donate in his memory, and why it was a Sephardic Torah as opposed to the more common Ashkenazi Torah, I'm not quite sure. I suspect because it was so beautiful and unique. It was certainly an unusual, precious gift.

Maybe the fact that his name was Abraham had something to do with why he chose a Torah to donate. In representation of the father of all nations, perhaps he just wanted to spread the words of the Torah, the body of historical learnings and principles that provides a foundation on which the Jewish religion is built. Containing the five books that God handed down to Moses (Genesis, Exodus, Leviticus, Numbers, and Deuteronomy), the Torah, for which the translation in English is to teach or instruct, consists of God's various teachings and guidelines for the Jewish people to follow.

It takes a while for someone to craft and assemble a new Torah—many months, sometimes more than a year. It requires the work of an artist of sorts, a professional scribe called a *sofer*, who has impeccable handwriting skills, steady hands, and has rigorously trained under strict calligraphic guidelines for the creation of such a masterpiece. And of course, beyond all else, the scribe must be pious of the highest order, taking the utmost pride and devotion in both his religion and his work. In fact, to show his devout level of piety and commitment, it is customary for the *sofer* to immerse himself in a *mikvah*, a bath of natural water to purify his body, before embarking upon this work.

Further, it's then customary for the scribe to continue to submerge himself into the *mikvah* every day throughout the whole process prior to writing the name of God. Specifically, as he writes the text each day, he leaves a space for every time God's name is to appear. And then at the end of the day he immerses himself in the *mikvah* before going back and filling in God's name.

The Torah scripture is composed on sheets of specially cured parchment or vellum known as *klaf* that comes from the skin of a kosher animal, which are sewn together with sinews to create one long scroll. The sofer dips a quill pen into a receptacle of black ink before he carefully and artfully details each letter on the parchment, using another Torah as a guide from which to copy each letter the exact same way. When completely finished, the *sofer* will have written a total of exactly 304,805 letters. Supposedly, if one letter is off or missing, or if there's any kind of smudge or incongruity, the entire Torah scroll is not kosher and needs to be reworked.

It wasn't until over a year later, late in 1961, that the new Torah arrived at Temple B'nai Israel. It was quite a bit different from the traditional Ashkenazi Torah we had been used to seeing, which is dressed in a decorated and embroidered velvet cloak that serves as its mantle and has two wooden shafts or rollers called the *atzei chayim* that extend beyond the top and bottom of the scroll and are used as handles to hold the Torah and scroll it from portion to portion. Rather, with this being a Sephardic Torah, there were no extended handles, but instead its scrolls were encased in a silver cylindrical shell and topped with an ornate, resplendent silver crown. With its shiny, gleaming silver casing and majestic crown, this Torah was so exquisite and unique that the temple gave it top billing, placing it right in the middle of the four other Torahs in the ark within the main sanctuary. It was unlike any others I had ever seen.

The Sephardic Torah donated to Temple B'nai Israel
in memory of my Dad's best friend Yale

The inside of the Sephardic Torah, which does not have any scroll handles

I remember, every time the ark was opened, looking in from the congregation, I would marvel at how that Torah clearly stood out on among the other Torahs, adorning the *bimah* (pulpit) with its glistening silver shell. Seeing that beautiful, majestic Torah stand out and shine the way it did left me with a sense of pride knowing that my father was the lead guy in bringing this magnificent masterpiece to the temple and that I was his son, the son of Abraham, and that our family would forever be linked to it.

This Torah was brought out of the ark and used only for special occasions, one of which was my bar mitzvah in 1965. As is traditionally the case in a bar mitzvah service, after a Torah is initially taken out of the ark and prior to the reading of it, the bar mitzvah boy is handed the Torah to hold it up in front of the congregation and then carry it up and down the sanctuary (a procession called the *hakafah*) to give the congregation an opportunity to kiss the Torah with their tallit or prayer books and give the bar mitzvah boy a little congratulatory pat on the back. In my case, however, the Sephardic Torah was a little too heavy for a small guy like me at the time to hold it up and walk with it throughout the sanctuary. So for the processional, I ended up holding and carrying another Torah, one of the Ashkenazi Torahs in the ark that was much lighter. But lo and behold, parading right in back of me was my father carrying that beautiful, glimmering Sephardic Torah. It was only appropriate that he marched with it, given that he was the one who was instrumental in acquiring it for the temple.

Chapter 9

STRAIGHTENING OUT THE BOW TIES

SOME OF THE EARLIEST MEMORIES I HAVE of my father date back to me sitting on the cover of the toilet seat in my parents' lime green-colored bathroom staring up at him, the guy who I always looked up to, standing at the sink looking into the mirrored medicine cabinet. He had the same routine all the time. First, he would fill up the sink with warm water, almost right up to the edge but always making sure to turn off the faucet just in time before there was any chance of overflowing. Then he would pick up a white aerosol can of Rise shaving cream in his right hand and, using circular motions, he would squirt out the thick, white soapy substance into the palm of his left hand and then proceed to smear it all over his face, making him a little scary looking. Then he would make all kinds of funny faces as he painstakingly glided his double-edged Schick razor across the contour of his facial terrain until every patch of whiskers had been accounted for, taking a break every so often to dip the razor into the sink of warm water and swish it around to clean off any accumulated gunk. When he was content that he had mowed down all of his stubble, he'd splash his face a couple of times with the soapy water from the sink to clear off any remaining shaving cream. He'd then open up the drain to get rid of the puffed-up bits of floating shaving cream and whisker-infused sink water, turn on the faucet to splash his face once more, this time with fresh water, and let the water continue to run in the sink to clear out any leftover traces of his shave. Then, as one final test to confirm that he had plucked out every whisker and was completely clean-shaven, he did the old two hands-over-the-face gesture, followed by a couple more pats on the cheeks, and then it was onto his next routine.

Dad would then pick up this apothecary-type bottle of a cloudy, greenish hair tonic called Trol that was almost the same color of the bathroom, give it a couple of hard shakes, put it over his head, turn it upside down, and gently shake out a couple of droplets onto his disheveled hair. And then with some of the stuff sometimes dripping down the side of his face, comb in hand and one eye half-closed, he attentively and meticulously went about trying to part his hair down the middle, which is the way he wore it back then.

Trol Hair Tonic that Dad used

Hair tonic was very popular back in the '50s and '60s. In addition to Trol, there were brands such as Vitalis, Jeris, Reuzel, and Clubman Prinaud. Today, hair tonic tends to be "old school," given way to the much hipper styling crèmes, mousses, and gels. But back in Dad's day, hair tonic was one of the major hair styling products of choice, claiming as well to remove dandruff, reverse baldness, and make hair grow longer and thicker. Trol's advertising slogan back then was ***Removes loose dandruff as it conTROLs the hair***.

As for me, I never really liked the stuff. For one thing, I was rather turned off by the color—had a hard time putting something green in my hair. Plus, I wasn't particularly keen on having some slime-like stuff dribbling down from my hair onto my face. Instead, for my pompadour, I opted for Brylcreem, which came in a red and white tube.

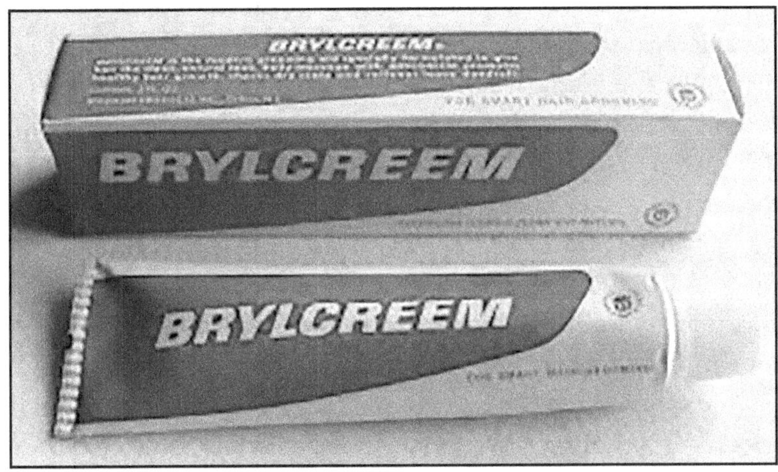

Brylcreem, the styling crème I used

As promoted in its tagline, ***A little dab'll do ya***. I specifically remember this one advertising campaign it had…

Brylcreem—A little dab'll do ya!
Use more only if you dare.
But watch out—The gals will all pursue ya!
They'll love to run their fingers through your hair!

When Dad wasn't travelling and on weekends when he wasn't playing golf, sitting on the covered toilet in his bathroom was how I would often start my day. That's where we would have a lot of our father-and-son chats. I would listen intently as he shared his ways of the world and answer a lot of my "why" questions about life. It's also where he would talk about his stores and teach me a little bit about business. And that's where I would share any problems or frustrations I had encountered in my young life. Where it would all come out if I was sad or bothered by something, to which Dad always used to tell me to keep my chin up and stay in there pitching. I liked that he used a baseball metaphor. Anyway, that's where I first learned about his interest and vision to go into the men's and boys' discount clothing business.

Starting in the 1950s, one of the major retail phenomena that was quickly evolving was the onset of mass retail discount outlets. But unlike the traditional discount stores of today like Target and Walmart that own and run all the respective departments within their stores, back then there were these fast-growing mega discount store chains that functioned more like landlords or shopping mall companies and leased out their individual departments to other owners to run. As such, there would be separate operators for each department within the store… for the men's and boys' department, women's apparel, hard goods, toys, and so on.

And so it came to pass, after several years of gaining valuable specialty retail experience via running his haberdashery Regal Menswear stores and having the vision that the men's and boys' apparel industry was going to be trending more and more to these fast-growing mass retail outlets, Dad jumped on the bandwagon. He began operating a men's and boys' department within one of these outlets that had just opened up less than a five-minute drive from our house in New Britain. It was originally called Palmer Mills, but for some reason shortly after its opening, changed its name to Trio. I figured there must have been a change of ownership, in which three guys bought the place.

At first, while Dad concentrated on getting this new retail format off the ground and testing the waters, he still kept his haberdashery stores open. The stores were still doing pretty well, so it was difficult to walk away from them. Plus, they provided a good fallback, should the new concept not pan out. But it didn't take very long to prove out the concept. From the very start, Dad's discount business took off like gangbusters and was taking up most of his time. Within a year of opening up at Palmer Mills/Trio, he bowed out of his Regal Men's Shops specialty stores, closing the store in New Britain and selling the one in Middletown, in order to focus all his efforts on this new discount retail operation.

It's fair to say I spent a considerable amount of my childhood at Trio. Either I would just go there with him and hang out while he worked, or whenever I'd be in the car accompanying him on errands around town, it seemed as though we would always make our way over there for him to check something out. Consequently, I was always waiting for him to finish something up, which most of the time would take much longer than he'd originally tell me.

While I was waiting, I would invariably go to the bow tie display, which I took on as my personal section of the store to oversee and manage. These were clip-ons, the least expensive type of bow ties that clip right on the shirt collar. They were individually packaged in a plastic pillow pack with cardboard backing. Not really sure why I chose bow ties, but I guess at the time, as I still do now, I just thought they were kind of cool-looking, even though I seldom had occasion to wear them. Bow ties were fairly popular in those days, and they had their own 4-foot-wide section. Yet it was one of the smaller sections in the store, which made it more manageable to oversee. Although I hadn't even reached my teens, I felt it was my responsibility to maintain the section. It was my contribution to the store and it made me feel important. Plus, it helped make the time waiting for my father go faster.

Incredulously, just about every time I would check on "my" department, I would find it in a complete state of disarray, with all the individual packs of bow ties mixed up and strewn all over the place. I would get so mad at all the shoppers for messing things up so much and not having the courtesy to put the bow ties back in the orderly position that they found them, that I had so fastidiously put them in the last time I was there. I could never understand how the shoppers could be so inconsiderate. If they only knew how much time I spent fixing up this section. Still, each time I was there, despite my disappointment and frustration, I would relentlessly assume my responsibility and take it upon myself yet once again to organize and put things in order. And so this cycle would continue.

After starting out with Trio, over time my father began to branch out and make his way west from Connecticut and expand his operation. First to upstate New York and into Pennsylvania, and then burgeoning all over the US, either buying out existing men's and boys' departments or opening up new ones in a variety of mass discount stores with different names like Big Ben, Miracle Mart, Treasure City, Two Guys (as opposed to Trio), and Twin Fair. But he still kept the same Regal name for his firm.

Dad's departments opened in quite a few locations in upstate New York, including Poughkeepsie, Kingston, Watertown, Jamestown, and Buffalo. There were even more stores in Pennsylvania, mostly in mid-sized cities like Reading, Lancaster, Pottsville, Allentown, Harrisburg, York, and Johnstown. Other locations included Cincinnati, Ohio; Fort Wayne, Indiana, home of WOWO, the high wattage station I used to pull in late at night on the radio; Fargo, North Dakota; Brownsville, Texas; and even as far west as Phoenix, Arizona.

Other than Trio, the Pennsylvania stores were the ones I spent the most time in, as my family, including Spice of course, went to Pennsylvania at least once a year on vacation to visit my Uncle Hank and his family, who lived in Reading. Hank Schenck, my mother's brother, was the manager of the Reading store. He and his wife, Marge, had two girls, Kathy and Colleen, both a little older than I, and a set of twin boys, Robbie and Paul, who were seven years my junior. Having had their share of struggles, they had lived in a lot of places over the years with my Uncle Hank holding a bunch of different jobs to try to make ends meet. As he had done for his side of the family, being the compassionate "Al-truistic" guy that he was, my dad brought his brother-in-law into the business to manage the Reading store, even though my Uncle Hank never had any retail experience.

Every time we went to Pennsylvania, in the interest of combining business with pleasure, my father made sure to stop at each of his stores there to check on them and take care of any unsettled operating issues. This was one of my favorite parts of the Pennsylvania trips, in that I got to see different cities and stores and be on the road with him, while my mother, sister, and Spice would stay behind with my cousins.

It felt like an adventure of sorts, just us two, father and son, on the road together. It was our time together. The type of bonding experience every son, at least this one, longed for. I vividly remember, each time we would embark upon on one of these store check journeys together, just as he was turning the key to start the car, he would bellow out the phrase that the entertainer Jackie Gleason always used to say at the end of his opening monologue on the popular Jackie Gleason Show, his famous so-called signature phrase… "And away we go!" It was akin to a bugle call, a kind of call-to-action, an official signal that our adventure was about to begin.

We'd start out with the store in Reading, our home base, and then take a half-day trip to go north to the Allentown store, near where there were a lot of steel mills. Then we'd take a good part of another day to head south to hit the Pottstown, Lancaster and York stores, passing through Amish country in Lancaster County, where it felt like we were taking a big step back in time. We'd be riding along and see these one-horse drawn covered buggies with a triangular red hazard reflector in the back, clip-clopping along on the side of the road. As we would pass by, the Amish man inside, with his broad-brimmed black hat, would give a nod or wave hi in a neighborly way, as though he understood and was acknowledging our expected takeover on the road.

An Amish horse-drawn buggy

Then finally, we'd take our big full-day trip, across western Pennsylvania to visit the Harrisburg and Johnstown stores, which back and forth from Reading included a total of over six hours of driving, mostly on U.S. Route 22.

Once at the stores, Dad got right down to business. He was a man on a mission, making the rounds of the men's and boys' department in each store, visiting with the respective store manager, and reviewing the merchandise and the way it was being displayed. It was impressive to watch the guy in action. He sure had a knack for retail, an uncanny ability for knowing what was going on in each store; a knack for knowing what was selling and what wasn't; and a knack for uncovering any problems and what actions needed to be taken. Even though he only went to each of these stores periodically, he seemed to be on top of everything going on there. I could only hope that perhaps by just watching him in action, some of his flair for business would rub off on me.

While he was doing his thing, I would make my way over to the bow tie section to do my thing. Apparently, when it came to bow ties, shoppers weren't any more considerate in Pennsylvania than they were in Connecticut. The section was always in shambles. After a while it finally dawned on me that shoppers were shoppers, no matter where they are. But still, even though I realized it was probably an exercise in futility, whether it was force of habit or a disheartened, uneasy feeling that I couldn't leave the disheveled bow ties this way, I found myself straightening up the section.

Practically every time we went on one of these store circuits throughout Pennsylvania, I came back with a lot of clothes, as of course I had my choice of whatever boys' merchandise was in the stores. All we needed to do was to make a list of what I picked out, so my father could account for the merchandise. It worked out pretty well, except for this one time.

I must have been about 10 years old or so. We were in the Reading store, late at night just before closing time. After having tried on countless pairs of pants, shirts, and jackets in the back room under my mother's supervision to see what I liked and what fit, we together had selected a large stockpile of merchandise for me to take home. Accordingly, for inventory purposes, my mother made a detailed list of all the items we were taking with us. Since we had picked out so much stuff, it was going to necessitate two trips out to the car. So I grabbed as many items as I could hold, not even bothering to put the stuff in a bag, and started making my way out of the store into the parking lot. I was just about at the door when the two security guards on duty, one male and one female, stationed at the door stopped me in my tracks. Having startled and scared me, they immediately started to interrogate me on what I was doing and where was I going. Thinking they were suspecting me of stealing, I immediately broke down and started crying. I couldn't even get any words out to defend myself.

To this day, I'm convinced that maybe the only thing that saved me from getting into trouble was that my pants zipper was down.

At that age, my zipper tended to be down more than it was up—at half-mast with shirt sticking out. At that point, I didn't know what was more embarrassing, being caught for stealing or being caught with my zipper open. But maybe in this case having my zipper open was a blessing in disguise, as they must have figured that someone with his zipper down couldn't be that much of a hardened criminal.

After being zipped up by the female security guard and realizing that they were probably going to let me off, I was able to compose myself enough to explain the situation. In a daze of embarrassment, I was escorted to the back of the store to find either my mother or father to corroborate my story. From then on, I made sure that any merchandise that I ever took out from one of his stores was always in a bag and that, most importantly, I was always zipped up.

Chapter 10

THE KID WHO LOOKED BACK

LIVING IN NEW BRITAIN HAD ITS DRAWBACKS. Oh sure, it was a nice combination of a bustling city and quaint New England town and all. Not too big that it took a long time to get into and around downtown, but just big enough to feel like you had everything you needed. And it certainly was a warm community that offered comfort, safety, and security. But unfortunately, it didn't have the greatest schools. While the high schools, Conard and Hall, in the nearby, more affluent community of West Hartford, were among the best public schools in the Northeast, somehow, with New Britain being a more blue-collared town, its high school was barely accredited. More than once, my parents seriously thought of moving to West Hartford, but given that our house was only a stone's throw from the Trio store and Regal's office above the store, they were hard-pressed to make the move.

Accordingly, after going to the public Vance Elementary School in New Britain, my parents thought it best from an education standpoint that I then go the private school route. So from sixth through ninth grade, I went to a small middle school called Mooreland Hill in Kensington, less than a half-mile from my house. It was so close that I could walk there. It had kind of a country day school feel to it. In addition to a separate gymnasium, it consisted of only two buildings. One that housed just classrooms and the other that had more classrooms and a cafeteria, which also served as our assembly hall and our study hall where some of the more memorable spitball fights I've ever participated in took place. And when I say the school was small, I mean small. When I went there, there were only 67 kids in the whole school and only 15 kids in my class, 8 girls and 7 boys. That might have been the only time in my life that I was in an academic environment with more girls than boys. But talk about a small, individual-based program, this was it. It was so small that my mother, as I suspected many of the parents of the other students as well, was on a first-name basis with the school principal, Oscar Steege.

After Mooreland, starting in tenth grade, I went to Kingswood, an all-boys private day school in West Hartford. While it was a little bigger than Mooreland as it included grades seven through twelve and had slightly bigger classes consisting of 40 or so students per class, it still felt very small and limited in a number of ways. Of course, one of the biggest limitations was the lack of members of the opposite sex, especially coming off of the much more desirable ratio at Mooreland where the girls outnumbered the guys, even if only by one. Shortly after I graduated from Kingswood, it became coed as it merged with its sister school Oxford, an all-girls private school also in West Hartford, where my sister had attended. That change to a coed population was certainly poorly timed, if you asked my teenage self back then.

No doubt I got a great education from these private academic institutions that arguably set me up on a successful path to go on to a respectable college and what not. But to this day, I still can't help but feel I missed something by not going the public-school route, missing out on the experience of a typical public high school and overall a more real-world type of education I would have had— sharing classes with members of the opposite sex as well as being exposed to some socioeconomic diversity.

But getting back to Mooreland, there were a number of experiences there that were quite memorable, ones that have stayed with me all these years. There was the time, I think it was in the eighth grade, when in the spring, early in the Major League season, my favorite team at the time, the Atlanta Braves, and favorite player Hank Aaron were coming to New York to play the Mets at Shea Stadium. It was a weekday series, two night games, followed by a day game on Thursday that coincidentally fell on my birthday. Thanks to my never-ending pleading, and knowing how much it meant to me to see Hank Aaron in person up at the plate, my parents agreed to take me out of school for the day to drive to New York and take in that final game of the series.

About a week or so before the game, upon picking me up from school at the end of the day, my mother stops in to talk to Mr. Steege to tell him that my birthday was coming up and that to celebrate she and my dad were planning to take me out of a school for a day to go to New York for a ball game as my favorite team was coming into town. Although in the spirit of making it seem as though she was asking him his permission by starting the conversation with an acquiescent phrase such as "Oscar, I hope it's ok" or "If you don't mind," clearly in her mind she was just giving him the heads-up and covering him off as a courtesy, expecting him to give her a perfunctory nod and maybe say something like "I appreciate you telling me." But instead, Oscar responded to her soft request with a negative shake of the head saying, "Nikki (he called her by her first name too), I wish you hadn't come to me on this, as I'm afraid I can't approve it. You should have just kept him out for the day and said he was sick or something." Which yes, perhaps we should have done that. But somehow, something was wrong with that picture. Here we were coming to the school in an honest way, and the school, the headmaster nonetheless, was not respecting this honesty but telling us that we would have been better off telling a little white lie. What kind of message was this sending? What kind of lesson were they teaching us here anyway? Sadly, I ended up not going to the game, in fear that the cat was out of the bag and therefore that Mr. Steege and my teachers were somehow going to hold it against me if I ended up not showing up for school that day.

And then there was the time I had an assignment to write a story in my ninth grade English Composition class taught by Mr. Brown. He himself came from a literary family or at least had married into one, as his wife's family owned the town's newspaper, The *New Britain Herald*. In fact, it was through Mr. Brown that our class was given the exclusive opportunity and honor to take a tour of the newspaper and learn the intricacies of how a newspaper is put together and produced. Certainly, an experience a kid doesn't get every day. And for sure, that field trip turned out to be very interesting and educational and then some, as our class had the dubious distinction of being the worst-behaved group that had ever taken a tour there. I think that might have been the last time Mr. Brown took his class on a tour of his family's newspaper.

Anyway, getting back to my assignment. It was one of my first forays into writing a story. I wish I had saved it. I forgot the title and can't really remember all the details, but suffice to say it featured a business-related mystery plot with some twists and turns along the way, plus a surprising ending along the lines of an O'Henry story.

While I tend to be my toughest critic and I'm never really satisfied with my writing, for an initial submission, I had to admit it wasn't all that bad, especially considering I was only an eighth grader. Basking in my adolescent grandiosity, I figured I'd get a pretty good grade on it. I had more than delivered on the assignment, in terms of number of pages and content. And given his connection to the literary world, I felt Mr. Brown would appreciate my attempt to take a little creative license to make the story more engaging and exciting. I was so confident that I would get a good grade that I was actually looking forward to getting the paper back.

Well, when I got the paper back, I was crushed when I saw that I had received only a "C+" on it. I couldn't believe it. But it wasn't just the grade. It was Mr. Brown's handwritten comment that was the killer, which explained why, in his view, I came up so short: "Well written, but too imaginative."

I came back home that day, thoroughly lamenting to my parents about the situation. How could this be? Here was a school that I liked to think in principle was trying to get me to expand my mind and be creative, and here they were telling me that I was being too imaginative.

I don't think I've ever gotten over it. In fact, to this day, the infamous Mr. Brown lives on. For after that, every time my mother and/or father and I would watch a movie together that had a bizarre plot or theme to it or was really far-fetched, of which there were many, we would shout out the name "Mr. Brown" to each other, implying that he should only be here to watch this. That if Mr. Brown were to see this movie, he would realize that my story wasn't in any way near as preposterous as this movie, that it paled in comparison, and that he was totally out of line to penalize me for being what he considered to be too imaginative.

But perhaps my favorite Mooreland Hill story happened out on the gridiron. Because Mooreland was so small, we had six-man football. That is, instead of the typical 11 players on the field, our team only had six. On offense, it was a quarterback and two half-backs, plus a center and two receivers up on the line. I was one of the team's centers, who, in addition to hiking and blocking, was also eligible to go out for a pass. And on defense, it was three rushers up front on the line, and three guys back, two cornerbacks on each side and one safety deep in the middle. Most of the time our defensive backs played man-to-man, but sometimes zone.

We played in a league against various Catholic and other comparably sized private schools. And even though it was only six-man football and we were only middle-schoolers, it was tackle. Accordingly, we were all decked out in all the required equipment, complete with a jock strap, padded football pants, shoulder pads, and helmet.

It was our first game of the year. And for me, as a first-year middle-schooler, it was my first-ever six-man tackle football game.

We were home against McTernan, a small private boys' school, coincidentally out of nearby Waterbury, my father's old stomping grounds. Not knowing if he'd be in town or if I'd even get into the game, I debated whether or not I should invite my dad. But I did. He said he'd try to make it.

On the bench, my starting position, I was on the lookout for Dad, assuring myself that he's probably been detained, but wondering if he would make it at all. But sure enough, fathers have a way of sneaking in without their sons noticing, sometimes at crucial moments.

As I would later find out, he arrived just about the time this rookie on our team caught a bullet of a pass at about midfield and was heading toward the goal line. I guess I was too caught up in the moment myself to notice the new spectator on the sideline.

To the 45, 40… 35, 30… 25, 20… With no defenders in front, only the goal line, and the end zone clearly in sight just a few steps away, the touchdown was a cinch. Well almost. With a McTernan speedster rapidly following on his heels, our player, even though he was pretty fast, committed the cardinal sin of a rookie. He peeked back to see how close the competitive defender was. If only he hadn't looked back, which of course slowed him down, I'm sure he would have made it. But instead… kaboom, he was tackled from behind. No touchdown!

Now my father, having just arrived at the game and witnessed this exciting but rather frustrating play and having always had a knack for "calling a spade a spade" and speaking what was on his mind, wandered over to our neighbor Marilyn Slater, the Slater boys' mother, and curiously asked, "Who is that idiot?" To which she nonchalantly replied, with I'm sure a little bit of a giggle, "Why, that's your son Bruce!"

Chapter 11

AL LEVINE THE PUTTING MACHINE

OUT AT HIS COUNTRY CLUB, Cliffside in Simsbury, Connecticut, Dad was known as "Al Levine the Putting Machine," as fellow club members took a little creative license with his last name. He was a master with the putter. He seldom three-putted. And if he was within 10 feet of the cup, he was deadly. If only this could have been a trait I inherited from him.

As long as I can remember, he used the same putter, the Tomahawk. Nothing fancy like the ones out there now with all kinds of aerodynamic shapes and thick grips, all designed to guarantee success on the green; but rather just your regular, run-of-the-mill thin, flat-blade, straight-edged putter. To him, there was nothing like the ole Tomahawk.

Dad was first introduced to the game of golf in his late teens when he was in Florida. But he didn't really take it up until quite a bit later, when he opened the Bond Cut-Rate store with his partner Teddy Schwartz, whom he would play with out at Stanley Golf Course in New Britain. And then he really started to get a feel for the game and hone his skills while at the Berkshires on his many trips up there with his buddy Yale.

During the spring, summer, and fall, practically every weekend, both Saturday and Sunday plus at least one day during the week, he'd be out on the course. He was pretty easy to spot. He'd be out there wearing all different bright-colored pants—red, kelly green, light blue, even turquoise. He didn't wear a hat often, but if he did it would usually be just a visor.

Every part of his game was good. At one point, he had gotten down to a 7 handicap. It's not that he hit the ball all that far. He didn't have to. Most of the time, with his short, compact swing, he was easily straight off the tee in the middle of the fairway, whether it was with a wood or an iron. But it was his short game that really stood out. And as they say, "It's the short game that separates the men from the boys." That's what saved him the strokes. That's what he became known for. If he was within 50 or even 75 yards or so off the green, he was often up and down with a chip and a putt.

Dad won a lot of club tournaments that way: member-member, member-guest, and club championships in his respective handicapped-based flight. And he had a lot of trophies in our basement to show for it. About the only thing in golf he never attained was a hole-in-one. He came close a bunch of times, as close as a couple of inches, but never quite in.

Al Levine the Putting Machine accepting one of his many trophies at a Cliffside Country Club tournament

We played quite a bit together out at Cliffside. That's one of the great things about golf… it's one of the few sports activities that lends itself to fathers and sons. It was something we could go out and do together. Sometimes we'd go out for nine holes during weekend afternoons after he already had played 18 as part of his weekend routine, or at the end of the day during the week. And we'd play together on vacations in Florida.

Plus, every year on Father's Day, we would team up together in Cliffside's Annual Father and Son Tournament. We would play as part of a foursome with another father and son team. It was set up as a Scotch foursome format, specifically Chapman style, where on each hole he and I would both drive, then hit each other's drive, and then choose which of the two balls we wanted to go with. From there, we would proceed to hit alternative shots until the end of the hole. That was a fun tournament. I looked forward to it every year. I loved that he was my partner, that we were a team together. Actually, we teamed up pretty well together, as one year we won low net and another year we came in second. Hence, a couple of more trophies for the basement.

Our trophy for winning low net one year in
Cliffside's Father and Son Tournament

While most of the time Dad played out at Cliffside, he had the opportunity to play at many other courses, particularly in Connecticut, either in a member-guest tournament at another club or later on when he was retired as a member of the Nutmeggers. Named after Connecticut's nickname the Nutmeg State, the Nutmeggers was an elite group of retired executives who once a month during the summer played different championship-caliber courses all around Connecticut.

After a game of golf, at the end of the day at home, usually during cocktail hour with a gin and tonic in hand, Dad would take me through his round. He would be able to recount every stroke he took. When it came to remembering golf shots, he had a photographic memory. It was uncanny how he could recall the detail of every shot— where the ball was, how far away from the green he was, and what club he used, as well as the shots of everyone else in his foursome. Plus, he could remember the layout of just about every hole on every course he had ever played.

On weekend afternoons, he would be watching the weekly golf tournaments on TV. A lot of the time, he'd be working while watching. Even when he wasn't in the office or on the road, he would be working in some fashion. He'd be in his recliner, with pencil in hand and a pad of paper on his lap, mostly attending to inventory management, transferring product from one store to another. With all the stores he had to manage, it was a lot of paperwork for him back in those days, a never-ending process. Today, I think to myself, poor guy, if only he had had a computer, it would have probably cut his workload to a tenth of what it was.

Yet even when Dad was making his inventory adjustments, his eyes were still on the TV, following the tournament and watching just about every shot. His favorite player was Arnold Palmer, as he was clearly a part of Arnie's Army. Actually, I always felt my dad was a lot like Palmer. He resembled him in so many ways. Same mild-mannered, gentlemanly demeanor, same gracious personality, same high level of professionalism, same likeable type of guy, and above all else he had that same magic with the putter.

Chapter 12

A MAN OF HIS WORD

THERE I WAS, SQUISHED IN THE MIDDLE of the front seat and starting to get a little squeamish, in between my dad driving and one of his business associates on the right smoking a big stogie. I guess I should have said something when he first started to light up, but being a tag-along and having just met him, I was intent on "being one of the guys" to show I wasn't a boy among men. Plus I didn't want to be rude, although I had to admit it was kind of rude of this guy to smoke in our cramped situation.

I was accompanying Dad on one of his frequent trips to the Big Apple, which I did on occasion, mostly in the summer when I wasn't in school. I would go along with him to some meetings he had, and then we would go out for lunch, usually for Chinese, and then later in the afternoon we'd go to FAO Schwartz, one of my favorite go-to stores for my electric train collection. We would make a day of it. Normally we would take the New Haven line train to New York. So given my love for trains, just going on the train with him was enough to make it a good day. But this time, since he had a bunch of cartons to bring with him, shipments of some damaged product he was returning to one of his vendors, he needed to drive. And with the back seat down in the station wagon packed to the gills with all the boxes, we had to go with three in front.

Things kind of snuck up on me. Suddenly, I was at the point of no return. Clearly it was too late to say anything, except to shout out in a terrified, panic-stricken tone, "Dad you gotta pull over… now! I mean now!"

Fortunately, he didn't ask me why, as his paternal intuition must have somehow kicked in, but quickly slowed down and drove onto the shoulder. Even before the car stopped, I was tapping the cigar aficionado to my right to move out of the way, and once the car stopped I basically climbed over and steamrolled the guy in order to get out, and then right when I did, boom… I deposited my breakfast onto the shoulder of I-91. That was a close one. Luckily, I didn't have to say anything as the guy got the message and extinguished his cigar, and we rode with all windows open for the rest of the drive.

While it wasn't quite as extreme as the rigors of being a full-time salesman on the road, having to travel every week by leaving first thing Monday morning and returning late Thursday night or Friday, Dad was almost constantly on the road. It seemed as though he was always either taking the car, a train, or a plane to go somewhere. As such, while he did make it out to my memorable rookie debut on the football field at Mooreland Hill and a few of my other games here and there, he wasn't around all that much during the week to cheer me on in person.

In addition to his usual one-to-two-day trips to New York City just about every week to meet with his vendors, Dad was always making store visits. He tried to make it to each store at least once a quarter. Having as many stores as he did, that meant a lot of trips. He was able to visit a number of his stores, the ones in Poughkeepsie and Kingston, as well as all those in Pennsylvania, by car. But there were quite a few stores he had to fly to.

When he flew to Buffalo, where he had a number of stores, he would take Mohawk Airlines, or "Slowhawk" as we liked to call it. It was a small, regional airline that basically served the Mid-Atlantic region, mostly New York and Pennsylvania. I just remember that airline having these drab, nondescript prop planes that were a generic white with yellow and black stripes going down the middle. Between its tardiness, its nickname, and its unattractive planes, it was easy to make fun of. It was later acquired by a slightly bigger regional airline called Allegheny Airlines, thus starting a string of different airline generations, becoming US Airways in 1979, merging with America West Airlines in 2005 under the US Air name, and eventually merging with and turning into American Airlines in 2015.

In addition to Mohawk, Dad took other airlines that have since folded in their wings or merged with other airlines. He flew TWA, which was later acquired by American in 2001, to Cincinnati; Northwest Orient, which was absorbed into Delta Airlines in 2010, to Fargo; and Braniff, which filed bankruptcy and ended up biting the dust in 1982, to Texas and Phoenix. The thing I remember about Braniff was that its fleet sported different-colored planes —blue, green, red, and orange—and it had nice leather seats.

And then there was Dad's eventful flight to China. I think it was the only international business trip he ever took. He needed to go there to check out a number of different clothing manufacturers to see if they could be potential vendors. It was a multi-leg trip that took him through a few different airports, starting from Bradley Field in Hartford to Chicago, then to Hawaii, and then into Hong Kong. He had a full-day layover in Honolulu, so he ended up renting clubs and playing a round of golf before flying to Hong Kong that night. He always managed to fit in a round if he could.

So, there he was on the plane in Hawaii about to take off, with the Northwest Orient 747 barreling down the runway when all of a sudden, just as it's about to leave the ground, it comes to a screeching halt. The aborted takeoff must have been harrowing. But what was even more traumatic was when the brilliant captain came on the intercom to tell his passengers that they had just received a call from the tower that there was a report of a bomb on the plane. As one might expect from such a boneheaded remark, complete pandemonium broke out, with screaming and passengers getting up and going every which way to try to get off the plane. My dad described it as total chaos. It was all the crew could do to try to calm the passengers down and restore enough composure to get people off the plane in a somewhat orderly manner, which they finally did as they corralled everybody off the plane and into a designated waiting area.

Now my father had always promised my mother that if he ever had to get off a plane, no matter what the reason, he would never get back on it. I guess just one of those superstitious-type pacts that husbands and wives make to each other. He gave her his word. And with honest Abe, his word was his word. So when he was sitting there in the waiting area with all the other passengers amidst the airport authorities and the airline staff all scurrying about to organize things and get all the luggage off the plane for a thorough search of each piece, he went up to an airline representative and told her he didn't want to take this plane anymore but instead would like to take another flight. The rep acknowledged his request and said she would see what she could do, but told him to go back to his seat for now until things settled down and then the airline would try to accommodate him.

So he proceeds to go back to his seat and continues to wait there patiently. And then, about ten minutes later, two men in plain clothes come up to him and one of them takes out his badge and says, "Abraham Levin, we're with the FBI. Would you please come with us?"

My father naturally replied, "Would you mind telling me what this is about?"

"We just want to talk with you, sir. Have a few questions for you," said one of the agents, whereupon they escorted him to a small interrogation room with just a desk and some chairs on each side. Once the FBI guys started in with their questions, it didn't take long for my father to realize he was being considered as a prime suspect behind the bomb threat. Apparently, his innocent request to change his flight was being taken out of context, making him a possible perpetrator. They asked him for all kinds of identification and thoroughly searched the briefcase he was carrying with him. Then they grilled him with all kinds of questions on where was he from; where specifically in China he was going and his purpose in going there; what luggage had he checked; and why he wanted to change flights.

Knowing my father, he kept his cool. He was really good in terms of going with the flow. It seemed nothing ever really fazed him. Or if it did, he never let on that it did. He always took things in stride and made the best of the situation. I know he had his share of bad days, like when he lost his dry cleaning business down in Florida due to the catastrophic hurricane in 1926; or the time when driving home from Tom McAn's shoe store with his brother Lou after having just come back to Connecticut from Florida, his suitcase fell out of his brother's car and he ended up losing everything he had brought back with him including the deed to the 50-acre piece of land he had bought in Florida that who knows might have made him a millionaire; or on his first day working for Allen Cut-Rate when he made a simple deposit of the Company's weekly sales at the bank only to find out there was a run on the bank minutes later, which resulted in the company losing all that money he had deposited; or during his stint in the Army when he found out that he was going to Fort McClellan on the brink of being sent off to war, as opposed to having a lightweight assignment stateside that his friend Davey Melnick had led him to believe was the case. And now here he was, the number-one suspect of a bomb threat, and still I'm sure he didn't let it bother him and just went with the flow.

Applying his knack for getting out of things, he kept his cool and provided obligatory answers to all their questions, although I would imagine that the FBI didn't entirely buy into his whole excuse for why he wanted to change flights. But, after an hour or so of intense questioning, he was able to make a case for his innocence and clear his name, and they returned him to the waiting area.

It turned out that the bomb threat was just a hoax, and the plane eventually took off six hours late. But, as per his pact with my mother, Dad wasn't on it as he ended up changing his flight to the following evening. Which for him wasn't all that bad, as it meant another round of golf in Hawaii.

Unlike the Berlin train station, which wasn't even five minutes from our house, our local airport Bradley Field was about 45 minutes away, making it kind of difficult as I got older, to go with my mom to pick him up. But still I liked to go with her when I had time. And when I got my license, sometimes it would be just me who would pick him up.

But whether it was picking him up at the train station or the airport, even if he had been away for a long time and I hadn't seen him in a while, he would always greet me with a "Hi ya Tiger" and a handshake, never a kiss or even a hug. I can't remember ever kissing my father. Maybe it was a guy thing, but it was always a handshake. As he always said to me, "There's nothing like a firm handshake."

Chapter 13
GOING PUBLIC

THROUGHOUT THE '50S AND '60S, Dad's business continued to flourish. Still under the company name Regal, he continued to open more and more men's and boys' departments in discount houses around the country to the extent that he was in over 40 stores throughout the U.S.

As Regal expanded, Al-truistic continued to be good to his family. In addition to his brother Lou and brother-in-law Harry in the business, he brought Lou's son Arthur and son-in-law Earl into the operation as well.

With the rapid expansion and success of mass retail discount stores, the higher-end specialty stores such as my dad's original Regal Men's Shop were left far behind. It wasn't only the advent of the discount business that was a factor, but the explosion of shopping malls that housed department stores such as Macy's and Lord & Taylor. There was also a lifestyle trend away from business suits to more casual clothing. These factors all took its toll to the point where specialty stores were on the decline.

It should be noted, however, that the two Regal Men's Shops that Dad had sold, the Middletown store and the one in Manchester, had withstood the test of time and continued on into the twenty-first century with their new owners under the same Regal Men's Shop name. Even though he no longer had any affiliation with those stores, it was, in essence, a great tribute and testament to my dad to see the Regal Men's Shop name live on.

Clearly, my dad had made his mark in the business world. From that one small haberdashery store he opened in New Britain in 1939, he had built up an impressive, multi-store, mass-merchandising operation that accounted for $8 million in volume, which was pretty respectable in those days. No doubt many of the jobs he had engaged in throughout his career, from running the grocery and dry-cleaning businesses in Florida, to managing various sundry stores in Connecticut and Boston, had played a major role in shaping his business acumen.

In the '60s, many of the discount operations were going public. Likewise, Dad thought the time might be ripe for his company to do the same. Yet, upon looking into this opportunity, the Wall Street firm with whom he consulted told him that his $8 million total revenue wasn't quite substantial enough for that endeavor. But if he could team up with another company doing roughly the same amount of volume or so, he could maybe make a go of it. So that's what he did. He approached a number of other potential suitors, and finally happened upon a company called Meadows, Inc., which like him leased departments in discount houses, only toy departments instead of men's and boys'. It was also somewhat similar in size with volume of about $7 million.

And so it came to pass, around the time of my bar mitzvah in 1965, Regal teamed up with Meadows and went public under the name Regal-Meadows. Quite an accomplishment for a guy who started out with just that one store in New Britain. Then, a couple of years later, his company was bought out by a chain of discount department stores out of Buffalo called Twin Fair. Unlike other discount houses in which my dad had operated his men's and boys' departments, Twin Fair owned all of its individual departments in its eight-store chain.

Twin Fair in turn was actually a subsidiary of a conglomerate called Unexcelled, Inc. While a strategic connection with Twin Fair made sense, the parent Unexcelled seemed to be a strange suitor. It had a lot of diverse companies in its portfolio. Originally starting out as a small chemical company back in the 1880's, Unexcelled got into the foundry and meat packing business; and then after it purchased Twin Fair in 1962, it ventured into the aerospace industry. Oddly enough, in 1965, it had acquired a company called Aero Spacelines, which manufactured a so-called Super Guppy Plane that was a huge, wide-bodied aircraft that carried oversized cargo. Believe it or not, this Super Guppy Plane was so humongous inside that it was used to transport rockets for NASA. It looked like a plane on steroids, kind of a cross between a blimp and a plane. Some even described it as a plane that was pregnant.

Part of his deal was that Dad would stay on and work for Twin Fair, continuing to manage all of his previous stores as well as Twin Fair's original eight stores. Between going to the home office and visiting his newly inherited stores, he would be taking his ole standby "Slowhawk" Airlines and shuffling off to Buffalo a lot more.

And so, after more than 25 years of running his own show, Dad found himself working for someone else. But he didn't let up on the gas pedal, and went about his job in the same determined and diligent way as if he still owned the business himself.

Chapter 14

THE SOCKS GUY

DAD CONTINUED WORKING WITH TWIN FAIR until he reached the formal retirement age of 65. It was part of the acquisition agreement he had made with Twin Fair to stay on with the company until at least that time. To commemorate his service with Twin Fair and celebrate his illustrious retail career, Twin Fair threw him a big retirement party in the summer of 1973. It was held in a New York hotel, so that as many of his business associates, managers, buyers, and wholesalers as possible who he had worked with over the years could attend. Of course, our whole family was also there.

With Dad's departure, I'm sure Twin Fair must have missed him. Its business continued to exist for a while, but by 1982 its retail operation had dwindled down to only 14 stores, all in western New York, as it sold off some of its stores to another retail chain called Meijer and closed the others. Shortly thereafter, the remaining Twin Fair stores were acquired by Federated Department Stores, which later bought Macy's.

And in terms of Twin Fairs' parent Unexcelled, it eventually disbanded. However, its Super Guppy Planes, having been taken over by Air Bus, continue to exist today but are now referred to as Beluga Planes. Supposedly the Beluga can now carry two times the weight of the original Super Guppy Plane.

The Airbus Beluga Plane

Although Dad formally retired that summer, he couldn't seem to completely walk away from the action. So he decided to become an account rep for Mobil Socks, his long-time wholesaler for all the socks he sold in his stores and the same company that arranged for my Hank Aaron letter. His job was to be the account guy for several of the firm's major discount client retailers it serviced in the Northeast Corridor. Most of these accounts were nearby, so he wouldn't have to travel that much.

More than anything, it was just a way my father could keep his head in the game and foot in the door so to speak, and still experience some connection to the business world that he thrived on. Of course, it was also an opportunity to bring home a little revenue on the side.

So naturally, being in the socks business, Dad had to have an ample inventory of product samples at his disposal. Athletic socks, crew socks, tube socks, thermal socks, dress socks, you name it, he had them in his possession, at least several boxes of each item Mobil offered in its product line. This meant dozens of socks boxes lining the walls of our garage in Connecticut, basically turning it into a socks warehouse. The cartons of socks were even starting to take over my ole sacred Train Room.

Not only did he use them as samples to bring to accounts, but he also gave them out as gifts as a thank-you or token of appreciation. If somebody had done a favor for him, he would return the favor by giving them a half dozen pairs of socks. Or he would just give them outright as gifts, perfect for the mailman, trash guys, and others to be recognized at the holiday season. Or he would give them out to "grease the skids" with someone to try to establish a rapport. Kind of like he did with the colonel back when he was in the army. Dad was a master at that. Or really there didn't even have to be a reason, he just wanted to show people that he was thinking of them. One time he brought socks out to the Stanley golf course to give to an older gentleman who was always out there on the 7th tee selling used golf balls.

Having accompanied my father on many business trips, I knew early on I wanted to go the business route as well. Like father, like son, I guess. So when it came time to choose a college, I went with Babson College in Wellesley, Massachusetts, a four-year liberal arts college with an emphasis on business. It was a small school of only about 1,500 students and mostly guys as it had just started to go coed. Coming off of my high school days at Kingswood, this was the scene I had been accustomed to, as I continued to deprive myself of female classmates. You would think I would have learned my lesson.

But Babson had a solid reputation within the business world, at least in the East. Plus, it wasn't too far from home, close enough that I could easily jump in the car and come back for a weekend, but far enough to feel as though I was going away to school. What's more, it was just outside of Boston, certainly a popular college town. And while there weren't that many girls in my classes, there were many all-female academic institutions for us "Camp Babo" guys to tap into, such as Pine Minor or "Pine Glamour" as we called it, which was known for its attractive student body, Laselle Junior College, Reed Junior College, Wheelock, and Mount Ida, to name a few. There was also Wellesley College, which was literally right across the street from Babson, but the Wellesley women were rumored to be "off limits," instead preferring the likes of the Harvard men.

Given its business-oriented curriculum, Babson gave me the opportunity to be exposed to most if not all the major facets of business. So, while I majored in accounting given my interest in numbers at the time and thinking maybe that was going to be my profession, I got a good dose of other business courses such as marketing, management, operations, and finance.

At Babson I had some of the best teachers I ever had. There was this one guy in particular, Professor Bruno, my Intermediate Accounting teacher, who I'll always remember. Given that his class was an elective, Professor Bruno didn't want anybody enrolled who didn't want to be there. Not that any of us really wanted to be in there, but if you were an accounting major you had to be in there. During the first couple of classes, he would start out by waving a pad of pink slips in our faces, saying, "For those of you who want to get out now, before the going gets tough, I've got these slips ready to go… anybody want one? Don't be bashful".

Being majors in accounting, my friends Jim and Henry and I were among those who unfortunately couldn't take him up on his offer. We were in there for the duration. But it wasn't long before he started to call us "hear no, see no, and speak no" for the obvious reason of our nonparticipation. I'm not sure which one I was, as I could have qualified for any of the three.

Early on, I realized that accounting wasn't really where my interests lay anymore and I was leaning toward the marketing route, but I stuck it out and got through the class. Although it wasn't without getting the chalk thrown at me. The unorthodox Professor Bruno would be at the front of the room intently writing on the blackboard and at the same time asking a question of the class. And if he spotted you out of the corner of his eye looking in the book for the answer, what he termed using the "educated thumb," he would whip around and throw the chalk at you. There were quite a few times when I would have to duck, which the guy in back of me didn't really appreciate. Professor Bruno would say, "Accounting is nothing more than brute logic," as he clearly frowned upon anyone using the "educated thumb" to get the answer. Rather, he wanted you to think through the logic to come up with the solution. I suppose the course was worth taking just for that common-sense lesson.

I also liked how Professor Bruno would use our names in exam problems. Some of our exams were four hours in length, which in and of itself certainly should have been enough for me to question majoring in accounting and reconsider signing one of those pink slips. But I guess one of the motivators that helped get me through these interminable tests, was when I would see my name pop up in one of the problems. "The Bruce Levin Plumbing Supply Company used the LIFO method of accounting..." and then it would go on to describe some of the accounting challenges the company was facing that needed to be resolved. To this day, I always wondered how Professor Bruno found out about "my" plumbing supply business back in Berlin, Connecticut, across from the railroad station.

While at Babson, starting my junior year, my dad arranged for me to get a part-time job at Mobil Socks. At the time, with both of us on their payroll, I was, pardon the pun, following in my father's footsteps. I guess I was becoming a socks guy as well.

The job wasn't all that grueling—just a few hours a week to get out a little bit, earn a little money, and gain some exposure to the business world to complement my business-oriented academics with some real-world experience. Given that it was Mobil Socks, I would have probably worked for free, if for nothing else in gratitude for setting up the letter from Hank Aaron. But of course, it was nice to have a little cash rolling in. My general job description was basically to service some discount stores in the greater Boston area, specifically to straighten up and organize their sock section and take stock of the inventory to see if the stores were out of any items. Given my experience with bow ties, this was right up my alley. My former pride of ownership of the Regal bow tie sections had provided me with excellent training, as I took on the sock sections in much the same way, with the same kind of passion and determination.

As I had found with the bow ties, shoppers were just as brutal in terms of interacting with the sock section of the store. Socks were constantly in disarray. Being sold in packs of three pairs, some pairs were separated from the pack and strewn all over the place. Some individual pairs were even separated into single socks and mixed up with each other. These sections were always a mess. Again, while I understood that shoppers will be shoppers, I still couldn't help but get mad at them for not being considerate enough to put the socks back where they found them. Not surprisingly, even though I was now committed to socks, when passing by the bow ties I couldn't help but stop and straighten out a few here and there. Just force of habit I guess.

Chapter 15

A "VAN"TASTIC LUNCH

Having bought a condo in Palm Beach, Florida in 1976, my parents had been ongoing snowbirds ever since. They finally sold the house in Connecticut in late 2001 and became full-time Florida residents. I suppose it was only fitting that my father was planning on living the rest of his life in Florida, the land of sunshine and opportunity, where he had first made his mark.

So here it was August 2003, and I hadn't seen the folks for almost six months, since March when my family was down there for spring break. I was only going to be in Florida for a couple of days, as it was a just a quick, spur-of-the-moment trip down there mainly to see Dad.

I had reserved a full-size car, but apparently that day the rental car company I chose at the Ft. Lauderdale airport must have run out of inventory of that class of car, so they offered me a free upgrade. It was a van. I liked vans and was used to driving one, as we had a Chrysler Town & Country at home. Besides, the offer of an upgrade is always tough to pass up, so I went with it.

Like our van at home, this one was gold as well. But, unlike our Town & Country, which had automatic sliding doors and a state-of-the-art interior, this was your standard, no frills van—a Ford

104

Econoline, more suited, in my opinion, for running local deliveries, not carting around people. Certainly not attractive or luxurious in any way, but rather more functional in nature and kind of rough around the edges. I guess that's why they must have been offering it up as an upgrade. But it was its simplicity, its "plain Jane" kind of makeup, its lack of any contemporary features that made it somewhat endearing in its own right. So endearing in fact that it deserved a nickname right off the bat. I immediately thought of the name "Bully"—I guess because it was so rugged and tough-looking and as far as vehicles go, it kind of looked like a bully or what I imagined a car that goes after other cars would look like.

Not only was my family big on adopting nicknames for ourselves, but we applied them to our cars as well. The first car names I can remember as a kid were "Wags 1" and "Wags 2" for our wood-paneled station wagons. We got a little more creative when my mother, Nikki, originally Bernice, who had a reputation within the family and among my friends for having somewhat of a lead foot, got a light-blue Cadillac convertible that we referred to as "Blue Lightning." And then my first car, which I shared with my sister Lexye, originally Deborah, was a gray Chevy Malibu that we formally dubbed "The Gray Ghost" but often just called "Boo," which cleverly tied in with both the ghost concept and the "bu" in Malibu.

Upon graduating college at Babson but still staying in the Boston area and embarking upon my first full-time job as a marketing research analyst at the Shawmut Bank of Boston, I finally got my very own car, a royal blue Audi Fox with white interior. Couldn't really call it a sports car per se, but nonetheless it was hot-looking. So hot-looking that I called it my "Foxy Lady." Still doing a little moonlighting for Mobil Socks in the evenings and on weekends, I was certainly riding in style as I used it for my sock runs.

I drove my Foxy Lady for almost two years in and around Boston, which was a feat in itself given that I was driving in the perilous state of Massachusetts. With all its antiquated roads and rotaries plus its share of reckless drivers, Massachusetts had a reputation for being one of the most challenging states to drive in. Upon describing what it's like to drive in Massachusetts, someone once summed it up best when saying, "if you're a pedestrian in Massachusetts crossing a one-way street, always look the other way first to see if traffic is coming."

Plus, Massachusetts drivers seemed rather bullish by nature, especially in the eyes of an out-of-state driver. It was almost as if there was an unwritten code among them to go after those with out-of-state license plates. And unfortunately, I was on the wrong end of things, as even though I was up in the Boston area for six years, I still kept my Connecticut plates. This was partly because I considered my stint in Massachusetts only temporary and didn't want to incur the added expense of a new license and registration, but more so because I didn't want to be labeled as a "Massachusetts driver."

No doubt about it, I had a number of close calls. I swear they tried to get me on a number of occasions and indeed those bullies almost drove me off the road at least a couple of times. But by some miracle, my Foxy Lady and I escaped unscathed. That is until the last day of June, the last day of my apartment lease, and my last scheduled day in Boston as I planned to go home to Connecticut for the rest of the summer before heading off to Cornell to start graduate business school. Sure enough, they must have been holding out on me, waiting until my very last day in town to get me.

There I was, in the parking lot of the Natick Mall, just trying to nose my way out from one of the rows of cars and take a right onto the main thoroughfare in the lot. When all of a sudden on my left, this big old behemoth of a vehicle, kind of the same ilk as Bully but even older, driven by a 16- or 17-year-old male teenager, who was looking the other way perhaps distracted by another foxy lady, the human type, started to veer to the right. By the time he realized what was happening, it was too late. He looked at me in despair and I looked at him in more despair. It was inevitable. My Foxy Lady didn't stand a chance. Much bigger in length and girth, he plowed into me, causing my Foxy Lady to start to fold in like an accordion. My head hit the rear-view mirror, but luckily I was ok. I couldn't say the same for my car.

Foxy Lady had to be towed to the nearest Audi dealer, where she was on the verge of being declared totaled. It could have gone either way, as I could have opted to have the repair shop declare it totaled, get reimbursed by the insurance company, and put the payment toward a brand-new car. But no. As though I was deep into a romantic relationship, I loved the car too much and didn't want to break up with her. So, against my better judgment, given that the Audi dealer had to practically rebuild the whole engine and outer body, I decided to have them give her a total makeover. Somehow, they were able to put her back together, and sure enough she ended up looking like the same good-looking, hot Foxy Lady I knew and loved.

I ended up taking my Foxy Lady up to Cornell for my wheels. While up there in the land Far Above Cayuga's Waters, she was ok for a while, but pretty early on in the first semester the steep hills of Ithaca started to take their toll on her and she started to show signs of breaking down. On more than one occasion, her engine would all of a sudden just die, and she had to be towed in. After countless times of having to call the tow truck, it got to the point that I wouldn't even say anything to the tow truck driver when he arrived at the scene. I would just shake my head, and he would give me a nod and a wave and proceed to tow it to Ripley's Motors, the Audi dealer in Ithaca. That's right, can you believe that was the name of the place? Actually, it turned out to be a perfect name, as I used to call it "Ripley's Believe It or Not Motors." As every time I picked it up there after it was supposedly repaired, I didn't know whether or not to believe them that this time the car was really, truly fixed.

After a while, the name of the place morphed into "Ripoff Motors" as they were never really able to fix it and my Foxy Lady was never the same. She didn't make it through the first semester. Ithaca's cold, blistery winter, along with its insurmountable hills, just did her in, and she had to be put to rest for good. So much for my Foxy Lady.

For my next car, I went with one that had a little bit more stability, a silver Oldsmobile Cutlass. Compared to my Foxy Lady, the car was huge. I guess because it seemed like somewhat of a whale of a car to me, I called it "Mobi." Mobi turned out to be quite a workhorse as I drove it for five or six years or so, at which time I turned it in for a silver Honda Prelude that I ended up calling "Honduras."

To this day, in my own household as well, I have carried on this, some might say, "sick" Levin family tradition of naming cars. At the time, our current van at home was called "Le Van," a takeoff on our last name. We actually went so far as to try to get that for its license plate, but that vanity plate was already taken. Our other car, the one I drove most of the time, was a royal blue BMW 525i, about the same color as my Foxy Lady, that because I considered it to be a sort of preppy, I nicknamed "Biff," which sometimes I affectionately called "The Biffer."

As I made my way up I-95 toward my folks' condominium, it didn't take me long to realize that Bully provided anything but a smooth ride. It was almost as if I was actually riding on a real bull. Even on the smooth paved surface of the expressway, I could really feel the bumps as let's just say its suspension system wasn't the greatest. But Bully got me to their place in one piece.

Dad was looking pretty good. While sure he was slowing down a little bit and his golf handicap continued to creep up by a few strokes over the years, he was a lucky guy when it came to his health. Here he was 95 and never had any diseases or major medical problems to speak of. He did have a hip replacement, some back surgery, and skin cancer on the outside of his ear, which while removed had weirdly enough later found its way inside his ear that in turn ended up precipitating a more involved procedure. But other than those hiccups, he withstood the test of time.

Throughout his whole life, Dad had aged remarkably well. Nobody ever believed he was his actual age. Even though during my days at Mooreland Hill I would call him "Senex" on occasion, he always looked at least 10 years younger than his actual age. In his mid-90's, he could have passed for low-to-mid-80's, maybe even late 70's.

The guy seemed to drink from the fountain of youth. It must have been all those gin and tonics he drank, one or sometimes two every day, but never more, that contributed to his longevity and youthful look. Cocktail hour was big in our house, and for my dad, gin was his liquor of choice. Specifically, Gordon's Gin. My mom would opt for rye and soda, with either Canadian Club or Crown Royale.

I had to wonder if Dad's routine G&Ts were truly the secret elixir to his good health. There had to be something that sustained him all these years, so I did some research. Gin is made from juniper berries, considered to be "super berries" that are full of antioxidants and packed with infection-fighting properties, making it therapeutic in more ways than one. Furthermore, juniper berries contain flavonoids, which have been found to protect against heart disease and improve blood flow and circulation. Plus, I read that juniper berries help to stop water retention in your body and enable you to pass more water than any other alcohol, thus helping to flush more toxins and bacteria out of your system. And with its antioxidants, gin is known to regenerate cells in the body, resulting in smoother, healthier skin. It's even associated with reducing inflammation and being an effective treatment for arthritis and other types of chronic pain. It seemed like I perhaps had unearthed part of the answer to Dad's good health all these years. Needless to say, one could certainly make a strong case for having a G&T or two every day.

But now there were signs that he was starting to slow down, not really eating that much, not doing as much financial administrative work as he was always used to doing, not following the stock market as much, which he so loved, and not wanting to go out anywhere. I was hoping that I could at least get him out for lunch. We tentatively set something up for the next day. The plan was to go out for some Chinese, his favorite. There was only one Chinese place around that we liked: The Singing Bamboo. We tended to go there when I was in town. However, when he got up the next day, he was moving kind of slow and was hinting that maybe we should have lunch at home.

"How about we just bring it in or have it delivered?" Dad asked. "You know Chinese is perfect for takeout." He always seemed to put forth some good rationale to defend his position. But I wasn't about to let him off the hook. Somehow eating at home just wouldn't be the same. After all, it was about us going out together, just him and me, which made it a true father-son lunch. Besides, I had a father-son type question for him that I couldn't envision asking in front of my mother, who undoubtedly would be at the table with us while we were eating or somewhere in the apartment within earshot. So at my encouragement and insistence, telling him that it would be good for him to get out of the apartment, take a little drive, and get a little sunshine, coupled with him sensing that I would be disappointed if he backed out of it, he acquiesced.

As Dad went into the bedroom to get dressed with my mother trailing behind to help him, not to miss a beat in his paternal, thorough way, he suggested, "Why don't you call the restaurant to make sure they're open?" Whether it was stopping for directions or some other logistical matter, he was always thinking ahead and wanted to take that extra step for reassurance. Didn't want to ever to leave anything to chance.

Feeling this extra step of calling was unnecessary and overkill, I was tempted to put in my two cents of questioning his doubt and expressing my confidence that we were all good, implying that there wasn't any reason to take things any further. But just the same, to avoid any confrontation and not wanting to seem lazy, I found myself always going along with his request.

More often than not, his premonition and follow-up paid off, which was the case this time. It turned out it's a good thing we called The Singing Bamboo before we went out, as unfortunately, according to their phone recording, it was closed for lunch. It seemed that a number of restaurants down in Florida weren't open for lunch during the out-of-season summer months. So, in keeping with the Asian cuisine, we pulled an audible and opted for Thai instead. There was a place we had been to a couple of times before that was pretty good, Orchids of Siam, not too far away on Forest Hill Boulevard. I called and they were open.

Dad came out dressed as though he was headed out to the golf course, in his typical, colorful "Al Levine the Putting Machine" style with white sport shirt, red golf pants, and kelly-green V-neck cardigan sweater, sporting kind of a Christmas look. Even in this unbearably hot, humid, sultry summer month of August in Florida, whether he was inside or out, he always insisted on wearing a sweater. The temperature could be in the high seventies in their apartment, which it was most of the time, he would always have a sweater on. As you get older and your skin gets thinner, I guess always being cold comes with the territory.

Everything looked a little large on him. His red pants were kind of baggy and draped over his shoes, his sweater was a little big in the shoulders, and the collar of his shirt was oversized for his neck. Over the years, he had gone from a large to a medium on almost all his shirts, sweaters, and jackets. And now even the medium was looking too big. I'm sure I was destined to follow the same progression. Come to think of it, some of my large sized shirts were already getting to feel a little loose on me.

If I wanted them, I would become the recipient of his hand-me-down shirts and jackets that he had outgrown. A lot of them weren't really my style as I tended to go for the more understated basic colors of black, navy, tan, and gray, but there were a few items I decided I'd inherit. I still have a forest-green colored nylon jacket of his with the Cliffside Country Club logo on it, which is currently rolled up and stuffed in my golf bag. Somehow it has withstood the test of time, as those types of jackets seem to have remarkable longevity. Nothing really special about it, only that it was his and I wanted to continue to keep it as part of my ongoing golf wardrobe. I don't have the occasion to wear it much, but it's comforting to know that it's always there. When I do wear it, I can still make out a trace of his smell.

It was just about noon when he grabbed his state-of-the-art walker stationed near the front door and was ready to go. Dad's walker was this sleek, lightweight metal, V-shaped three-wheeler that could be folded up into a thin accessory for easy travelling and storage. When open to the full extent, the three legs created a triangular leather pouch in the middle of the walker, into which he could put books, magazines, glasses, snacks, and other paraphernalia. If one needed a walker, this was clearly the way to go.

We took the elevator down to the lobby and made our way to the visitors' spaces just outside the front door on the left side of their condo building, where Bully was parked. I probably should have opted to take him out in style and go with my parents' Cadillac, one of a long string of family Cadillacs that all started with my mother's Blue Lightning. But somehow it seemed like taking the van would be much more fun. For Bully seemed more like the type of wheels that father and son adventures are made of. A Cadillac just wouldn't cut it.

Although just getting into Bully proved to be an adventure in itself. It had a big step up. For a 95-year-old guy with a walker, clearly this would be no easy task. Unfortunately, I hadn't thought about that when I rented it. We tried a few times, but it was evident that there was no way Dad was going to make it up to the seat without the aid of some type of intermediate step. Trying not to get too discouraged, I told him that I had an idea and that I'd be right back.

I temporarily left him standing outside the van and ran back up to the apartment. A few minutes later, I came back with the little step stool that he used every day to step up into the shower. Even with the step stool it took several attempts, but we were determined. With my left hand, I ended up kind of pushing him up from the stool with a little boost on the left side of his behind, and at the same time steadying him with my right hand on his right hip. And sure enough he made it into his seat.

Of course, we weren't on easy street yet, as what goes up has to come down. He was going to have to get out for lunch, and then repeat the whole process of getting up and down one more time on our return trip from the restaurant. But for the time being, we celebrated our accomplishment, as I shut the passenger door, folded up his high-tech walker, threw it in the back seat along with the step stool, and then climbed up on the driver seat to take the wheel and head out. As we made our way out of the parking lot, I shouted out "And away we go!" and we were off.

In no time at all, we were cruising on I-95 North, the road that broadcasted his age, bouncing our way to our Thai destination. Quite a different experience than the smooth ride of the Cadillac, that's for sure.

My father suddenly piped up… "heh…heh, I feel as though I'm riding in my ole dry cleaning delivery truck. I used to be in the dry-cleaning business you know. This ride kind of reminds me of those days when I used to drive a truck like this to pick-up and drop off dry cleaning. I used to bounce around like this, heh…heh."

Of course, I remembered all of his various stints in the dry-cleaning business. The first being one of his early ventures in Florida, when he traded the small grocery store he owned for a dry-cleaning business. Then, later on, after he had returned to Connecticut, he went back into that same type of business working with a small mom-and-pop dry-cleaning establishment.

"Did I ever tell you about this one dry-cleaner I worked for out of Waterbury, called Hart's Dry Cleaning?" he asked.

"I think so, but I'm not sure," I replied. Even though I knew the story, that's what I would always say to him so that he would tell it again.

"Well, it wasn't your traditional dry-cleaning pick-up. It was really a high-end operation. I used to drive up to these extravagant what-you-macall-its in Connecticut."

"Estates?"

"Yeah, estates. It was unbelievable, a butler would answer the door, invite me in, and escort me right upstairs into these people's closets and have me go through and pick out the garments that needed cleaning or pressing. Some of the walk-in closets were so big that they were like regular rooms. Can you imagine going into these rich people's closets and just picking out whatever clothes you felt could use some cleaning or pressing. Long evening gowns, men's suits, fedoras, you name it. They were there for the picking.

"Well, I don't have to tell you that was a pretty good gig, and I was doing fairly well, especially considering the country was still in the throes of a depression at the time. But unfortunately, there was, should I say, one little wrinkle in the operation, heh…heh! Hart had a daughter a little younger than me, nice enough girl but not really a looker per se, whom he was trying to marry off, and I was heh…heh candidate number one. I endured the situation for a while, but I finally couldn't stand it anymore, even though I liked the job and the old man was a nice guy. I remember we would drive into Hartford together once a week and he would tell me stories of the old country. But anyway, I wasn't that interested in her and it was getting kind of awkward and embarrassing for me, so I ended up moving on to something else."

We took the Forest Hills exit off of I-95 and headed west. If I remembered correctly, it was just a little way down on the right. "It should be coming up soon," I said reassuringly.

"Why don't we stop somewhere and ask for directions?" Dad asked. "Here, pull over to this gas station. I'm sure they know where it is."

"I think we're good, Dad," I said, a little bit abruptly trying to curb my impatience. "We just haven't gotten there yet. We're only at the 2500s and its address is 3027 Forest Hills. It's got to be just up ahead."

And sure enough there it was, Orchids of Siam, right there on the right in the strip mall, of which Florida had so many. It had to be the strip mall capital of the world. I'm sure if Florida hadn't been known as the Sunshine State, it could have been called the Strip Mall State.

Getting down was much easier than going up. It usually is. With me steadying him, it was just a little bit of a reach with his foot onto the step stool, and then another step down. When we walked into the restaurant, not so surprisingly given the slow summer season, we noticed that we were the only customers in there. It was actually kind of cool that we had the whole place to ourselves.

We started out each ordering a cup of Tom Kha Gai, or as we called it "coconut soup." We both loved coconut, which tends to be one of those flavors you either love or hate. I wondered if my love for coconut was in any way hereditary. In addition to the soup, we ordered spring rolls and Pad Thai with shrimp, which came with rice.

Our conversation got off to a slow start. It wasn't always easy to come up with stuff to talk about. We had a strong bond and all, but like a keg of beer, this bond often needed to be tapped from time to time in order to get the conversation flowing. Sometimes the communication was sparse, not always there. Other times, I was afraid that more was left unsaid than said, that there might have been some missed opportunities. I suspected that this was the case with a lot of fathers and sons.

Sure, Dad liked to tell stories, to share and sometimes even will his opinion and rationale on you. And he could certainly hold his end of the conversation. But he wasn't what I would call a talker, nor was I for that matter. He was more of a cut-to-the-chase kind of guy. He didn't really use more words than he had to. He certainly wasn't the type of guy who was going to share his innermost feelings with you, or the type with whom you'd have deep philosophical conversations.

The kids were always a good kick-starter for conversation. He loved to hear all about them. My dad had waited a long time for grandchildren, as he was over 80 when my daughter Danni, alias Danielle, was born. And even though he lived far away from them and didn't see them all that often, the kids were his pride and joy. They were always the first topic of conversation whenever we got together. While we had already talked all about the kids in detail the day before, rehashing everything now was a good way to get the conversation going.

I talked about how Danni, who was soon to be 11, was going to be a sixth-grader this year. It was hard to believe that she would be starting middle school. That it just seemed like yesterday that we were celebrating her first birthday party at my parents' house in Connecticut, during which she had to take a nap halfway through.

And about how Mac, now 7, who Dad used to refer to as "a little cockroach," was getting to be, as Dad called him in Yiddish, a "Big Macher." He had just finished his summer baseball house league, and was getting ready to go back to school in a week or so as a second-grader.

Danni and Dad share a special kiss

Mac and Dad take time out of their storybook to smile for the camera

While sipping our soup, we managed to continue to maintain some small talk of sorts, about what the stock market was doing these days, what business projects I was working on, and what time my return flight was scheduled for the next day as I could always count on logistics to be part of our conversation. All this time I was rather preoccupied and getting a little nervous about the big, burning, father-son type question I was intending to ask him. I still wasn't sure on how exactly to broach it. What was I going to use as a lead-in?

It wasn't until we were eating our spring rolls when I ended up springing the question on him with no lead-in at all, instead just kind of randomly throwing it out there.

"So Dad, if you don't mind me asking, uh…uh…how long did uh…you know…uh..uh…your pipes last? You know…your pipes down below?"

"Why, you having some problems down there?"

"No, it's not that so much. Other than maybe of course my pipes are beginning to get a little rusty from lack of use. No, I was just kind of curious as to how many years you were able to…you know…have sex with mom?"

As if just the thought of one's mother and father having sex together wasn't enough of a hurdle to get over, here I was pressing the envelope of imagining the two of them getting on in years trying to get it on together. I mean sure I knew they had had to do it at least twice, once in conjunction with my sister and once for my conception, but beyond that it was hard to conceive that there could have been much more activity than that in their bedroom. You just don't think of your parents that way.

Finally, after a bit of silence, leading me to begin to question myself whether I should have even brought the question up in the first place, he came back with "Uh, I don't know, I think maybe around 80 or so."

A smile broke out on my face as I nodded my head in acknowledgement, while at the same time giving myself a little fist pump under the table. Not that there were any guarantees or anything that

that would be the case for me, but his answer was along the lines of what I was hoping for and was encouraging in terms of what I could possibly expect in that department down the road. And so it was onto our next course… Pad Thai with shrimp and a bowl of rice.

I was hoping that my last question would have been somewhat of an ice-breaker, that perhaps that question would open up a treasure chest of more father-and-son type questions and topics that would take us down a road of uncovering and sharing the meaning of life, to explore the roads that fathers and sons don't always find it easy to travel down together. That maybe this lunch would serve as a launching pad to crack the surface and take a deeper dive toward bringing to light some valuable nuggets or fatherly tips I could take away. But instead, our conversation fell into a bit of a lull, as we each seemed to focus our attention more on the Pad Thai than on each other. It was as though we had kind of tapped out, at least temporarily. But it didn't really matter. It wasn't as though we had to say something to each other. To me, it was enough just to be together. I liked to think our deep-rooted bond was always there just the same.

When the check came, I took care of it. I guess it was sometime just after college, whenever we went out to lunch together, Dad and I had this tradition where we would alternate picking up the check. For me, as his son, it was an opportunity to show him that I had become established and that I had officially entered adulthood. And to reinforce our relationship of not only being father and son, but also being genuine friends. And it was an opportunity, maybe more like an offering, for me to start to kind of pay him back for all that he had provided for me over the years of my upbringing. A lot of times we would forget who last picked it up. Rather than quibble about it, I would always assign myself the default guy.

Getting back home was no sweat. With the help of the step stool, we had the whole process down of getting in and out of the van. On the way home, we stopped for ice cream of course. We both always had a strong hankering for ice cream, especially after Chinese or really any other Asian cuisine for that matter. I wondered if that was a hereditary thing as well. But it was kind of an unwritten rule between us, if we had Asian we had to top it off with ice cream, whether as dessert at the restaurant or as a second stop. We had to have it.

It was a drive-through Baskin-Robbins. He usually went with butter pecan, unless of course the place had coconut, which was the case on that day. I was also tempted to go for the coconut, but instead I opted for my standard vanilla. I always thought it was the finest of the flavors.

Ice cream was kind of a bonding agent for us. When we were home together, it was something we shared almost every night. An after-dinner, before-bedtime snack that we would both indulge in and enjoy together.

While driving back, with my ice cream cone in hand and my father sitting next to me, I started to wonder how many more of these cherished lunches, how many more ice cream cones, how many more car rides, and how many more of these precious moments we would have together.

Chapter 16

HANGING UP THE STICKS

The next time I saw Dad was a couple of months later in November for Thanksgiving. Because it was difficult for him to travel, in addition to spring break, my wife Gail, the kids, and I typically went to Florida for Thanksgiving every year, and around Christmastime as well most years.

Having always been captivated by Dad's stories, my sister Lexye and I over the years had talked about getting his stories recorded, but we never got around to it. We were intent on making sure that we captured all his captivating anecdotes so that we'd always have them for us kids, our kids, and their kids. It was one of those good-ideas, nice-to-do kind of things that with everything else you have going on, falls through the cracks. But finally, starting sometime around 2002, thanks to Lexye, who lived in West Palm Beach, close to my parents, she took the initiative to sit down with Dad and start the ball rolling. She did such an assiduous job of interviewing and bringing out the best in him, getting him to relive his past and share so many of his adventures. It's great to have cassettes of all of these priceless stories, as well as transcriptions of them.

While Lexye did most of the interviewing with Dad herself, we tried to carve out a little time when we were all together as a family to hear him firsthand add to his memoirs. So whether it was at my

120

parents' condo or Lexye's house, we would all gather around the table after dinner, kids included, and turn the floor over to him. He seemed to love it, and so did we.

It was on that Thanksgiving weekend of 2003 when we listened to and recorded what turned out to be among his last recordings. It was regarding the first time Dad met Mom in the summer of 1948. The session was actually more of a collaboration between the two of them.

Mom:

I knew I was going to marry him once I met him, although he ended up having to go away on a cruise to make up his mind.

Dad:

Well, I was a dyed-in-the-wool bachelor. I hated to give up my status as a bachelor, because you know I had nobody to answer to except myself. I had a fairly good business, and wherever I wanted to go, I could go. I could take a week off, a few weeks off, a month off. It was a difficult decision. Although after I had been with your mother for a couple of days, I sort of loosened up and I thought maybe she might be the one for me. But then I wasn't sure she would accept.

Mom:

What do you mean? He bought the ring before he proposed; he was pretty sure of himself.

Dad:

Well, I had to buy the ring – what did you want me to do, say, "Do you want to get married" and then say, "I'll go and buy a ring?"

Mom:

But the jeweler told him he could return it.

Dad:
Where did you get that?

Mom:
We met at Berkshire Country Club on the 4th of July in 1948. First of all, when he met me, he said, "I'm never getting married." And I said, "OK, you don't have to get married," although I said to myself, "You want to bet, buster!"

Dad:
And I said something like, heh...heh, "We'll just go to bed together, that's all."

Mom:
And then, he told me he couldn't travel out to Great Neck.

Dad:
What was that? What did you say?

Mom:
You told me you weren't coming all the way out to Long Island, to my house.

Dad:
I don't remember that.

Mom:
And when I met him in July in the Berkshires, when we left, he took my phone number and he said he comes to New York all the time and he'd call me. So, then he announces to me that well it's July now and I don't come to New York until September, in the fall. So part of me thought to myself... goodbye, I'll never see him again.

And there was a storm that night going home and when I got home, my mother asked, "Do you know an Al Levin?"

I answered "Yeah, why?"

He called to see if you were home. I got a little alarmed because of the storm, and he said "Oh no, you left late," which I didn't of course.

I kept raving about him to my mother. I told her he was quite a bit older than me, but when I met him at first I didn't know how much older. My mother married a man 16 years her senior, but she thought maybe he was too old for me, which of course he was [giggle].

And then the following week, I got a call from him that he had to be in New York unexpectedly, and could I meet him. I had another date, which I broke.

Dad:

Yeah, we had a few dates in New York, didn't we honey?

Mom:

Oh, we had quite a number of dates. You would always take me to Lum Fung's for dinner.

Dad:

Yeah, that's right when I came to New York on business.

Mom:

And then sure enough he came to Great Neck for dinner.

Dad:

Yeah…heh heh, I wasn't sure what to expect. I imagined her father was cleaning the gun, and her older brother was polishing the sword, so I don't have to tell you, heh, heh!

The first night I ended up sleeping on the porch, didn't I honey? You made up the bed for me on the porch.

Mom:
It wasn't the porch, it was the sunroom! It was in the house.
Dad:
Yeah, yeah, that's right not outside.

Mom:
I made dinner. I remember I served broiled grapefruit, and my brother wanted to know why I put the grapefruit in the fridge all night and then took it out and broiled it in the morning.

Dad:
Yeah, I had never had broiled grapefruit before, in all the years that I had been wherever I went… Grossinger's, Concord, Berkshires, nobody had ever mentioned broiled grapefruit.

Mom:
Spice liked him right away. And my father liked him too. But my older brother Bobby, he was a little skeptical, and actually became very annoyed when your father felt he needed to go on a cruise to think about whether he wanted to get married. He said, "Well, he couldn't really be interested in you if he's got to do that."

Dad:
Yeah but you know I almost killed the shittach, the deal, on the night before the wedding. We were getting married on a Sunday, and the day before, Saturday, I had gone out to Great Neck and spent the day there. Yale and I had checked into the Warwick Hotel in New York earlier in the day. Bobby, along with Nikki, had picked me up and then drove me back to the hotel, and I say to Nikki… "You want to come up and say hello to Yale?" But Bobby wouldn't let her go up!

Mom:
He said, "Oh no!"

Dad:
I almost killed the deal right then and there!

Mom:
He was so wonderful, my brother Bobby, what a guy he
was. He was the male edition of Spice.

That Thanksgiving, I noticed how Dad was really starting to
slow down. While he clearly still had his wits about him and these
recording sessions seemed to bring out the best in him, there were
continuing signs that he was slowly regressing.

Gone were the days when he played golf. He actually was able
to play longer than most, through his 80's and even into his 90's.
Along with playing gin and drinking gin, the game of golf might
have been one of the key factors that kept him so young at heart. No
doubt, it was part of his lifeblood that kept him going. I remember
playing with him on his 87th birthday, and he shot his age, a lower
score than me. And then when he got into his nineties, even though
he lost a few shots due to distance, he still was able to pretty much
shoot his age. He still had the magic with his putter.

But when Dad reached 94, his legs were beginning to give out
and even though he always took a cart and didn't really have to do
a lot of walking, it just got to be too much for him. He had to put
away his sticks.

But from time to time he still played gin. When it came to
cards, his mind was still very sharp and he didn't miss a beat. I
remember the kids used to play with him when we came down
to Florida to visit. It was their thing to do with Pop-Pops. He
had taught them the game, and each one took turns playing with
the master. They even had some round robin tournaments together.

As he eased into his mid-90's, he was becoming quieter and more reclusive, a sign that he was starting to withdraw. His appetite continued to diminish, he was sleeping more and more, and overall his interest in things was waning, as he just didn't seem to have the motivation to do much of anything. His body functions were becoming less controllable. And because of all that, he didn't ever want to go out. He would just sit in his recliner in the den and keep to himself, watching TV, and continually dozing off.

It was getting to be too much even for my diehard mother to take care of Dad. It was to the point that it was time for him to cash in on his long-term care policy, as he couldn't shower himself, had difficulty dressing himself, and generally needed help in getting around from one place to another within the apartment and using the bathroom. Except for the fact that he was able to eat for himself, he pretty much qualified on all of the rest of the major prerequisite conditions for long-term care eligibility, so we initiated that insurance policy and he was able to have an aide come to their place.

His aide was this big dude from Haiti named Jude. He was studying to become a nurse, and in the meantime was working as an aide to help pay for school. Jude would come to my parents' apartment every weekday at 9:00 am, putting in an eight-hour shift until 5:00 pm. My mother was still her beloved husband's go-to aide during the evenings and on the weekends.

Dad and Jude immediately hit it off, as Jude provided companionship as much as care. Every night when Jude left, my father would say, "Good night, my friend," with Jude repeating the refrain.

As hurricane season took hold that year, in 2004, the storms seemed particularly abundant in Florida. It became dubbed as "the year of the hurricanes" down there. The four that impacted the state the most were Charley, Frances, Ivan, and Jeanne, all of which hit during the four-week period of mid-August through mid-September. These storms were relentless. They kept pummeling some of the same areas of the state, and all told, they accounted for at least 30 deaths and over $30 billion in damages.

One of the most intense of these storms was Hurricane Frances. As it approached the Palm Beach area in early September, warnings went out for those living on the coast to evacuate as preparations were setting in. While it wasn't an easy process for my parents to pick up and leave, the portentous severity of the situation dictated that they needed to get out of there, so Mom and Dad packed up the car and went to my sister Lexye's house, about a half hour or so inland from where they were.

My sister suddenly had a full house, as her place became a refuge for several others in addition to my parents. In total there were seven of them. There was Lexye and my brother-in-law Gianni; Mom and Dad; Gianni's son-in-law Mosomo, who lived in Italy and was here on vacation, this being his first trip to the U.S.; the grandmother of actress Gwyneth Paltrow, Dotti Paltrow, whom my mother had grown up with in Great Neck, New York, and now lived in Palm

Beach; plus a good friend of Lexye and Gianni's. It turned out that all these guests were at her home for a couple of days before the storm actually hit, as the slow-moving forecasted storm took its time to make its way to landfall.

But sure enough, as expected, on the evening of Saturday, September 4 (I remember the specific day because it was my daughter Danni's birthday), the storm rolled in and started hitting the east coast of Florida, including West Palm Beach, battering the area with 102 mph winds. While quite a bit less than the Category 4, 150 mph winds the storm had previously attained while out at sea and fortunately less than what was expected at landfall, it still wreaked havoc on the area. Trees were uprooted with big branches strewn all over, causing extensive damage to both residential and commercial properties in the area, especially right near the coastline.

While not nearly as devastating, to my father this storm must have been reminiscent of another Florida storm, the catastrophic hurricane of 1926 that he had lived through back in his teenage days when he was first in Florida. Even though he slept through much of this devastating 2004 storm, which he did back in 1926 as well, it still seemed to take a toll on him. As if uprooting and displacing Dad away from the comfortable surroundings of his own home and forcing him to make a sudden migration to another environment wasn't enough, Hurricane Frances, with her own gusty, howling winds and relentless force, had powered her way in and seemed to somehow zap him of whatever strength he had left, and cause him to become a little disoriented.

The storm lasted all day Sunday. They had no water and the electricity was out. All told, the seven of them were at my sister's refuge for almost a week, much of the time without any water or electricity. And while they must have been anxious to get back to the comfortable environs of their own condo, my parents waited things out, staying even a couple extra days after the water and electricity came back to make sure that all the debris had been cleaned up from the streets and they would have a clear path for a safe, uneventful trip back home.

A little over a week later, late Friday afternoon on the 17th, I got a call from my mother that Dad was failing, that he wasn't eating, that he wasn't very coherent, and was pretty much sleeping all the time. And that a nurse from hospice, who was now checking in on him almost every day, felt it was the beginning of the end.

I had played 18 holes of golf that afternoon and had just gotten home when I got the call. I had had quite a round. On the front nine, I played my usual inconsistent game... some good holes, some not so good holes, and some in between. As is the case even today, it's always a challenge for me to put a string of good holes together and put up a decent score. But then on the back nine, something magical happened. Something seemed to all of a sudden kick into gear. I was on fire! My game went to another level, a level I wasn't accustomed to, a level I had never before attained but could only dream of. By some fluke, I was getting par after par, as I found myself questioning if this was really me playing. I couldn't help but think that perhaps someone else was swinging the club for me. I ended up bogeying the last whole, just missing a 10-foot putt for my par, and ended up with a one-over-par 37 on the back nine, which, to this day, has been the best nine-hole round of my life.

The phone call, of course, put a damper on my exhilarating high coming off of the golf course, as I quickly forgot about my round and jumped on the computer to see how quickly I could get down to Florida. Unfortunately, there weren't any more flights down there that night, so I booked a flight out the first thing in the morning.

Because it seemed like my dad was in the on-deck circle of leaving this earth, it didn't feel quite right to be going to a baseball game that night. But several weeks before, I had promised my son Mac that I would take him to a Chicago White Sox game on the South Side that Friday night. He had never been down to a ball game at U.S. Cellular Field, which just the year before had changed its name from Comiskey Park, and he had been really looking forward to going.

Mac and I had recently made a pact that one of our father-son bucket list items would be to go to every Major League ballpark together. It didn't count if one of us went to a stadium without the other. It had to be together. So far we only had gone to a few with each other, as we had a long way to go to complete our goal. So, U.S. Cellular would be one of the initial ones we could add to our list.

Even though my heart wasn't in it, I didn't want to disappoint Mac. Plus, I didn't want to bring attention to his Pop-Pops' situation sooner than I had to. So, since I couldn't get down to Florida that night anyway, I figured we might as well go to the game as planned.

Still hemming and hawing to myself as to whether or not we should actually go, we got off to a little bit of a late start. And, with the typical rush hour Chicago traffic, by the time we got to the stadium and into our seats, it was already the bottom of the first inning and the visiting Tigers were winning 1-0. We had some great seats, about 10 rows or so right behind home plate. Since it was the first time Mac had been to the stadium, I figured it was worth it to pay a little extra to get down near the field.

As we sat down in these choice seats, Mac noticed that this older fellow wearing a White Sox cap sitting next to him was keeping score on one of those formal score sheets that the most diehard baseball fans fill out throughout the game. And so being the consummate fellow baseball fan that he was, Mac proceeded to ask him how the Tigers scored their run.

Seeming as though he appreciated Mac's attentive interest in the game, the man popped his head right up, pointed to the score sheet, and with somewhat of a half-smile on his face said "Omar Infante, the Tiger shortstop, hit a home run off my son." It turns out the guy's name was Steve Grilli, father of the White Sox starting pitcher for the evening Jason Grilli, who had broken into the majors with the Florida Marlins in 2001 and was now in his first year with the Sox.

What's more, in talking with Steve, we learned that he himself was in the majors, having pitched for the opposing Tigers back in the mid-1970s and then the Blue Jays in 1979. Coincidentally, he had made his final Major League appearance on September 17, 1979, exactly 25 years ago to the day.

You had to love that the dad was in the stands to see his son pitch, no less keeping the scorebook for him. I figure he must have been keeping track of his son's balls and strikes, which the two of them would no doubt recap and analyze at the end of the game. He told us that he tried to make it to White Sox games whenever he could, especially the games when his son was scheduled to pitch. In this case, given that the White Sox were playing the Tigers, it must have been difficult for Steve to root against one of his former teams, but a father's love for his son is unconditional.

Since we got a late start and didn't think we'd be getting there in time to get any autographs, Mac didn't bring a ball to the park this time. But like he always did, he still brought his glove, in the event he got any foul balls hit near him or any balls that players might throw up to the stands between innings. He also brought with him a few baseball cards of some of the Tigers and White Sox players he had in his collection, with one of them being that of Jason Grilli. And so, Mac asked Steve to autograph his son's card.

What made this game even more special was that later on in the sixth inning, in comes this relief pitcher for the Tigers named Al Levine. I'd had never heard of this guy before, but his name obviously hit close to home. I guess it was only apropos that he made an appearance that night. He only pitched one inning, giving up two hits and one run, with no walks and one strikeout. But it looked like he had some pretty good stuff.

The game ended up being a slugfest, a real barn-burner as they say, with the lead going back and forth and the Tigers finally winning it 11-10 in extra innings. We saw a lot of hitting, that's for sure. Between the two teams, there were a total of 10 home runs in the game that included another one from Omar Infante.

On the way home from the stadium that night, Mac and I couldn't stop talking about that whole experience of meeting former Major Leaguer Steve Grilli, the father of the starting pitcher. I actually used this happenstance as one of those life lesson opportunities for a father-son teaching moment… that wherever you are in life it's always good to seize the opportunity and strike up a conversation with the person next to you, as you never know who you might meet.

On the flight to Florida the next morning, I began to work on my dad's eulogy. On one hand, I couldn't help but feel a little disrespectful and guilty, that it was too premature to be doing this. I mean in good conscience how can one really start writing a eulogy before the person passes? I was afraid that might precipitate the process, that I might be giving him a *kinehora* of sorts (a Yiddish term meaning an evil eye), maybe the worst *kinehora* or jinx somebody could give someone. But still I knew it would take me a long time to come up with just the right words, so I figured that I should get a head start on things. I had to get it right, or at least as right as I could possibly get it.

As soon as I walked in the door of my parents' apartment, my eyes caught the makeshift hospital bed that hospice had set up for him in the living room. Rather than going to hospice, hospice had come to him.

Dad had slipped into a coma-like state, that from my understanding for some is the initial step that starts the gradual transition of easing into a permanent deceased state. A kind of a bridge toward the other side.

I would just sit there by his bedside and watch him sleep. I wanted so badly to talk with him. For a guy who usually wasn't that loquacious, all of a sudden it seemed as though I had so much to say. It made me think of all those times, in the car, at lunch together, at home, or wherever, when perhaps we could have said something more to each other but didn't. It makes you realize just how precious simple communication is.

They say when a person is in such a comatose-like state, even though he has his eyes closed, can't talk, and virtually has little or no signs of life, he can still hear you. But it just didn't seem that way. There seemed to be an impenetrable barrier. I was hoping that he would come out of this sleeping funk for at least a few minutes, long enough for me to get a few words in.

I wanted to tell him about yesterday's back nine, take him through each hole, each shot, just like he always used to do when he would give me a detailed, shot-by-shot account of many of his rounds. How the putts were falling, except for the last hole, that is. And how I actually even felt a little bit like Al Levine the Putting Machine out there. I suspect part of me was still trying to impress him with my stuff. I suppose sons never stop trying.

If nothing else, I wanted to somehow say goodbye to him. To give him a proper sendoff, a final farewell, however it is that one does that. I wasn't really sure what I would say, but I was hoping that the words would somehow come to me. And I wanted to see if perhaps he had any parting words for me that I was hoping might come forth, that I was still holding out for. Perhaps some last shout-outs, some pearls of wisdom, some final tidbits of fatherly advice, or some of life's secrets to leave me with to help put it all into perspective.

All the while, my mother would go back and forth, to and from his bedside, doing household chores and whatnot but always making sure to check on him every so often. But for much of the time, she stayed at his bedside as well. She and I would sit with him and every so often would bring up and relive memories we had all shared together. While we were hoping of course he was listening to these memories and they were resonating with him, they were more for our therapeutic benefit and to help us get through this difficult time. It was comforting nonetheless for my mother and me to be able to be next to him at his bedside during what seemed to be his final hour.

The only member of the immediate family we were missing was my sister, who was away on a business trip. Of course, we had gotten word to her on Dad's condition, but she wasn't scheduled back until tomorrow evening. We were just hoping that she would get back in time to say goodbye.

I didn't really want to go to sleep. I wanted to be by his side the whole time. But I ended up nodding off, as his sleep begat my sleep. When the morning came around, there was no change. Even though I knew in my heart the inevitability of it all, I was still hoping that somehow the Florida morning might bring in some rays of sunshine and improvement, that somehow the tide would turn.

But still I had hope. After all, it was Sunday, the last day of the weekend's PGA tournament, the Valero Texas Open, coming from LaCantera Golf Course in San Antonio. If anything could bring Dad out of his comatose funk, I figured it would be a golf match. So come the afternoon, I turned on the TV and blasted out the tournament for good measure, with the outside chance that perhaps his ears would pick up the sound and he would perk up.

Even though it was Sunday, knowing the severity of the situation, Jude had come in around 3:00 pm to be with him at his bedside. Like the hospice nurse who had previously come in a couple of days ago to check on him, he knew my father's systems were shutting down and that his time was drawing near. He had seen this type of progression before. I knew it was coming, but I was hoping that he would stay with us at least until my sister got back from her trip that night. But unfortunately, it wasn't to be.

Not that I wasn't prepared for it, but it all seemed so surreal when it happened. Like it didn't really happen. But with my mother and I by his bedside, in the late afternoon around 5:00 pm on that Sunday, September 19, he passed. With his stethoscope in hand, Dad's new friend Jude made the final pronouncement.

Before I knew it, two dubious-looking characters showed up at our door, holding a folded-up gurney. Both were fairly young looking and each was sporting a different hat. One guy was tall and skinny, wearing a baseball cap. The other guy was short and stocky with scruffy facial hair, wearing a battered chapeau. They were dressed pretty shabbily, and looked as though they might have been out drinking at a neighborhood bar when they got the call to come over. Except for their medical-grade type gloves, nothing seemed professional about them.

I wondered how they got here so fast. It was almost as if they had been secretly summoned from above. I found out later that my mother had called hospice, which had set up the plan. All my mother had to do was make a quick call, and an alert was sent out.

And who the heck were these guys? How was it that they were selected? I mean here they were, two complete strangers all of a sudden kind of coming out of the woodwork to take my father away. And where were they taking him?

I suppose I should have thought of them as special "messengers of God" of sorts, carrying out such a sacred and dutiful deed that not everybody, actually I'm sure very few, would be willing to undertake. Clearly, this was a mitzvah they should be commended for. But, taking one look at them, they were not exactly who you would expect or feel all that comfortable with entrusting a loved one to.

I had heard a little bit about the Jewish religious ritual called *shemira* (derived from the Hebrew root word *shin-mem-resh*, meaning guards or keepers), where a guardian called a *shomer* (if male) and a *shomeret* (if female), watches over the body of a deceased Jewish person from the time of death until burial. Supposedly, while on the job these *shomerim* aren't even allowed to eat or drink, in respect to the deceased who can no longer perform these actions. They tend to be volunteers, whose service is to be looked upon as being meritorious of the highest order, in that they are doing a mitzvah for someone who can never repay them.

But I wasn't exactly sure how these guys fit into the whole process. I didn't know if they were indeed the *shomerim* planning on staying at the funeral home to watch over him. Or if, as I suspected, they were merely transport guys, who would be handing the body off to a *shomer* if indeed there was a *shomer* for Dad. While they might have been volunteers, I imagined rather they were from a service agency who specializes in this kind of work that the funeral parlor uses.

These two guys didn't say much, not even a "sorry for your loss," just a nod of the head from one of them signifying an acknowledgement of the situation. They merely went about their business of transferring Dad's body from his makeshift bed to the gurney, covering him up with a few more sheets they had brought, and then without any pause, immediately started to wheel him out.

As they wheeled him out the condo door, I followed along right on their heels, partly because I still didn't really trust these guys, but more so because I wanted to stay with Dad as long as I could. It seemed as though they knew exactly where they were going with him, as they zipped down the hall gathering speed, almost like they were trying to elude me. They made their way to a back service elevator, which I didn't even know existed in the building. They had already scoped it out, as I figured they must have come up that way.

Meanwhile, given that there wasn't enough room in the service elevator for me, or these two transporters purposely positioned themselves and the gurney in such a way to make it seem like there wasn't enough space for all of us, I hightailed it down the stairwell and met up with them outside the building.

Still not speaking, they rolled him along the side of the building to their large, limousine-type black van. It was parked in the visitor's section, right about in the same spot I had parked that rented gold minivan Bully when my dad and I had taken her out for our last official father-son lunch a little over a year before.

Still feeling a little suspicious of these guys, I just stood there near the back of the van and idly looked on as these two strangers hastily placed Dad's body inside. Just as they were about to close the swinging back doors, I managed to get in a half wave and told him that I loved him. With that, both transporters gave me a reassuring nod in unison, and before I knew it they sped off, leaving me still searching for some words to say goodbye.

Chapter 17

A TRIBUTE TO AL PAL

AS IS CUSTOMARY WITHIN THE JEWISH RELIGION, one's funeral is a fast turnaround. According to Jewish Law, the immediate body internment of the deceased is sacrosanct and takes precedent pretty much over everything.

Jewish law dictates that the *kevura* or burial should take place as soon as possible. Initially, way back when, the protocol was that the deceased be interred within 24 hours of passing. As stated in the Torah… **"His body shall not remain all night upon the tree, but thou shalt surely bury him the same day" (Deuteronomy 21:23).** Supposedly, Jewish folklore has it that the interpretation of this is that the soul is in turmoil until the body is properly buried in the ground. But over time, the law has been relaxed somewhat as it doesn't necessarily need to be within 24 hours per se, but rather as soon as practical or logistically possible. So unless it's the Sabbath or a Jewish holiday or there are some underlying circumstances involved such as holding the service until a loved one can be there, it's planned for the closest day it can conceivably be scheduled. Which for us was three days away: Wednesday, September 22.

In the meantime, there was a lot of preparation to be done. First, we had to go to the funeral home in Boynton Beach to meet with the funeral director to make all the arrangements for the service and to reconfirm the casket that my father and mother had already picked out ahead of time. Then, we had to go to the nearby cemetery to review the specific location of the mausoleum in which his casket was to be placed, as my parents had opted to be above versus below. And we had to make time to talk to the rabbi, Rabbi Yellin of Temple Emeth in Del Ray Beach, with whom the funeral director had matched us up. It was important to each one of us—my mother, sister, and myself—to spend a considerable amount of time over the phone with the rabbi to provide some ample background information on our "man of the hour" in preparation for the service.

When it came to coming up with some accolades for our father, my sister and I had a lot to draw from and reflect on. After all, he had been presented with the distinguished "ABE" (short for Abraham) award by us kids in 1988 in honor of his 80th birthday for being the "Absolutely Best Ever" Dad, so there was a lot to share about him.

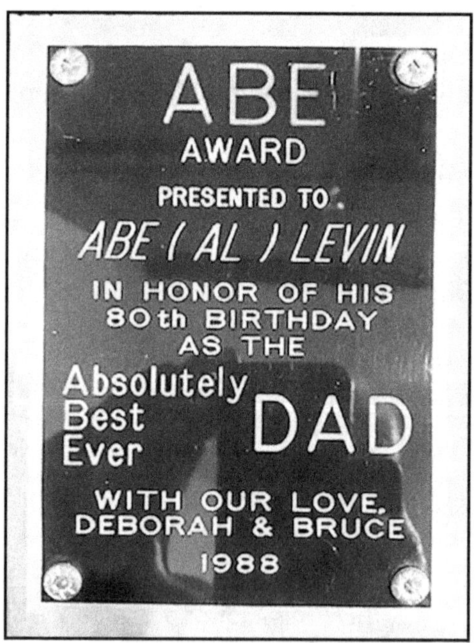

Dad receives the ABE (Absolutely Best Ever) Dad Award

Meanwhile, I was scheduled to go on a business trip to Seattle that Tuesday to conduct some market research for Starbucks. Postponing the project wasn't really an option. It would have been very costly to reschedule the research, and the client would have lost valuable time in its project schedule.

It was my first project with Starbucks, and here I was having to back out of it. Rather, I had to line up a replacement to fly out to Seattle and pinch hit for me, which while it wasn't easy to do given the eleventh-hour turnaround time, I was fortunately able to have a fellow market research freelancer help out.

Dad's service was called for 10:30 am, but as is customary for the immediate family we got there about an hour earlier to go over all the logistical details with the funeral director and then meet up with Rabbi Yellin in a private room designated just for the mourners. Rabbi Yellin couldn't have been nicer. He tried to put all of us at ease, including Mac and Danni, for whom this was their first funeral and I'm sure it must have been very scary for them. In his understanding and comforting tone, he went over the agenda of the service and the general content of what he was going to cover in his introduction.

He then had my mother, me and Lexye, and Dad's brother Harry (my father's only living sibling) stand up for the pre-service *kriah* or black ribbon ceremony. *Kriah* is the Hebrew word for "tearing," and refers to the act of tearing one's clothes as an expression of the sorrow and grief for the loss of a loved one. It's memorialized by having the rabbi affix a black ribbon on one's clothes and then tearing the ribbon.

According to Jewish law, all immediate family members of the deceased—children, parents, spouse, and siblings—are to partake in this ritual. It dates back to an ancient tradition when Jacob, who believed his son Joseph was killed somewhere out in the field, was so torn to pieces over his death that he tore his own garments off his body. As it is written...

> **And they took Joseph's coat, and killed a goat**
> **and dipped the coat in its blood; and they brought the**
> **coat of many colors to their father Jacob and said…**
> **"This have we found. Know now whether it is thy son's coat**
> ** or not." And he knew it and said…**
> **"It is my son's coat; an evil beast hath devoured him; Joseph**
> **is without doubt torn in pieces." And Jacob rent his**
> **gaments, and put sackcloth upon his loins, and mourned**
> **for his son many days.**
>
> **(Genesis 37:31-34)**

Supposedly, it also has traces of other biblical references when King David did the same upon hearing of the death of his predecessor King Saul and his friend Jonathon, Saul's son. As it is written…

> **Then David took hold of his clothes and rent them;**
> **and likewise all the men that were with him.**
> **And they wailed, and wept, and fasted for Saul,**
> **and for Jonathon his son, and for the people of the Lord,**
> **and for the house of Israel; because they were fallen by**
> **the sword.**
>
> **(Second Samuel 1:11-12)**

Kriah is always performed with the recipients standing up, as the act of standing signifies strength during the time of one's grief. As such, for each of us standing up, the rabbi pinned a little black button with a dangling ribbon on our clothing, on the left side of our chest right over our heart, and then tore it. The placement over the heart is to symbolize a broken heart from within, and this torn ribbon is to be worn during the funeral and then on through the mourning period called the shiva for the mourner to express their continued grieving and make visible for all others to see.

As we got closer to the start of the service, as part of his repertoire, to give us one final opportunity to say our last goodbyes, the funeral director asked if anybody cared to see my father in his casket. I had thought about it ahead of time and questioned myself… that if and when the time came would I actually want to go ahead and do this, as I had a lot of apprehension about seeing him in this state. I wasn't sure how I would react and if this was something I really wanted to go through.

I probably wouldn't have decided to go through with this option to peek into the casket for a final goodbye if it wasn't for the deep-seated compulsion that I had to leave him with something. I figured he could maybe use it where I thought he would most likely be going. So when it came time to being asked, with still some trepidation and reservation, I motioned to the funeral director that I would, as he started to escort me to the adjoining chapel, where the service would be held and where the casket was located. But as we entered the chapel, I hesitated and asked him to give me a minute, as I excused myself and proceeded to walk back out to the vestibule as though I had to go to the bathroom or something. But instead, I went outside to the car and grabbed my dad's prize possession that I had snuck in there the night before, just in case I had gotten up the nerve to go through with this. When I came back into the funeral home and reunited with the funeral director waiting for me in the chapel, I tried to conceal it on the side of my body as I followed him right up to the casket, which he had just opened while I was out in the car.

There was Dad in his peaceful state, still looking young for his age. It was difficult for me to bring myself to look at him. But I made it quick, as I gave Al Levine the Putting Machine a kind of a half-smile and a little wink, as I slipped in the ole Tomahawk putter and placed it right next to him. Then, one last "I love you," and I was gone, not wanting to prolong my farewell more than I could muster up. And then I returned to the private room where the rest of my immediate family was waiting.

Just before the service was set to commence, a few minutes after all the visitors were settled in their seats, our family emerged out of the private room together, as the rabbi escorted us into the chapel, and we sat in the front row that had been reserved for us.

Rabbi Yellin started the service with some opening remarks about why we were gathered here today and then recited *Psalm 23…*

> *The Lord is my Shepherd; I shall not want.*
> *He has me lie down in green pastures,*
> *He leads me beside the still waters.*
> *He revives my soul;*
> *He guides me on paths of righteousness for His glory.*
> *Though I walk through the valley of the shadow of death,*
> *I fear no harm,*
> *For you are with me.*
> *Your rod and your staff do comfort me.*
> *You set a table in sight of my enemies;*
> *You anoint my head with rich oil; my cup overflows.*
> *Surely goodness and mercy shall follow me all the days of my*
> *life,*
> *And I shall abide in the house of the Lord forever.*

The rabbi continued on, taking the congregation through a brief chronology of my father's treasured life, talking very eloquently about the type of man he was and how he had touched so many people's lives.

Then it was my turn to deliver a eulogy. Of course, as is always the case when I have to stand up and give a speech to an audience, I was nervous. My legs were a little shaky as I ambled up to the pulpit, took a deep breath, and took a moment to gaze out at the congregation.

As expected, the congregation was pretty sparse. There couldn't have been more than a total of maybe 40 folks out there, if that. Other than our immediate family, there wasn't much in the way of family representation. Most of my other relatives on my father's side still lived in Connecticut and given the long distance they weren't able to make it down. Only his younger brother Harry, my Uncle Doc, who was a spry 94 at the time and still going fairly strong, flew down from his home in Waterbury to be there. As an aside, my dear Uncle Doc ended up living to the age of 98, outlasting his brother by two years. Those Levin boys sure had some longevity. I was just hoping that longevity would transcend down to the next generation.

Meanwhile, other than my mother, the only one from her side of the family was my cousin Robert Schenck, my Uncle Hank's son. Hank himself had recently passed, as had his wife, Marge, and their other kids couldn't make it in.

In addition, there were a handful of residents from my parents' condo building, the Barclay; plus some friends, who had permanently moved down to Florida from Connecticut and lived nearby in the Palm Beach area. But unfortunately, all told there weren't that many. Truth is he had outlived most of his friends and acquaintances. I also noticed that his caretaker and new friend Jude was out there as well—our family was really touched that he took the time to attend.

Somehow it just didn't seem fair that only a modicum of people were there to celebrate Dad's life and pay tribute to him, to a guy named Abraham who was so caring, so generous, so revered, and so loved. A guy who had the wherewithal to be the father of all nations. I felt that if only half of everybody he had touched and positively impacted in life were around, it would have been standing room only.

As I looked around, I wondered if perhaps my father was out there as well, somewhere invisible in the audience, perhaps in the front row. I always felt that you should be given the opportunity to attend your own funeral and take it all in, to see who shows up, to hear what they have to say about you, to kind of bring it all together for you, and hopefully end it all on a positive note. It would be a good way to wrap things up, a proper send-off for the newly deceased. It could serve as a compendium of your life, a leave-behind that you could take with you to wherever you're going.

Analogous to the tradition during Passover when you place a cup of wine for Elijah on the Passover table and leave the front door open for him to come in and partake in the festivities, I always felt the door of the funeral parlor should be left ajar and there should be an empty designated chair in the front row, next to the immediate family, for the deceased to come in and sit down during the service and take it all in.

I cleared my throat and began…

There's a great little saying people use to describe those whose parents they also happen to know, that being "The apple doesn't fall from the tree." I know if I was fortunate enough to have someone say that about me, it would be the sincerest form of flattery that someone could possibly give me.

For my dad was quite the tree… as solid and sturdy as a mighty oak, as brilliant and colorful as one with full foliage in the fall, especially when he would wear those flashy colors on the golf course, and as tall and majestic as one would ever come across. He clearly stood out in the forest.

He was a tree that never wavered in the wind, but always stood its ground… a strong decision maker and man of his word. He was a tree that could withstand any hurricane, the 1926 one, the 1928 one, and even the more recent Hurricane Frances. He was a tree that had a strong inner core that was rock solid. And he was a tree that had a lot of branches that bore an abundance of fruit, which he shared with many people. For he was very generous with his family, his friends, his business associates, and even strangers.

I'm reminded of one of the days I played golf with him at Stanley Golf course in New Britain, Connecticut. As you know, my dad loved golf and fancied himself as quite a golfer. He definitely had a magic putter in life. In fact, so much so that they called him "Al Levine the Putting Machine". While he was a member of Cliffside Country Club for many years

and played a lot of different courses over his lifetime, he ended up playing his last few years of golf at Stanley, which appropriately enough was one of the courses where he first started to play. And, when I was in town, I'd often play with him, as I loved being out there with him every chance I got.

Anyway, I remember on this one particular day, we were on the 7th hole and there was this very elderly man sitting at the tee, selling golf balls. Upon seeing each other, they exchanged waves and started talking to each other as though they knew one another. After my dad bought a few balls from him, he explained to me that this fellow was a nice man that he had met a few weeks ago out here and in the interest of trying to help him out a little bit, he told me he had brought him some socks (apparently the Socks Guy still had quite an inventory of socks in our garage to work off of) as well as some of my dad's old clothes. Giving to others wasn't uncommon for my dad, in fact he's probably given all of you some socks at one time or another. In fact, you may even be wearing them right now.

Ever since I can remember, I've thought of my dad as a role model and have tried to fashion my life after his. I like to think I've done a pretty good job in following in his footsteps so far. You know, like father, like son. After all, like him, I married late in life, as we both robbed the cradle so to speak and married beautiful younger women, much younger, who were terrific beyond compare; and we both had our daughter and son at about the same age. Now if I could only get to a 7 handicap in golf, which he had gotten down to at one time. Or better yet, I really just hope I can get to the ripe old age of 96.

Dad had a special place in his heart for his grandchildren, Danni and Mac. They lit up his life, especially these past few years. He called Danni his princess, his sweetie pie, and his pumpkin. While he called Mac… Little Tiger, and The Big Macher.

So, this generous father of mine, who gave his all to those around him, was fortunate to receive tremendous love as well. Certainly from all of those friends and strangers he helped along the way, but most of all from his unbelievably dedicated wife Nikki, for whom words can't express the love and devotion she showed for him. Al and Nikki enjoyed life together for 55 years, and I want to thank and recognize her for the love and support she has given him for all of these years. I know that the last few months have been difficult ones for all of us, but especially for you, being by his side, caring for him the way you did, to keep his roots intact, and keep him standing tall.

I know my father was very appreciative of everything my mother Nikki did for him, and he told me that many times. And he also had a lot of appreciation for others, always managing to say thank you. In fact, during his last several months, whenever his aide Jude would leave at night, my dad would say… "Goodnight, my friend and thanks for everything!"

So today, on this day of tribute to him, I'd like to use my father's own words that he always used to say to his aide Jude at the end of the day, and say… "Goodbye, my friend and thanks for everything! "We love you!"

My sister followed with her eulogy, imparting some beautiful and loving words about him. Having practically been born on a stage, majoring in theatre, and having a flair for the dramatic, she was a natural up there on the podium.

Lastly, my Uncle Doc went up to the podium to say a few words about his brother. Having the same Levin brother charm as my father, he was liked by everyone. He was very personable and had a great way about him. Plus, he was very sociable, the type of guy who was involved in a lot of local community organizations, including being the president of his local Lions Club. Even though they lived in different cities—Harry had stayed in Waterbury for his adult life and they didn't get together all that often—the two were very close. Harry shared a bunch of lighthearted stories about his brother, mostly ones harkening back to when they were growing up in Waterbury.

Our eulogies were followed by the *Mourner's Kaddish*, a prayer in Hebrew honoring the deceased and praising and thanking God for the experiences and value of life. Upon the conclusion of the service, the pallbearers, which included myself, assembled and we carried his casket out to the hearse and then followed behind in our car to the cemetery.

While in my mind there should have been a long parade, there wasn't much of a procession to the cemetery, only a few cars, as we had a very small service there, that included mostly family along with the rabbi. I had very mixed feelings about the kids coming with us, exposing them to the scary finality of it all.

Once at the cemetery, the rabbi said a few prayers, and then his casket was hoisted up into the air, up into the blue sky, to the uppermost row of the mausoleum.

After the funeral, we sat *shiva*, the tradition where the mourners are greeted by friends and loved ones, at my parents' condo for the rest of the day and through the evening, as well as during the next evening. Both nights Rabbi Yellin came to the *shiva* to officiate the *minyan*, a prayer for the mourners, to which we needed to invite some neighbors in order to have the requirement of at least 10 men to hold the religious evening service.

That next week when we got back to Chicago, before the seven-day mourning period was up, Gail and I held our own *shiva* with our friends, most of who never even met my dad. It was so nice that so many of them came to pay their respects to him.

Chapter 18

THE CALL FROM ABOVE

As it came to pass, in early September 2007, just before the Jewish High Holidays of Rosh Hashanah and Yom Kippur, I got a call from above. It was clearly from a higher order.

The call was from my mother! Calling from her permanent residence in Palm Beach, Florida, she informed me that from out of the blue she had just received a call from Estelle Bernstein in New Britain, Connecticut, a name I recognized from the past as part of our local temple community when I was growing up. Estelle was someone I'm sure I was introduced to at some point but didn't really know, but I remembered that she and her husband, Abe, another Abraham, had been active members of our temple, B'nai Israel. Still a current temple board member, Estelle had called my mom with some disheartening news: our former 111-year-old temple was unfortunately planning to close its doors for good. Apparently, the normal attrition of members and the continuing decline of the population of New Britain had taken a toll on the congregation over the years. Membership had dwindled to the extent that there were only a handful of current members and a lack of new members to keep it running, barely enough to support a minyan. So the temple had no choice but to close down. It was to become a Greek church.

But from this closure, there was a silver lining… an opportunity of sorts posed to my mother. As Estelle explained, when a temple closes, it's customary for the temple to pass along all the Torahs it owns to other temples. B'nai Israel had six or seven of them, one of which was of course the beautiful, ornate, silver-encased Sephardic Torah that my father and company had brought over from Israel and donated to the temple back in the early '60s in memory of his good friend Yale Sabel.

Remembering that my father was the one who was most instrumental in bringing this Torah to the Temple B'nai Israel family, Estelle wanted to be sure to contact my mother to see if perhaps there was another temple that she or anyone else in our family was currently affiliated with, where we would like to see the Torah passed down for posterity.

Until this call, I had almost forgotten about that special Torah. But it quickly came back to me. It took me back to those days of growing up in New Britain and going to temple during the High Holidays and on other special occasions, where this unique Torah would take center stage. In particular, it took me back to when I had the opportunity to read from it during my bar mitzvah.

Living alone in Florida, my mother wasn't affiliated with any temple, nor was my sister. So when it came down to it, I was the only one in our immediate family who was currently a member of a temple and who could conceivably seize this opportunity.

Having discussed the matter with my mother and sister, we all thought this would be a wonderful opportunity to honor my father, while continuing our hometown ties with Temple B'nai Israel and keeping its memory and spirit alive. What a mitzvah it would be to pass along this beautiful Torah from Temple B'nai Israel, where our family had established our roots, to the temple my family currently belonged to, where my daughter Danni had recently became a bat mitzvah and my son Mac was scheduled to have his bar mitzvah in a year and a half. We envisioned that Mac could read from this Torah for his bar mitzvah, the same Torah that his grandfather had brought over from Israel and that I had read from during my bar mitzvah. From generation to generation, l'dor v'dor, we would be sharing the bond of this Torah.

It was certainly an unusual and coveted opportunity, one you don't come across every day. But who was I, with my limited Jewish affiliation, to be worthy and deserving of this honor and privilege, to be part of "The Chosen" so to speak to care for this Torah and arrange for its new home? For when it came down to religion, I tended to be more of a "seasonal" guy. For the most part, my Judaism only really kicked in on the major Jewish holidays—Rosh Hashanah, Yom Kippur, Hanukkah, and Passover.

Not that I didn't love being Jewish. I certainly relished the additional holidays from school in celebration of the Jewish New Year, eight days of presents on Hanukkah, and an abundance of delectable Jewish "soul" foods such as chicken soup with matzo balls, lox and bagels, potato latkes, beef brisket, and all those epicurean delights starting with "k": knishes, kishka, kasha varnishkes, and kugel. Plus, all the dessert delicacies that Jewish cuisine is known for, such as babka, rugelach, hamantaschen, mandelbrodt (mandel bread), macaroons, and of course chocolate Hanukkah gelt.

In their High Holiday sermons, rabbis often rhetorically ask "What does it mean to be Jewish?" While they impart to us their own definitions as what it is to be a good Jew… to support the temple, to maintain strong ties with Israel, and to give of ourselves, I have to admit my existence and association with the Jewish religion had mostly revolved around and were limited to those perhaps juvenile perks of holidays, presents, and sweet treats.

Indeed, I was a religious school dropout. I hung in there up until the time of my bar mitzvah, taking in some Jewish history and learning enough basics of Hebrew to get me through my *maftir* or Torah reading and my subsequent *haftarah* portion. But as soon as that momentous event signifying my passage into manhood was over, I was out of there. Since then, I had basically shed whatever Jewish skin I had developed, including my knowledge and ongoing ability to be able to decipher and speak the Hebrew language. Truth is, beyond my bar mitzvah, my tenuous religious school days, and my going to temple on the High Holidays, I had little to show to demonstrate my Jewish heritage.

After my bar mitzvah, probably the most religious I had become was at my own wedding, as my wife, Gail, and I were married by an Orthodox rabbi. While Gail wasn't Orthodox, which if she was probably would have been a deal-breaker given my love for bacon and other treyf staples of the American diet, her family was affiliated with a conservative synagogue in Lincolnwood, Illinois, which happened to have an Orthodox rabbi as the head of the clergy.

As such, we had an Orthodox-influenced ceremony, which made for some interesting activities. First off, by Orthodox law, we had to have two witnesses as part of the ceremony, who, in order to qualify as legitimate witnesses, had to keep kosher as well as be *shomer shabbos*—someone who observes the Sabbath. So in addition to counting himself as a witness, the rabbi brought along another qualifying witness, a complete stranger, to observe and participate in the signing of the *ketubah*, our written marriage agreement, essentially detailing our responsibilities to each other as a husband and wife; i.e., mostly my responsibilities. As it is written…

On the second day of the week, the twentieth day of the month of Cheshvan in the year 5752, corresponding to the twenty-seventh day of October in the year 1991 the holy covenant of marriage was entered into in Chicago, Illinois between the bridegroom, Bruce Robert Levin, son of Abraham and Bernice, and the bride Gail Delores Rapoport, daughter of Morris and Masha.

The bridegroom made the following declaration to his bride. "Be thou my wife according to the laws of Moses and Israel. I faithfully promise that I will be a true husband unto thee. I will honor and cherish thee; I will protect and support thee, and will provide all that is necessary for thy sustenance

> in accordance with the usual question of Jewish husbands. I also take upon myself all such further obligations for thy support as prescribed by our religious statutes." And the bride has entered into this holy covenant with affection and sincerity, and has thus taken upon herself the fulfillment of all the duties incumbent upon a Jewish wife.

The *ketubah* or prenuptial agreement I have with my wife

This other witness turned out to be quite the character. For a guy we didn't know, he sure left a lasting impression. First off, he never smiled or never even flinched. It was all business for him. As a total stranger trying to fulfill his Jewish duty of being a formal witness, perhaps he was intent on displaying and preserving his serious, professional character. I even tried to interject a few jokes here and there, partly to try to break up all of this serious formality on an occasion that I felt should be a little more convivial, but also to see if I could somehow get this guy to show some expression of emotion. But nope, he was steadfast in his staid manner and approach, certainly not showing any sign of the joy we were feeling on this most happy day of our lives.

Meanwhile, the formality of the *ketubah* signing made for a lengthy pre-ceremony event causing us to be late to the ceremony itself, and all I was thinking about through this arduous process was that our guests were probably getting a little restless and perhaps wondering if I was getting cold feet. I had always had a reputation for being a little late to things, and here I was true to form, at my own wedding no less, being late again. Only this time, it wasn't my fault.

Finally, we appeared on the scene with our guests waiting in what I imagined at this point had become some anxious anticipation, making our way in the traditional wedding processional fashion to the *chuppah* (canopy under which a Jewish couple stands during their wedding), albeit about half-hour late thanks to our drawn-out ketubah signing.

We began with one of my favorite parts of the Orthodox

ceremony: my lovely bride proceeded to walk slowly around me seven times in what seemed to me more of a mating call, or "Jewish foreplay," rather than a symbolic tradition of the ceremony. According to Jewish folklore, there are several possible meanings behind the bride's seven laps around her groom. One explanation is that it represents the seven days it took to create the world, thus symbolizing the creation of a new world formed by this marriage. Another explanation is that it commemorates the act of Joshua, the son of Nun, when he led the people of Israel against the city of Jericho and circled the city seven times, causing the walls to come tumbling down. This would symbolize the potential walls that two people may face between them as they enter into marriage, which would need to be broken down, so they can find their way to share and communicate with each other. Another interpretation having a wall theme is that the bride's seven times around represent a magical wall of protection from evil spirits and the glances and temptation of other women. Or that it symbolizes the bride as keeper of the household, creating a new family circle and providing overseeing love and protection from any outside harm. But the explanation that resonated with me the most was that it simply demonstrated that the groom was now the bride's center of her world, an idea I could certainly buy into.

But the pièce de resistance of our quasi-Orthodox wedding ceremony was the *Yichud* (meaning "seclusion") Room. After the rabbi's pronouncement of us as husband and wife, the stomping and breaking of the glass officially signifying the covenant of the marriage and the subsequent shouts of *"mazel tov!"* from the observing crowd of guests, and our procession from the *chuppah* as the newly deemed Mr. and Mrs. Levin, we were escorted by the rabbi to a nearby room. In this room was a nondescript couch and some folding metal chairs plus a few tables with all kinds of petits fours and other bite-size traditional delicacies, including some rugelach, mandelbrot, and macaroons, and an assortment of beverages including some wine. As part of the Orthodox service, the first stop for the new married couple is the *Yichud* Room. This is where the two can spend a little time together alone, typically 10 to 15 minutes or so, but really as long as they want, to bond, share, and celebrate their marriage in private—to eat, drink, and do whatever else together as they see fit.

Tracing back to earlier times, "celebrating the marriage as the couple sees fit" actually included physically consummating the marriage right then and there in the *Yichud* Room. Apparently this was standard practice. While in theory this seemed to be an exceptional idea that I could definitely see myself partaking in and indeed was certainly a tempting opportunity and one that God knows I could easily complete in the prescribed 10- to 15-minute time frame, with perhaps even a couple of minutes left to spare to enjoy a few postcoital petits ~~fours~~ together, it would have been too much of a production to get my new wife's dress off. Plus, given the small couch and its limited space, the room wasn't that conducive to making whoopee.

Furthermore, there is supposed to be someone stationed right outside the door as a guard to make sure no one else enters the room during the entire sacred period that the bride and groom are in there. After all, the newly married couple certainly wouldn't want to have someone barge in on them during a compromising moment that could result in coitus interruptus. In our case, of course, the guard was none other than our stoic second witness. The whole time we were in there, I had this vision that he was outside holding up a glass between the door and his ear, trying to listen for any sound effects.

By the way, as an aside, it should be noted that we later discovered that the expensive fountain pen that we had used for the signing of the *ketubah*, which we had bought especially for this momentous occasion, was missing. The proverbial fountain pen, a traditional symbol associated with the Jewish religion, harkening back to the "I Am a Fountain Pen" days when a fountain pen is what a 13-year-old boy or girl would typically receive for a bar or bat mitzvah present, was gone, nowhere to be found. We thought that the rabbi had perhaps picked it up to keep for us as a memento of the *ketubah* signing, but upon learning he didn't have it we couldn't help but suspect our beloved second witness was behind the pen caper. To give him the benefit of the doubt, maybe he didn't do it or he absentmindedly or accidentally stuck it in his pocket after the signing. But still I could only imagine that this inconspicuous guy must have accumulated quite a collection of pens that he had confiscated over the years.

Beyond my wedding experience, I must admit I hadn't really taken any steps to further indoctrinate myself into the Jewish religion. But when the subject of moving such a meaningful object as that Torah came up, I felt that this was a unique, once-in-a-lifetime opportunity and privilege that even a seasonal Jewish guy like myself couldn't pass up. I looked at this opportunity as a way to perhaps find a deeper sense of religion, and as a mitzvah that maybe could even help to seal my fate in the book of life. I therefore made an appointment with our rabbi at our temple, Temple Beth-El, in Northbrook Illinois, to discuss the prospect of bringing in a new Torah there.

Chapter 19

TORAHS AND TELEPHONE BOOTHS

RABBI SIDNEY HELBRAUN HAS AN EASY-GOING, mild-mannered, approachable way about him that always makes it a pleasure to chat with him. The fact that many congregants called him Rabbi Sid told you something about the guy. For me, compared to the rabbis of my generation, he seemed to represent a new wave of clergy who were more informal and flexible.

Rabbi Sid was quite a bit different from the rabbi I had grown up with in Connecticut, Rabbi Isadore Zaidman, who let's just say I never heard anybody call him Rabbi Izzy. While Rabbi Zaidman was a very caring man of the cloth who you could always turn to in times of need and count on to be there for you, he was certainly a little more old school in his philosophies and behavior. And I must admit he had a bit of an aura of intimidation about him, whether he intended to or not, and could instill a feeling of fear in you. I recall him always being on guard during his service, to the extent that if there was a slight bit of commotion during the service, he would know exactly where in the con-gregation it was coming from, and as such would give the perpetrator(s) involved one of those deprecating stares that would freeze you right in your place. He must have had really good hearing, as I swear this guy could even hear if a *kippah* fell off your head and dropped on the floor.

My meeting with Rabbi Sid started out talking about the Cubs and whether they were going to finish up at the top of their Central Division. Baseball was always a good conversation starter. He seemed to be a big fan of the Cubs and baseball in general, another reason that endeared me to the type of rabbi he was. The Cubs were having a good year, and it sure looked like they were going to make it to the playoffs and maybe go all the way. They actually did end up winning their division that year.

Transitioning from the topic of baseball, we got around to talking about the Torah, as I gave him all the background I had on it and how this opportunity came to be. I even had a picture of the Torah to show him (it was the only picture of it that I had at the time), which my mother had passed along to me. It was a black and white photo of my father, along with a fellow temple member, standing next to the Torah, which evidently must have been taken at B'nai Israel in the early 1960's, just after the Torah was donated. I didn't know the particulars of the situation, nor did my mom, as it was a picture she had come across among stacks of many other photos stuffed in one of her dresser drawers in her Florida condo. But from the looks of it, I imagine it could have perhaps depicted the original dedication of the Torah at Temple B'nai Israel.

Picture of the Torah presumed to be taken at the time it was originally donated to Temple B'nai Israel in New Britain, Connecticut in the early 1960's. My father is the one on the left.

I told Rabbi Sid our family would be honored if Temple Beth-El would consider adopting this Torah into its family of Torahs. I explained that I had read from this beloved Torah at my bar mitzvah, and mentioned to him how my son Mac's bar mitzvah was coming up in March 2009, and how I was hoping he could read from it as part of his service, that it would truly be a blessing to pass on this privilege from one generation to another... *l'dor v'dor.*

Rabbi Sid immediately embraced the idea of accepting this Torah with open arms, and gave me his blessing. For one thing, Beth-El didn't have a Sephardic Torah, so he felt this would be a good addition from that standpoint alone. Plus, regardless of the type of Torah, I'm sure he felt it was always good to have another Torah on hand, as I gathered that a temple could never have enough Torahs. But in particular, he seemed to be very taken with its unique, decorative look, and appeared excited about having this beauty among the temple's Torah assortment.

He shared his thoughts on where he felt the Torah could potentially be housed in the temple. He suggested one of three locations. One spot was in the ark in the main sanctuary, where like Temple B'nai Israel in Connecticut, it would share space with a number of other Torahs. Or, it could be placed in the ark in the smaller sanctuary that was used for services on occasions when there tended to be small congregations such as for minyans, and where it would share space with only one or two other Torahs. Lastly, with an enlightened face as though a bulb just went on inside his head, he came up with the option of putting it in the little alcove in the vestibule, where there used to be a pay phone. As such, it would be next to the coatroom and across from the social hall where the temple held *Oneg Shabbats* and other gatherings. He further added that this alcove could be encased in glass to provide a so-called ark for the Torah, which it would require. He envisioned that the Torah would still perhaps be used from time to time for various b'nai mitzvahs, like Mac's upcoming bar mitzvah as well those of Sephardic families, but that its home would be out in the open for everybody to see.

Rabbi Sid asked if I had a preference. Even though I told him I thought any of these locations would be great and would think more about it and get back to him, I had already pretty much decided. Of course it would be ideal to have it as part of the Torah line-up within either of the sanctuaries' arks, especially the main sanctuary where everybody in the congregation would see it when the ark was opened on High Holidays, b'nai mitzvahs, and other major temple services. But I was especially intrigued with the idea of putting it in the abandoned phone booth space where it would stand alone in its own specially built glass-encased ark, where it would be show-cased for members and guests alike to see, walking through that high-traffic area.

Now all I had to do was figure out how I was going to get the Torah from my former temple in Connecticut to my current temple in Illinois.

Chapter 20

HOW TO GET TO THE PROMISED LAND

Still feeling charged up coming out of my meeting with Rabbi Sid, the first thing I did when I got home from the temple was to Google "Torah shipping." Not sure there was going to be anything there, but I thought it might be a good place to start. Sure enough there was. Thank God for Google. One of the search items that initially came up was the *The Code of Jewish Law*, also known as *shulchan aruch* (meaning "set table"), which is where I figured I should probably start. The fact that this popped up on the search made me suspect that there might be some restrictions or limitations involved when it came to handling and shipping a Torah, which indeed there were.

I had no idea there was such a doctrine as *The Code of Jewish Law* and how extensive it was. But when I went to the library to check it out, I found a big, ole compendium dedicated to the laws of Judaism. It comprised a total of 4 volumes, 221 chapters, and 562 pages of laws. I don't know who came up with these laws—supposedly various venerable rabbis and sages put them together over time—but the code contained literally thousands of different laws covering everything under the sun and then some. Apparently, these guys must have had a lot of time on their hands.

How could one religion have so many laws? I couldn't believe that something like this existed. You name it, there was a law dedicated to it, starting with the Rules of Conduct upon rising in the morning (**Be bold as a leopard, light as an eagle, swift as a deer, and strong as a lion, to do the will of thy Father who is in heaven**); to attending the temple (**Upon leaving the synagogue, one must neither run nor walk with great strides, because this would indicate that his stay at the synagogue was a burden to him**); to customs associated with all the Jewish holidays (**It is forbidden to eat, drink, bathe, anoint, wear shoes, or have sexual intercourse on Yom Kippur**); to laws relating to marriage (**It is the duty of every man to take a wife to himself, in order to fulfill the precept of propagation. This precept becomes obligatory on a man as soon as he reaches the age of eighteen. At any rate, no man should pass his twentieth year without taking a wife. Only in the event when one is deeply engrossed in the study of the Torah, and he is afraid that marriage might interfere with his studies, may he delay marrying, providing he is not lustful**); to laws of sexual intercourse (**When having intercourse, the husband's intention should be not to satisfy his personal desire, but to fulfill his obligation to perform his marital duty, like one paying a debt, and to comply with the command of his Creator and that he may have children engaged in the study of the Torah**). Those are merely just a few examples, which barely begin to scratch the surface. One has to wonder how many of these laws are actually still being observed today, but nevertheless the roots are certainly there.

As one might imagine, there were quite a few laws relating to the Torah itself, ones associated with *The Code of Jewish Law* as well as other Jewish sources. Laws relating to not only reading and studying the Torah, but holding it, carrying it, transporting it, storing it, and conducting oneself when in its presence. Here are a few laws I came across that I felt I should be aware of in terms of planning for the transference of the Torah:

Handling the Torah

- A Torah scroll should never be placed on the ground
- A Torah should always be placed upright; never upside down
- A person should not handle the Sefer (meaning scroll) Torah without its cover or mantle
- If one should drop a Sefer Torah, even if it's covered by a mantle, one must fast; and it is customary that those who see it fall, also fast

Carrying/Transporting the Torah

- Is it customary to cover a Torah with a Tallit whenever it is transported
- The Sefer Torah should always be carried on the right arm or shoulder

Storing the Torah

- A man must treat the Sefer Torah with the utmost respect, and he must assign to it a special place which must be treated with reverence, and beautifully decorated
- When storing a Sefer Torah at home, it isn't sufficient to leave the Sefer Torah on a table wrapped in a Tallit. It should be stored in a cabinet with nothing else inside

Conducting Oneself in the Presence of the Torah

- When one sees a Sefer Torah being carried, he must rise and remain standing until it is brought to its place or is out of sight
- It is customary to kiss the Torah as it passes by
- A person should not enter a bathroom, a bathhouse, or a cemetery whilst holding a Sefer Torah, even if it is wrapped in a cloth or other covering
- It is forbidden to have intercourse in a room where a Sefer Torah is found, but it must be removed into a different room

One of the most interesting of these is the law that prohibits one from taking it into the bathroom. I mean why would one be inclined to bring a Torah into the bathroom in the first place? It's not like this would be somebody's first choice for reading material when on the throne, nor could you conceivably put it on your lap or even a little table in front of you while you go about your business.

Regardless of where the Torah would end up being placed in its new home, I was feeling confident that the Torah was going to be stored in a special and beautiful place. But I was a little apprehensive about the shipping of the Torah. While the code permitted shipping a Torah scroll when properly packed in a box or a case, it also noted that it is forbidden to place the Torah on the ground. I wondered how that would all play out, as I questioned whether the Torah being shipped on the floor of the truck would constitute a breach of Jewish law. I saw these provisions as being somewhat conflicting. But I figured maybe I was taking things too literally, and that as long as it was packed up in a box or crate, technically the Torah itself wouldn't directly be hitting the ground and therefore that would be permissible.

So, even though I might have been going against the code, I nevertheless looked into the option of shipping it. Initially, I considered FedEx. I would take the responsibility of going to Connecticut to pack up the Torah, and I figured I could package it carefully in one of their extra-large cartons that they use for golf clubs and the like. And I would of course take extra care to protect it with bubble wrap throughout to provide added padding.

I liked that it would be delivered the next day with FedEx and I would have tracking capability. But still, even though it would be well packed up, I was a little bit leery about the shipping conditions and what kind of shape it would be in upon getting to its destination. Plus, it's conceivable that it could get lost. Furthermore, the whole notion of shipping a Torah via FedEx somehow just didn't sit well with me. It just seemed too precious an item to entrust with them.

So maybe it was an ideological decision more than anything, but I nixed going the FedEx route.

I also checked into shipping the Torah with a professional trucking carrier, like a moving company, which I felt could perhaps provide a little more added protection. But the companies I contacted talked about having to build a special crate for it, which would necessitate a considerable amount of time and money to put together. And because it was only a single item, it would no doubt have to be shipped along with bigger loads, which in turn meant it would probably be transported through various cities and warehouses, where it would be handled excessively and could get lost. This whole scenario seemed too involved and fraught with potential issues.

If only I knew how my dad and company had originally shipped the Torah over from Israel. It would have been nice to be able to call him to find out. Knowing how good he was with logistics, I'm sure he must have researched it ad nauseam. Clearly, whatever method that was used worked, as it had arrived at Temple B'nai Israel just fine.

Of course, I also thought about just flying out there to Connecticut and then flying back with it. That way it would be in my sole possession and control the whole time. I could pack it up and check it like luggage, although that would be almost like shipping it with FedEx, being subject to the same perils of damage that could easily take place during the flight or the airline's mishandling of this precious cargo. And besides, as in the case of going with a professional trucker or even FedEx, the airline could lose it—just ask any random flyer about their experience checking luggage.

If I didn't check the Torah as baggage and instead carried it on, I'd have to take it through security. Just the thought of doing that seemed like a big undertaking, along the same order as Moses leading his people to the Promised Land. With the outer shell being made of sterling silver, the mantle of the Torah would probably need to be completely...um...dismantled. The crown would need to come off, the silver shell would need to be opened, and all of its components would probably need to go through the X-ray machine. Heck, knowing how difficult they can be, a TSA agent might even want me to sing a *bracha* (blessing) to verify its authenticity.

Then, let's say I was fortunate enough to part the Red Sea so to speak and get the Torah through security unscathed, it would no doubt be a challenge to transport it to the gate. I could just see myself trying to carry this 30+ pound heavy load, along with my carry-on. It was one thing to parade around the temple with the Torah as part of the processional during a bar mitzvah service. But to get it through the airport all the way to the gate, which would undoubtedly be at the very end of all the gates, would be a herculean task.

And what if by chance I had to go to the bathroom? I wouldn't be able to take it in there with me. There was no way I'd be able to go; I'd have to hold it. Not only the Torah, but my bladder!

What would everybody around me think, especially any Jewish travelers passing by? Would they think I had absconded with a Torah, that I had been walking around the congregation with it as part of a service; and then instead of taking it back up to the *bimah,* I did an about-face and walked out of the sanctuary, out the temple door with it and brought this runaway Torah with me to the airport, perhaps to insure safe travels. Regardless of what my fellow Jewish travelers would think, they would all have the obligation of standing up when I passed by. And no doubt they would be coming up to me to kiss the Torah with their hand, as they would traditionally do in temple during a Torah processional.

And what if, God forbid, I somehow dropped it? Not only would it be embarrassing, but it would be a major breach. Just think of how many people would have to fast on my account, including me.

And then once at the gate, there was really only one way I could potentially have pulled it off. Clearly, the Torah was too big to put in the overhead compartment. It would have to have its own seat, which meant I would need to get a separate seat for it and spring for another one-way airplane ticket, assuming the airline would even permit me to do that. I could just envision my religious companion occupying the middle seat all belted in, with me on one side in the window seat and another person on the other side in the aisle seat. Somehow, this seemed a little impractical, if not a little bizarre.

Net, net… I didn't really feel that comfortable with any of these options. When it came right down to it, there was really only one way to do this that would provide for my complete control of the Torah at all times, that would ensure the hands-on protection from damage or harm, that would alleviate any chance of it possibly getting lost, that would prevent it from coming in contact with the ground, and that would give it the special close attention it required and deserved. I would have to fly out to Connecticut, rent a car, and drive the Torah back with me. No doubt the long drive would be quite a schlep, but I was convinced that it was the best way to go. Yup, it was going to be a Torah Road Trip!

Chapter 21

GETTING A RIDER

MY PLAN WAS TO GO TO CONNECTICUT on Thursday, October 11, three weeks after Yom Kippur, the holiest of days when one asks forgiveness for his sins and is hopefully inscribed in the book of life for the coming year. Appropriately enough, that would be just one week after *Simchat Torah* (meaning "the rejoicing of the Torah"), which is the Jewish holiday commemorating the conclusion of the annual cycle of Torah readings and the beginning of the new cycle. I was actually cutting it kind of close in terms of timing, as October 11 was really the last day I could pick up the Torah, in that Temple B'nai Israel was scheduled to close its doors forever on October 12 and be converted to the aforementioned Greek church.

Accordingly, while my mother had already given temple board member Estelle Bernstein the news that we would be taking her up on her offer, I followed up with Estelle over the phone to thank her for contacting our family about the Torah and to coordinate with her on the pick-up date and time. I wanted to make sure she was there for the handoff.

I also contacted my longtime childhood friends Norman and Laura Kaplan, both of whom I had grown up with in New Britain and who were my religious school classmates. Norman and his

167

twin brother, Ronnie, who had become a rabbi in New Jersey, were just two days younger than me and our moms were in the hospital together when they gave birth. I was pretty close with the Kaplan boys as I was with Laura Hollander, who ended up marrying Norman. Since Norman and Laura still lived nearby there, in Milford, Connecticut, only about an hour away from New Britain, I thought they might want to meet me at the temple for the transfer of the Torah and give our last farewell to our former temple with so many, many memories.

There wasn't much preparation involved—I was ready to pick up and go. It was just a matter of getting my one-way plane ticket, reserving a rental car, and planning my driving route back home.

There were a few matters I needed to attend to, however. First and foremost, I needed to set up some documentation for the Torah, a covenant of sorts between the current acting rabbi of Temple B'nai Israel and myself, kind of a "will and testament" for it. This ended up being a handwritten note drafted by yours truly on the temple's stationary, stating that Temple B'nai Israel was giving me possession of the Torah to in turn hand down to the synagogue with which I was currently affiliated. I also wrote that this Torah should never be sold; but that should it no longer be used by its recipient Temple Beth-El, it would be in turn donated to another temple. And if that wasn't possible, it would be donated to and housed at the United Synagogue in New York City.

Also, given the Torah's high perceived value, I felt compelled to get it appraised. I was kind of curious to find out what its monetary value would be. I had no idea what a Torah, especially a beautiful, ornate one such as this, would be worth. Not that it really mattered, since to me it was priceless due to its sentimental value. But regardless, it certainly made sense to get that official assessment.

Beyond just my curiosity, I needed the appraisal for insurance purposes. Initially, I wasn't really sure where to bring the Torah to determine its value, but upon asking around I took it to a local jewelry store owned by a Jewish family, and they were kind enough to do an appraisal for me at no charge. While I assumed it would have significant value, I couldn't believe it when they gave me a letter valuing the Torah at $100,000.

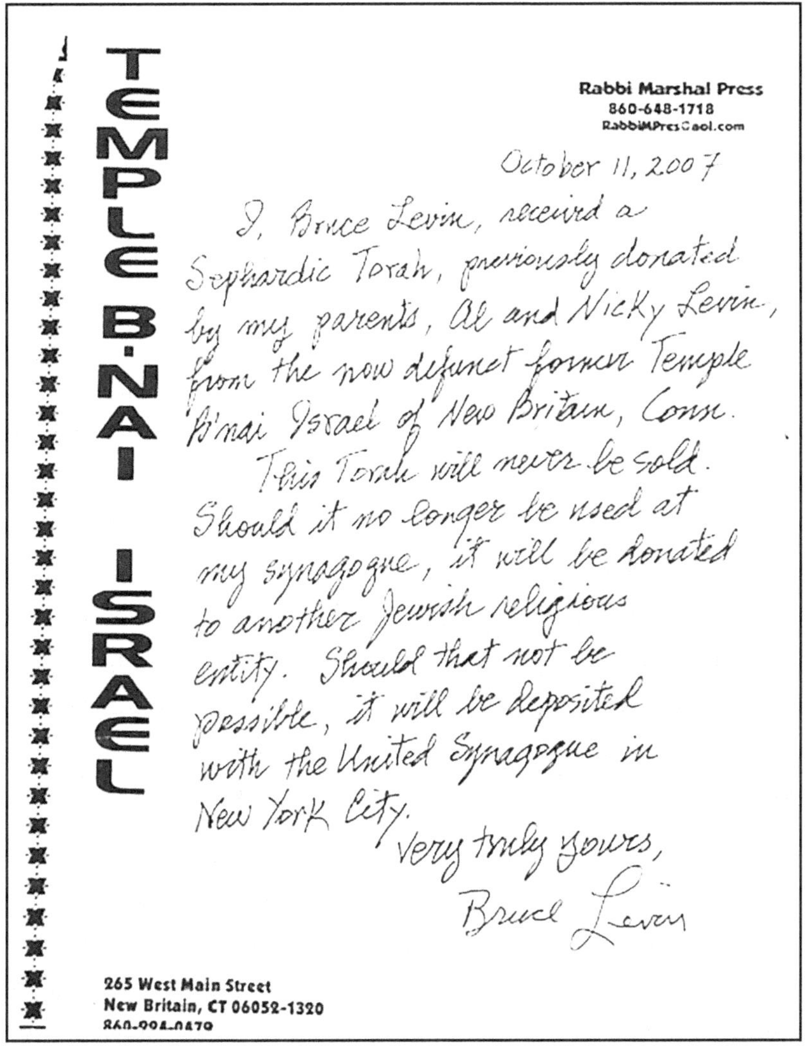

Handwritten covenant between Temple B'nai Israel and myself

Jewelry Appraisal

DATE: 10/12/2009
NAME: Temple Beth El of Northbrook
ADDRESS: 3610 Dundee Road
Northbrook, IL 60062
USA
847-205-9982

BY: X
Manuel S. Millman

VALUE PLUS TAX: $100,000.00

Torah

Torah, parchment scroll, hand scribed, 18 inches tall and 10 inches in diameter, incased in wood and entire sterling silver sheet that is tacked to the wood. This has Yemenite workmanship and hand chased design of flowers and other shapes. Set in handmade bezels are all colored stone consisting of aget, turquoise, gold stone, black onyx, green onyx, red and multi-color stones. This outer case is 39 inches by 24 inches and the crowns are on a 45 degree angle each has six bells. All the workmanship is all hand applied and all the silver wire is all handmade for this antique. This truly is a beautiful artifact that is given to the Temple by Bruce Levin.

Value... $100,000.00

These estimated replacement costs are based only on estimates of the quality of the stones. Mountings prohibit the full and accurate observation of cutting, color, clarity and weight of gems; therefore only a provisional grade may be assigned. We assume no liability with respect to any action that may be taken on the basis of this appraisal. Estimated current retail replacement value of comparable article excluding taxes. To be used for insurance and estate purposes only.

An appraisal of the Torah

I thought it would be good to have a rider. I don't mean a passenger in the car necessarily, although of course it would be nice to have someone to accompany me on my journey; but rather an insurance rider. After all, I would be in possession of some precious cargo and by taking it on a long drive, almost 1,000 miles, who knows what could happen. I mean, God forbid, what if I got into an accident and it was damaged? So I put a rider on our existing umbrella liability policy, just in case. I thought, if nothing else, it would serve as a comforting, assuring safeguard that would perhaps ward off any chance of misfortune.

Furthermore, I wanted to make sure to bring my father's *tallis* (prayer shawl) with me, which I had planned to use to wrap the Torah, along with a linen sheet as an outer layer. I had my mother ship out his *tallis* to me, which she had kept over the years.

A couple of weeks before I was to leave, Gail and I went out to dinner with some friends of ours, Mark and Diane Gluskin. Mark and I had become friendly with each other as fellow dads through our daughters in our "Me and My Daddy" Club, which was a social group consisting of about 10 or so father-and-daughter pairs that originated out of Danni's Hebrew school at Temple Beth-El during fourth and fifth grades. During the school year, we got together every other month or so to participate in some type of social activity. Plus, our wives were friendly with each other.

During dinner, we told them about my upcoming trip to Connecticut, and I noticed Mark's eyes light up a little bit. "You know, I'm going to be out on the East Coast in Raleigh, North Carolina, on business that week," he said, "so maybe I could meet you somewhere out there and can help with the driving." At first I thought he was kidding. But he kept saying, "No really, I could fly from Raleigh and meet you somewhere." After three or four "reallys," I realized he was really serious. I couldn't believe it.

We started to put our heads together, and over the next few days after looking at flight schedules, consulting AAA, figuring travel times, and considering a number of rendezvous spots, we firmed things up and decided we would meet in the Iron City. I would pick him up late Friday afternoon at the Pittsburgh Airport. What a friend! It turned out I would be getting the other type of rider after all.

Accordingly, I mapped out my route. While I might have gone a slightly different way if I wasn't going through Pittsburgh, it was adding only about 50 miles to the trip for a total of a little over 950 miles. Actually, it's funny, it turned out that the Pittsburgh Airport was 479 miles between both my point of departure and my destination, so it was exactly in the middle.

After picking up the Torah in the afternoon on the 11th, I would hit the road that evening and take I-84 West through Connecticut across New York state and into Scranton, Pennsylvania, pick up I-81 South, and then soon after stop in Wilkes-Barre for the night. Wilkes-Barre was about five hours from Pittsburgh, so it seemed like a logical spot to stop in order to connect with Mark at the end of the next day. Plus, my mother's friends down in Florida, Larry and Ruth Hollander (no relation to Laura), were originally from Wilkes-Barre and I figured they could give me a good hotel recommendation in the area.

That morning, I would get an early start and make my way across the expansive state of Pennsylvania on into the Pittsburgh Airport around 4:00 pm, a half hour before Mark's plane was scheduled to arrive from Raleigh. From there, he and I would drive together the rest of the way through the states of Ohio, Indiana, and Illinois for a late arrival back home no later than midnight.

Chapter 22

RETURNING TO THE HOMELAND

AS IT CAME TO PASS, Thursday, October 11, rolled around before I knew it, and it was time to start my trip. I was all packed up and ready to go. In addition to a change of clothes and my Dopp kit, my carry-on suitcase contained my father's *tallis* and a linen sheet, both of which I intended to use to wrap up the Torah. I also put in cassette tapes for the long drive, including those that had music on them as well as those that had the recordings of my Dad's life stories, which I thought would be only fitting to listen to during my journey. By listening to his stories, I could pretend he was there riding along with me. And last but not least I threw in some snacks for the road including a tin of freshly baked chocolate chip cookies courtesy of my wife, a big bag of barbecue potato chips, and a ziplock bag of both red and black licorice.

I took a mid-morning flight from O'Hare to good ole Bradley Field in Windsor Locks, Connecticut, located midway between Hartford and Springfield, Massachusetts, which served as the greater Connecticut airport. This had been my home-base airport where I had flown into and out of countless times myself as well as dropped off and picked up my father on many an occasion. Upon landing, I proceeded to the Hertz counter to claim the slightly souped-up

Chevy Trailblazer SUV that I had on reserve, complete with four-wheel drive, leather seats, sunroof, and an AM/FM radio with cassette player. I could have gone with a Ford Taurus or some other basic, standard four-door sedan, which would have been quite a bit less expensive. But I wanted to make sure there would be enough room for my precious cargo. Plus, I thought that Abraham, Isaac, Jacob, and company might want to ride in style. After all those years on their feet wandering around the desert, I figured they were entitled to an upgrade. Besides, it somehow seemed like the type of journey that called for a vehicle such as this. Just the model's name itself, "Trailblazer," sounded like it would be right for the part, something that our forefathers might have chosen for themselves.

Of course, in the Levin car-naming tradition, I had already come up with a perfect nickname for my new wheels: the "Torah Blazer."

The Chevy Blazer, alias the "Torah Blazer," I rented to transport the Torah

Behind the wheel of the Torah Blazer, I started to make my way on the 45-minute drive from Bradley Field to New Britain. But before I went to the temple, I had a little time to kill and thought I'd drive by my old house at 30 Windsor Road. I hadn't been back there in six years, just before my parents sold it in fall of 2001 and permanently moved down to Florida.

Upon approaching the house, in an attempt to be inconspicuous, I kept my distance, parking across the street. But no one really seemed to be around. Like always, it was a quiet neighborhood. There didn't seem to be any structural changes to the house. It was still the same 1950s-style split level with the same big bay window in the front, that same window that my blood brother David Goldstein had smashed into smithereens with a baseball on that glorious summer night. Plus, it was still the same overall, basic vanilla color. Yet somehow it didn't seem like the same house. It must have been the obtrusive, fire-engine red door and exterior shutters on the upstairs windows, which used to be turquoise and more subdued, that threw me off. These were only just slight changes that the new owner had made to the house, perhaps just to put their own mark on it, but somehow just those little changes clearly signified that the house now belonged to somebody else and seemed to almost erase the time that we had ever lived there. Whatever was behind the difference, it no longer seemed like my old house and I had a hard time even being able to identify with it.

I slowly moved the car up, creeping along the side of the road across the street, so I could get a glimpse of the backyard. The yard seemed much smaller. The row of bushes separating our yard from the Goldsteins', which had served as our home run derby wall, was still there, now more than ever, as those bushes were quite a bit fuller and taller to the extent that you could no longer see the Goldsteins' house anymore from the backyard. It was evident that you'd now have to launch the ball up really high to get it out of the yard for a homer. The big birch tree with its many branches hanging down, that had always been an obstruction in center field, seemed a little bit bigger and fuller as well, even though it was starting to lose its leaves. What's more, right in the middle of the backyard where the ad hoc pitching mound used to be, was now a little swing set. Maybe because I was now older and bigger compared to my playing years on this field, I had a different perspective on things—the taller bushes, the bigger birch tree, and the swing set all contributed to my perception of what seemed like a much smaller yard than I had remembered. Unfortunately, there was no trace of a baseball field anymore, leaving no vestiges of the many sandlot games that were played there. But nevertheless I wondered how many lost baseballs were still in the those bushes.

I stayed there in the car for a while, gazing at my old stomping grounds, taking it all in, and trying to recreate the many great memories of all those baseball games, the home run derbies, the Major League games that Dave and I would play along with our imaginary men, plus the nine-hole golf course we had carved out as part of the spectacular Levin Sports Complex. It was beginning to be an emotional afternoon.

By the time I got to Temple B'nai Israel soon after my neighborhood visit, Estelle was already there. Her kind face greeted me with warmth and enthusiasm, reflecting her happiness and satisfaction that the temple had found a suitable home for the treasured Sephardic Torah. To show my appreciation, I tried to return that same level of enthusiasm, as again I thanked her profusely for calling my family about the Torah and allowing us to pass it along to the temple I was now affiliated with.

Estelle escorted me to the Torah, which was still in the main ark. It was the only Torah left, as I presumed that all of the temple's other Torahs had found new homes as well. Maybe because it was by itself in the ark, its beautiful silver body glistened beyond my memory and was more impressive than ever.

Norman and Laura arrived shortly thereafter and it was of course great to see them. Before attending to the Torah, we decided to do a final walk-through of the temple and reminisce a little bit about our childhood days within these sacred walls, all the bar and bat mitzvahs that had taken place there, and particularly our nostalgic but chaotic religious school experience. We felt it would be a fitting tribute to our former temple, on this being its last official day. Recounting what seemed to be those never-ending days of religious school, we talked about all the eccentric teachers we had; the sneaking out between classes to a nearby convenience store to get snacks that we would consume during the subsequent class; and the time one of our classmates, who had been hiding in the coatroom closet in our classroom before class and didn't realize that the class had begun, suddenly popped out of the closet.

I found myself reflecting back to the scene of my own bar mitzvah on May 22, 1965. In particular there were a few things that stood out in my mind. First, my memories went back to two weeks before the event, when I was attending Saturday morning services with my mother as a warm-up to my upcoming big day. The cantor, who had gone through the arduous task of tutoring me on my *haftarah*, insisted on me coming to a Saturday morning service soon before my bar mitzvah so that I would be familiar with all the parts of the service. I had already sat through a bunch of b'nai mitzvahs before and felt I knew what to expect, which of course I had tried to point out to him. But as my tutor explained to me, I suppose rightfully so, he felt it would still be a good idea to take it all in from the perspective of a participant as opposed to just a casual observer.

Given that I was on the home stretch and admittedly wanted to be totally prepared, I went along with it. But little did I know that the guy had an ulterior motive. At the beginning of the service, a little bit after the *Shema* prayer, he snuck up on me from behind and encouragingly asked that I lead the congregation in the *Ashrei* prayer at the end of the service. Being caught totally off guard, as he had never mentioned to me beforehand or even given me any type of inkling that he was planning to call me up to the *bimah*, I rolled my eyes and froze. Particularly back in those days, I always wanted to know what was going to happen next and be prepared accordingly and thus was always in fear of surprises like this. I totally panicked and thought, how could he do this to me? I said to my mother, "No way I'm going up there."

Needless to say, after an extended period of carrying on, whining, and repeating the refrain of "I'm not going up there," I did in fact end up going up there. It wasn't smooth by any means, but somehow I got through it. Now looking back, it may have served its purpose and broken the ice for me, but I still haven't really forgiven the cantor for putting me through all that panic-stricken misery at the time.

I then thought about my formal debut, during the Friday night Shabbat service, when I was to be called up toward the end to lead the congregation in the *Ashrei*, the same prayer that I had so agonized over in front of the congregation two weeks earlier. Being so short at the time, I remember I had to stand on a little pedestal behind the podium so I could be seen up there on the *bimah*. While it wasn't quite as terrifying as the two weeks before when I was completely blindsided, I remember I was still plenty nervous. So much so that I spilled the wine up on the *bimah*, when I was rehearsing the *Kiddush prayer* recited over wine, before the service. And how, when it came to actually doing the *Ashrei* during the service, after the first three words of the hymn… *Ashrei yoshvei veitecha*, I suddenly paused for a few moments, and like a deer in headlights, idly stared out at the congregation. It had to be close to a full house of about 300, and I imagine given this sudden break in the action there must have been some edge-of-the-seats questioning whether I was going to be able to continue. Then, taking a deep breath and gathering my wits about me, I proceeded on with the words *od y'hallucha sela*. Once I took that deep breath and got through that first line, I was ok and on point for the rest of the prayer. At the very end of the service, I steadily held up a glass of wine and recited the *Kiddush*, just before breaking for the *Oneg Shabbat* celebration.

I thought about the next morning, the actual day of my bar mitzvah, when I read from the very same Sephardic Torah that I was picking up today to deliver to its new home. More so than any part of the main service itself, I thought about the end of the service, just after I had read my *haftarah* to the congregation, when I was behind the podium on the *bimah* one-on-one, face-to-face with Rabbi Z, sideways to the congregation. He presented me with some small gifts from the temple and the sisterhood, and then proceeded to give his bar mitzvah speech to me, imparting what I'm sure was intended to be some words of wisdom. I don't remember any of those words, as at the time I'm not sure they even registered with me. Rather his words were all going in one ear and out the other, as I wasn't really focusing on what he was saying but rather was in a state of idle consciousness just trying to get through it all. There I was, standing there on my little pedestal, swaying back and forth as if I was a bar mitzvah bobblehead, and as such needing to be constantly steadied by the rabbi.

I also thought about the special frozen fruit at the luncheon that followed. I couldn't remember what the main course was, but ahhhh… the dessert. In her attempt to make a unique splash at the luncheon that would be a hit with our guests, my mother had the caterer bring in some fancy iced fruit from New York for dessert that actually was served in the shape of the respective fruit. The options were oranges, apples, pears, and bananas. I had never seen anything like it and thought it was really cool. I had put in my request beforehand for a banana one.

Lastly, I thought about the goldfish bowls. As if the frozen fruit wasn't enough to impress, my mother, in her determined attempt to go the extra mile, got this wild idea of having a fishbowl as the centerpiece at each table, each one with two orange goldfish swimming around. Kind of kooky and a little bit out there, especially for those days. No doubt they were certainly a topic of conversation. I wasn't really a fan of this idea, but I went along with it. But just the same, as the bar mitzvah boy, I took it upon myself to make sure that those bowls all stayed on the tables. That's why when I noticed one of my female classmates scoop one up and head to the door, I made a beeline to try to stop her. If I remember correctly, her first name was Michelle, and I want to say her last name was Fishman, although I'm not sure. Anyway, like a fish in water she was pretty fast and was quickly out the door before I could catch her. Before I knew it, I was running down West Main Street chasing this girl with a goldfish bowl in hand.

I finally did catch her! There was no way I was going to let a girl, especially one carrying a goldfish bowl, outrun me. But when I got up to her, it turned out to be pretty much catch and release, as I found myself laughing, realizing how ridiculous the whole escapade was, and I backed down. I must have been caught up in the moment. I mean, what was the big deal? If she really wanted the goldfish memento so much, I thought to myself, let her keep it. To save face, I mumbled something to the effect about how my mother was responsible for returning all the bowls to the place we got them. But then I told her that it would be alright if she took it home, and let her go on her merry way with it.

After countless stories and a whole lot of laughs, my friends and I turned our attention back to the Torah. The three of us took the sterling silver-encased Torah out of the ark, carefully wrapped it up in my dad's *tallis* plus a layer of linen for extra protection.

I then carried the Torah out to my faithful chariot, the Torah Blazer. I had already put the backseat down, thinking that would provide the most room to accommodate the Torah. But upon surveying the situation and realizing that it would be difficult to secure back there and no doubt would be rattling around, I reconsidered my options.

I was tempted to open up the sunroof, as I briefly thought about resting it on the console in the front seat and standing it up such that it would extend through the sunroof. I could just picture the top of the Torah protruding out of the sunroof for everybody to see, as we forged our way down the road together. That would definitely be cool. But maybe too cool in more ways than one. Actually it would probably be freezing. Besides, it wouldn't be very practical. How would I secure it? And what about the atmospheric elements, including potentially rain and wind, that the Torah would be exposed to?

Rather, I ended up putting the backseat back up and laying the Torah lengthwise across the backseat. I figured that would be the most secure and practical way to go, in that I would be able to utilize all the seatbelts in the backseat and be able to extend them completely around the Torah to lock it in and keep it tightly in place. Also, by laying the Torah down across the backseat, I would be treating it more like a passenger than merely a piece of cargo. Certainly this plan seemed like it would be more in keeping with the spirit of *The Code of Jewish Law*. And no doubt it would provide my forefathers with a smoother ride.

Finally, we were ready to go. Leaving our former house of sanctity, and with the Torah buckled in safe and sound, Norman, Laura, and I, in the Jewish tradition, did what I'm sure Abraham, Isaac, and Jacob or any of their Jewish descendants for that matter would have done to celebrate this momentous occasion and kick off such a journey: we went out for Chinese!

Chapter 23
GREAT TASTE

THERE WAS REALLY ONLY ONE PLACE TO GO in New Britain for Chinese: Great Taste! Actually, it was the only Chinese restaurant in town.

Great Taste restaurant in New Britain, Connecticut

It was located on the outskirts of downtown, just about a mile down from the temple on the same street, West Main Street. While the location itself was nothing to write home about from a commercial standpoint, I always felt these guys were pretty smart to open up in close proximity to the temple. I'm sure it made for a popular choice to go for dinner on Friday night, right before Shabbat services—dine and daven.

Great Taste was considered one of the best restaurants in New Britain. That was not saying much, in that there really weren't all that many restaurants that had survived in town over the years. But indeed, it was a restaurant that seemed to live up to its name. The fact that it was still around in a city that saw the temple, many of its commercial enterprises, and a lot of its other restaurants go by the wayside, was a testament to how good it really was.

Actually, Great Taste did a pretty brisk business, not only on Friday nights but also Sunday nights, which seemed to be a popular night for Chinese food as well. And even on the other nights of the week, except for Monday when they were closed, most of the time they were able to fill the house. Their biggest days of the year, of course, were Christmas Eve and Christmas, when they tended to be the only restaurant open in the New Britain area. It was a smart strategy on the part of management to cater to the local Jewish community. In fact, during the Christmas holidays, in addition to one of those little silver artificial Christmas trees that stores or restaurants typically have on display, right near the tree as you enter the restaurant they even showcased a *menorah* on a little table next to the hostess stand. Nice touch… they knew their target market.

It was only fitting that we went there that night, as it was one of my dad's go-to places for dinner. When my parents would come back from Florida during the summer and fall months, it was snow peas for the snowbirds as they frequented the place more than any other restaurant. Dad especially loved their Lobster Cantonese, one of the more expensive items on a Chinese menu, made of lobster tails covered in a thick brown sauce composed of ground pork, smashed fermented black beans, egg, some garlic and ginger, and soy sauce. He claimed theirs was among the best he ever had.

The marketing guy in me thought it would have been cool if the restaurant took a local approach to its menu and honored some of their past and present customers by naming their dishes after them. What a posthumous tribute that would be: "Al Levin's Lobster Cantonese." I was tempted to mention something to the hostess, who I think was the wife of the owner.

When we got inside, like most Chinese restaurants I've been in, it was pretty dark. I always wondered why that was the case, whether it was merely to add some ambience or maybe it was that they wanted to keep you in the dark as to what you were actually eating. Also, consistent with the typical décor of many Chinese restaurants, there were several large aquariums along its walls, featuring all kinds of different fish including some big goldfish, which reminded me of the ones swimming around in the centerpieces at my bar mitzvah luncheon.

Here it was, still early on a Thursday, not even 6:00 pm, and the place was already getting busy. We requested a booth near the window, so I could keep the Torah Blazer in full view during the meal. Rain was in the forecast, and as I looked out the window, it was already starting to get a little windy and it seemed like a storm was brewing.

We ordered a lot of stuff. We were going all out. Hot & sour soup, egg rolls, spareribs, vegetable fried rice, General Tso's chicken, and of course "Al Levin's Lobster Cantonese." After telling Laura and Norman of my dad's love for Lobster Cantonese, they agreed that we had to get it.

Even though we hadn't seen each other in a while, none of us were at a loss for words. There was a lot to catch up on with each other. First, we talked about our kids, as I brought them up to speed with Danni and Mac; and they with theirs, Jonathan and Rachel. This included touching upon the kids' respective experiences with religious school, which, compared to our experiences, seemed very mundane and uneventful. We all agreed their experiences were much more subdued than what we had gone through. There were no kids popping out of closets during class; no teacher taking the popcorn away from you that you were eating in class and then proceeding to eat it in front of you during the rest of the class time; no kids getting thrown out of class and suspended for fooling around too much; and no food fights during bar and bat mitzvahs.

Every so often, like an overzealous mother attending to her newborn, I would take a glimpse out the window and make sure that everything was intact and that there weren't any suspicious characters looming around the Torah Blazer. That was my "baby" out there, and I wanted to be sure to protect it.

From our conversation about our kids, we jumped a few generations to talking about our parents, all of whom other than my mother had unfortunately passed on. We expressed to each other how we had been very fortunate and blessed to have the loving parents we did.

Norman would always ask about my mom when we saw each other, always referring to her as Nikki. He mentioned how he remembered her driving around in her light blue Cadillac convertible, alias the Blue Lightning. How she would drive fast sometimes when taking us in the carpool to Kingswood, the private high school we both went to in West Hartford. And how she would always dress in the latest fashions. He made her sound really cool, which of course she was.

Norm's parents were Henry and Rhoda. Henry had been my mother's and grandmother's OB-GYN, and had always been a very caring doctor throughout the years. Even though it was not his specialty, I remember how he went right up to New Britain General Hospital the night that Spice had her stroke in 1994, to make sure that the hospital was doing everything they could for her and to help if needed. And while Rhoda and my mother weren't in the same social circle, they were always friendly toward each other, having shared a special bond together as two moms being at the hospital at the same time giving birth to their respective sons.

Laura's parents were Dr. Frederick and Ruthie Hollander (that's right, another Ruth Hollander, the exact same name as my parents' friend in Wilkes-Barre). I was pretty close to this set of Hollanders as they were such warm people. A dentist by trade, Dr. Hollander always seemed to have a smile on his face, a fitting banner for his profession. Heavily involved in local activities, he was a pillar of the community. Both he and Norman's father Henry were some of New Britain's favorite doctors as well as favorite sons. Some called him Fred, some called him Rick, and some called him Doc. I called him Uncle Freddy, as he and Ruthie were family friends close enough to get the aunt and uncle nod even though we weren't related. When growing up, I had a bunch of those close family friends, contemporaries of my parents, like Aunt Reggie and Uncle Sig, and Aunt Hilda and Uncle Ben, who qualified under that aunt and uncle designation.

Uncle Freddy was very witty and liked to kibbitz. He would always tease me about my pursuits on the baseball and football fields. Just about every time I saw him, he claimed that he was going to get me a tryout with the New York Giants.

And while I was never invited to the Giants training camp, he did work some magic among his community contacts to line up a plum job for me working construction one summer while I was in college. I became a general laborer working as part of a small team putting in manhole covers in various suburban locations around Connecticut. It paid almost $7.00 an hour, way more than any other summer opportunity I could possibly get. In those days that was big money. Plus, it was a job that was outside, that would allow me to work on my tan. And it was one that would enable me to build up my muscles, which I figured couldn't hurt my chances with the ladies. By all counts, for a college kid, it was a dream job that was hard to come by. Not sure how he was able to finagle the job for me since everybody else I worked with was part of a union and I wasn't, but somehow he made it happen.

Not being the handyman or physical laborer type, let alone knowing anything about tools, I was clearly a fish out of water out there on the construction site. Even though you would think that someone from the "Hardware City of the World" would know something about tools, I was green behind the ears and didn't know the difference between a bucksaw and a hacksaw, which the foreman found out when he asked me to go get a bucksaw out of the truck. Luckily, the foreman, if I recall correctly his name was Les, must have realized early on that I was somewhat of a pitiful case, as he took me under his wing and got me through the summer. By the end of my job stint, I felt I had earned my wings as a bona fide construction worker. One day during my last week, when we put in a total of 11 manhole covers, our record for the summer, I had accomplished a noteworthy feat of mixing a total of 44 bags of SAKRETE Concrete Mix, which weighed 50 pounds each, with a hoe. I couldn't feel my arms afterwards, but it was certainly something I was proud of and that I continue to boast about even to this day. All in all, it turned out to be a great experience for me. Beyond learning about a variety of tools, it matured me in ways that only a job like that could do, especially for a kid who grew up in a relatively white-collar community and matriculated at private schools starting with sixth grade. And I owed it all to Uncle Freddy.

I should add that every morning during that whole summer working construction, my mother, God bless her, got up with me at 5:30 am to make me what we both termed a "Construction Guy's Breakfast": French toast and bacon. Not that I imagined too many construction workers actually started out their day with this type of cuisine. But that was my mom. This is something of course I didn't let on to Les or any other fellow members of my construction crew, as I felt it wouldn't do much for the "tough guy" image that I was trying to project.

We were enjoying our dinner but time was getting away from me, as the road was calling. I had to be on my way if I was going to make it to Wilkes-Barre, my destination for the night, before 11:00 pm. It was a good 200 miles away, which I estimated would take me three hours or so. I asked for the check, and of course, with that came our fortune cookies. I was hoping for something good—something that would give me a proper send-off, something that would perhaps be inspirational, that would speak to the journey I was about to embark upon. Maybe something like, **"Life is a journey, be sure to embrace it and enjoy the ride."** Or the Chinese proverb **"He who returns from a journey is not the same as he who left."** Or even something as simple and reassuring as, **"The road ahead may be long and winding, but you'll make it there safe and sound."** Some parting words that would be uplifting and at least give me a little comfort that I was destined to have a good trip.

I cracked open the cookie with great anticipation. And sure enough, it turned out that I did get a fortune that kind of related to my trip that I felt could certainly apply. It was a Confucius saying: **"Wherever you go, go with all your heart."**

As we stepped outside, it had already begun to drizzle. With the rain starting to come down a little harder by the minute, I hugged Laura and Norman, and we said our last goodbyes, and then I jumped up into the Torah Blazer to head west.

Chapter 24
THE JOURNEY BEGINS

AS ABRAHAM, ISAAC, JACOB, AND COMPANY, and I were about to begin our journey, I looked back one more time to make sure that the Torah was securely belted in. But before pulling out, with the rain starting to come down a little harder, I figured that this might be a good time to read the Traveler's Prayer. I wanted to do whatever I could to get off on the right foot. Also called the Wayfarer's Prayer (or *Tefilat Haderekh* in Hebrew), it's customary to recite this prayer at the onset of a journey, to protect the traveler from danger and deliver one safely to his destination. And with this storm popping up, potential danger was definitely looming in the air, calling for precautionary measures. So I went into my wallet and pulled out this little folded piece of paper that I had stuffed in there just before I left home, and read it out loud to myself.

> *May it be Your will, Lord, our God and the God of our ancestors, that You lead us toward peace, guide our footsteps toward peace, and make us reach our desired destination for life, gladness, and peace. May You rescue us from the hand of every foe, ambush along the way, and from all manner of punishments that assemble to come to earth. May You send blessing in our*

handiwork, and grant us grace, kindness, and mercy in Your eyes and in thy eyes of all who see us. May You hear the sound of our humble request because You are God Who hears prayer requests. Blessed are You, Lord, Who hears prayer.

Having read it, I felt more reassured to go ahead and proceed. I then popped in a cassette of Bruce Springsteen's "Born to Run" album to get the blood flowing and give me a little jump-start. Some of the titles of the songs, "Thunder Road" and "Backstreets," seemed to be rather appropriate for the occasion.

Then, with Torah in tow, I shouted out "And away we go!" commemorating the official start of my journey, and I was off, heading down West Main Street toward I-84 West, which I picked up about a mile away. As I made my way down the interstate, past the familiar towns of Plainville, Southington, and Cheshire, near where I grew up, the rain continued to intensify. By the time I was approaching the outskirts of Waterbury, my father's hometown and one that especially at this moment in time seemed to be aptly named given the current weather conditions, it was beginning to rain cats and dogs. This was something akin to the 40 days and 40 nights' passage in the Bible reminiscent of Noah and his ark (Genesis 7:12).

I had made my way over to the far-right lane and had really slowed down to the point that many others were passing me by. Between the intense rain and the passing trailer trucks spraying water, I had trouble seeing out the front window. Even the resounding vibes of The Boss couldn't drown out the tumultuous rain that was pattering on the roof of the Torah Blazer. It was so bad that I was contemplating pulling over and stopping to wait things out, which a lot of vehicles were beginning to do. That's what my father used to do in such conditions and what he would have wanted me to do. What's more, my cell phone battery was low. I should have charged it up at Great Taste since I had forgotten to bring a charger to use in the car. If something were to happen, I was leaving myself vulnerable to being cut off from any communication.

Here I was only a half hour out on the road, and I was already off to a precarious start. As I made my way through the torrential downpour feeling as though I was in the movie Indiana Jones and the Holy Torah, I wondered if maybe God was making some type of statement. I couldn't help but think, in his spirit of capturing the experience of it all, he was giving me just a little taste of the perilous type of conditions and challenges my ancestors had to endure when making their way to the Promised Land. I wondered what was in store for me, and if perhaps this was a portent for more adversity to come.

It was somewhat comforting that I had recited the Traveler's Prayer a little earlier and that the good word I had projected to the universe might put me in good stead. I was also beginning to think that it was a good thing I had put that rider on our insurance policy, as it was looking like it might possibly come in handy.

Some welcoming golden arches caught my eye. Perceiving this familiar bastion as a comforting safe haven, as though it was a temple unto itself, I pulled in to take a breather. Similar to the approach I had used at Great Taste, I parked near one of windows so I could keep my eyes on the parking lot while inside. Still pouring rain harder than ever, I made a mad dash to the door, getting completely soaked. I ordered a coffee and asked the cashier if she would be kind enough to charge my cell phone behind the counter. And so, strategically seating myself next to the window where I could see the Torah Blazer, as well as near the counter where I could keep an eye on my cell phone, I patiently sipped my coffee as I dried off and waited out the storm.

Not long after, with my cell phone fairly charged up and the rain just about to let up, I hit the road again. Hopefully it was going to be clear sailing between here and Wilkes-Barre, still about another two-and-a-half hours away.

I continued on I-84 West passing Danbury, Connecticut, and then on into New York state, through the towns of Brewster, Fishkill, Newburgh, and Middletown, and then Port Jarvis, on the border of

New York and Pennsylvania; and then on into Pennsylvania through the small towns of Lords Valley, Bloomington Grove, and Greentown, just outside an area of the Pocono Mountains coincidentally called Promised Land State Park; and then on into Scranton, where the road connected with I-81, which I took south toward Wilkes-Barre.

At around 10:00 pm, I turned on the ballgame, the National League Championship Series game between the Colorado Rockies and the Arizona Diamondbacks. Both teams were coming off a three-game sweep of their opponent in the Divisional Series Playoffs, the Rockies over the Phillies and the Diamondbacks over the Cubs, the latter of which I attended the third and final game at Wrigley Field where I watched the Snakes prevail over the hometown Cubbies by a score of 5-1. As I listened to the game, not really having a stake in terms of which team I wanted to win but rather just to keep me in the loop as a general baseball fan, my mind wandered off to another baseball game.

Chapter 25
SEE YA AT EBBETS

MARCH 15, 2003... THE IDES OF MARCH. More noteworthy, it was my father's birthday. His 95th! What a way to celebrate his milestone day... the three generations of Levin boys, spanning a whopping total of 88 years, had planned to take in a game together, a Grapefruit League rivalry between the St. Louis Cardinals and the Montreal Expos at Roger Dean Stadium in Jupiter, Florida, the spring training home field for both teams.

Talk about following in your father's footsteps—it was somewhat of a coincidence, not to mention a rarity, that my father had begat me when he was 44 years old, and I begat my son Mac just a month shy of my 44th birthday. I mean, how many families can boast 88 years between grandfather and grandson? Ok, maybe we weren't quite in the same league as Abraham, Isaac, and Jacob, who combined for a total of 160 years, as according to the Torah, Abraham was 100 when he begat Isaac, and Isaac was 60 when he begat his twin sons Jacob and Esau. But then you have to wonder just how accurate the records were back then.

The three generations of the Levin Boys spanning 88 years

Maybe his staying power was in the name, as I learned from my conversation with my father at the Orchids of Siam down in Florida that he was an example of another Abraham who was able to hang in there for many years. But it seemed inconceivable, no pun intended, that the original Abraham was able to do the deed at the ripe old age of 100, and procreate a child no less. I mean it wasn't like there was a little blue pill back in those days. I don't know, maybe while wandering in the desert, he stumbled across some testosterone-laden plant that gave him some added virility. That or perhaps God was able to pull some strings on his behalf. But at any rate, by modern-day statistics, our expansive span of three generations of Levins had to be right up there in the record books.

While maybe not quite the devoted fan as his son and grandson, my father was rooted in baseball long before he had me and I put him through all his rigorous fatherly baseball duties… from getting bombarded with continuous requests for pop-ups; to having to go to my school games when he could; to being dragged to Major League games or watching them on TV; and to serving as the behind-the-plate, lone umpire at my annual baseball birthday parties, at which he always ended up getting an earful from his argumentative son on his ball and strike calls and any other calls that didn't go my way.

To add to Dad's impressive job history, although it was only for one summer, in the early 1920s, a year or two before he wandered down to Florida to seek his fortune, he was a batboy for his home-town team the Waterbury Brasscos, named after all the brass factories there that dubbed it the "Brass City." At the time, the Brasscos were an independent, Minor League team in the Eastern League. While the team was only in existence for a short time, from 1918-1928, the Brasscos paved the way for Waterbury to bring baseball back into the fold. The city was later picked up starting in 1966 as a AA Minor League affiliate team for a number of different Major League teams. A total of seven different Major League affiliates came and went over a 20-year stretch, after which time Minor League Baseball went by the wayside in Waterbury, much like so many of its brass factories. Like New Britain, Waterbury was one of those industrial cities in Connecticut that had lost its luster over the years. But the fact that my dad had rubbed elbows with some Minor League–caliber players was pretty impressive and noteworthy, and showed that he had indeed put in some quality time on the field.

Dad had always talked about going to Ebbets Field back in the day to see the Brooklyn Dodgers play, that is before they moved out to Los Angeles in 1951. Every time he mentioned Ebbets Field, my mind flashed back to the black and white newsreels that I used to watch as a boy at the local theatre prior to the main attraction. These clips included shots of fans packed in the stands like sardines… guys wearing sport jackets, ties, and fedoras, and women in dresses and white gloves, looking as though they were attending church or temple. According to Dad, in those days people would dress up when they went to a baseball game, oftentimes in their Sunday best.

Even though the stadium doesn't exist today, we three generations of Levin boys had always joked about how we would eventually all meet up at Ebbets in our Sunday best to take in a game, as though that would be our heaven. To this day, a metal blue Ebbets Field sign, a little gift from his Pop-Pops, hangs in Mac's bedroom right above his closet, against a backdrop of wallpaper full of pictures of different baseball grips.

Ebbets Field sign above Mac's bedroom closet

Also hanging on Mac's wall, not too far away from the Ebbets Field sign, is another link to his Pop-Pops. It's an electric art landscape of a diner in Fall River, Massachusetts, called Al Mac's—a picture of a vintage stainless-steel diner originally built in 1953 that still exists today, which was photographed by Lucinda Lewis and featured in her book *Roadside America: The Automobile and the American Dream*. Of course, our interpretation of it was that my dad and Mac had teamed up together as the two proprietors who ran the place. In particular, under their duo partnership, the diner was known for its mac 'n' cheese of course as well as their crisp french fries, both of which were among Mac's personal favorites. It was established that the diner would always give away free mac 'n' cheese on Mac's birthday and free fries on opening day of the Major League Baseball season as part of its annual promotions.

Electric Art Picture of Al Mac's Restaurant in Fall River, Massachusetts, hanging on Mac's bedroom wall

In the photo, parked in front of the diner are some antique cars that include a big old turquoise blue Cadillac with a white trimmed top. And next to it is a flashy, red Corvette convertible. According to Mac, the Caddy belonged to Pop-Pop and the Corvette was Mac's wheels. And maybe we were reading into things too much, but the Massachusetts license plate numbers on Pop-Pop's Caddy was "2857," a combination of Mac's birthday, March 28, and my birthday, May 7.

There is an electric cord hanging down from the picture. When you plug it into the wall and flip the switch at the bottom of the picture… voilà, the whole photograph lights up, the Al Mac's sign up on top as well as some lights in the diner inside, plus the taillights on all the cars. It's really cool how it all lights up, especially how it glows in the dark.

I remember we came across this precious piece of nostalgic art in a touristy, souvenir store while on a family trip to Galena, Illinois. While for some reason we didn't buy it right away, we reconsidered after we left the store and ended up going back the next day on our way home in the pouring rain to get it, as we came to realize it was something that was made to order for us that we couldn't pass up.

The familial reunion at Ebbets would be down the road, hopefully long down the road. But for now, it would be the Cards and Expos at Roger Dean. As part of our annual, traditional spring break trip to Florida to visit Mom and Dad, the plan had been set for weeks, the tickets had been bought back in Chicago, and both Mac and I were counting the days until the big game.

But unfortunately, as the days got closer, even before we left for Florida, Pop-Pops was dropping hints that he wasn't sure if he was going to be able to make it. Being in his mid-nineties, he was no doubt getting into the late innings of his life, or at this point maybe extra innings, and as such had started to slow down quite a bit. We had to come to grips with the fact that going out to the ballpark, climbing up the stands, and fighting the crowds might be too much for our veteran and legend of the game. And sure enough that morning of the game, I could see he was moving kind of slow and while his heart was in it and he didn't want to disappoint us, he told us he just wasn't quite up to it. Naturally, Mac was pretty bummed out, as was I, for not only was I looking forward to the three of us in the stands together as a prelude to our eventual get-together at Ebbets, but I had planned a little surprise for Dad during the game.

The morning started out looking like a typical March day in southern Florida, with a bright sun and barely a cloud in the sky, and the temperature already climbing into the 80s—a great day for baseball. Or at least we thought. But being the Ides of March, perhaps we should have suspected that there was something in the air suggestive of a portent to come. As often is the case in Florida, the weather can turn on a dime, and by the time we got to the parking lot of Roger Dean, some ominous, blackish gray clouds were starting to roll in, with a faint rumble in the distance that, while you hoped it was a plane, sounded a little like thunder.

As we always tried to do for a spring training game, Mac and I got to the stadium about 45 minutes or so early, partly to see some batting practice and players taking their warm-ups on the field, but more so to get some player autographs or "graphs" as Mac liked to call them. That was one of the big attractions of spring training games. The more casual environment of these games provided a fertile ground for autographs. Sometimes you were even lucky enough to get signatures of some of the big-name stars of the game. You never knew who you were going to get.

Of course, most of the guys who signed were the spring training invitees from the Minor Leagues, many of whose names you had never heard of. These were the guys who typically wore really high numbers on their backs, in the 60s, 70s, 80s, and 90s, which signaled to fans that these players were probably a long shot to make the team. Even after they signed their name, be it their shorthand representation or illegible cursive writing style, you couldn't always make out who they were. And of course, you didn't want to ask. So, a lot of times, here you were getting an autograph of a guy who you had no recognition of at all, other than his number. You had to buy a program to match and identify these mysterious players with their numbers.

But still, it didn't really matter… it was an autograph of a professional player, a Major Leaguer, or perhaps soon-to-be Major Leaguer. Plus, who knew, any of these up-and-comers could turn out to be one of tomorrow's stars. Besides, it was almost as much of a quantity thing as a quality thing. It was about how many "graphs" you could get. That was where much of the whole sport of it came in.

Mac was a pro at getting graphs. He had a nose for finding the players who were signing. And he had a knack for knowing how to weave in and out of the seats, making his way through the crowd, and getting right in there in the ready position with his baseball and Sharpie. Not only did he have to contend with other kids who shared his enthusiasm, many of whom were much bigger, brasher, and more boisterous, but he also had to deal with memorabilia professionals who were there solely as part of their job to get a signature and then turn around and sell it. These guys were the most pushy and ruthless, for whom you had little patience as they were depriving kids of this thrill at the expense of their economic gain. But Mac was not to be denied, he was as assertive as can be, and practically always came away with his share of graphs.

While Mac would do his thing, I would follow him around, carrying his glove that he would always bring along to the games, so that he would be prepared in case a foul ball came his way or a player on his way back to the dugout between innings was in a position to flip him the ball. It was all I could do to keep up with him, as he would roam the whole stadium going back and forth from the home team side to the visitor's side of the field. Scampering from one guy to another, whoever was out there, he was determined to get as many graphs as he could right up until game time, at which point he'd have to curtail his efforts until after the game.

Even though I tried to keep up with him, sometimes he would be darting in and out so fast from one crowd into another that in all the hubbub I'd lose sight of him for a while and had to resort to the old family heirloom warbler-like whistle… "Whill, Whill… Whill, Whill" to get his attention and locate him.

All of Mac's efforts usually paid off. There were games when it wasn't unusual for him to come away with a dozen or so graphs. This included those that he got at the end of the game, when he would take one more final pass of the field on our way back to the parking lot to see if any players were signing as they strolled back to the clubhouse or the parking lot.

Mac always came prepared, with a brand-new shiny white baseball, along with a black Sharpie. It had to be black. He had learned this lesson the hard way. One time he brought a red Sharpie, which ended up being a big mistake in more ways than one. Not only did the red magic marker make the signatures look unofficial, but the red markings tended to smudge all over the ball to the extent it made it even more difficult to make out anybody's name, which was especially frustrating when you didn't know the names of many of these players to begin with. But worse than that, there was an incident with the red marker that came back to haunt him.

It happened at the end of a Cubs exhibition game in Arizona, when we were returning to the parking lot. Thanks to an assist from his sister Danni who spotted somebody signing at the fence in the back of the parking lot, Danni and Mac quickly ran to the scene of the opportunity before most everybody else got wind of it. Lo and behold, they found none other than legendary Chicago Cub and Hall-of-Famer Ferguson Jenkins doing some signing. The handful of fans, who were already there, were one-by-one tossing their ball over the fence for Fergie to sign and then toss back to them. Since it turned out that Danni happened to be a little closer to the fence than Mac and because when it came to getting a graph positioning was everything, Mac handed the ball over to her when it seemed like she was next in line. When Fergie gave the nod for the next autograph and Danni in turn tossed the ball over the fence, it immediately prompted a comment from the Hall of Famer, who evidently had seen the sibling exchange and said, "Hey, let the kid throw it over himself!" As if that wasn't enough to bruise Mac's ego, Fergie looked at the ball in wonderment and started laughing. "What is this, some kind of lipstick ball?" he joked, and the comment in turn elicited a roar of laughter from all the others waiting in line. But with a continuing snicker or two, Fergie signed the ball and tossed it back. Needless to say, this is the only ball with red markings on it in Mac's extensive collection.

Just before we got to the gate, there were several folks milling around asking fans if they had extra tickets, as apparently the game was sold out. While I had an extra ticket in my pocket, I didn't even think about selling it. For both Mac and I had decided, even if Pop-Pops wasn't going to be able to make it physically, he was going to be there in spirit with us, our imaginary man. In deference to him, his seat would remain empty. We would just pretend he was there.

It was becoming more and more ominous out, as we showed our tickets at the gate and entered into the stadium. While we both couldn't wait to hit the field, we had to make a pit stop.

Actually, even if you didn't have to go, it was worth going into the men's room at Roger Dean. Not that the bathroom itself was anything unusual… it's your typical nondescript bathroom with urinals and stalls on one side and sinks on the other. It's what was above and inside the urinals that made it so unique. For above each of the dozen or so urinals that lined the far-side wall there was a separate, tiny square white billboard, advertising a local exterminator called Nozzle Nolen. All the signs look basically the same, featuring the company's smiling little elephant logo on top next to a big bug, with the company name beneath in blue, along with a cute little smug advertising quip written in red. Then, to go along with the signage, inside each urinal, toward the bottom just above the drain, was a replica of a big bug with a bull's-eye on it that was evidently there for targeting purposes.

Nozzle Nolen ads hanging above the urinals
at Roger Dean Stadium in Jupiter, Florida.

This time, when I looked up, the message above my urinal read…

The sign in front of Mac's a couple of urinals down to my right read…

As a marketing guy, I marveled at those signs and had an appreciation for this approach. What a brilliant campaign! It capitalized on the benefit of a captive audience to ensure Nozzle Nolen got their message across. What's more it had some entertainment value, and was thoroughly engaging. In addition to being able to read a funny blurb while taking care of a boring task, there was a sporting element to the whole process as you'd find yourself really wanting to hit that big bug target down in the urinal spot on. Furthermore, the janitorial crew at the stadium must have loved it as well, as I imagine it minimized any spillage that ended up trickling to the floor. A "win-win" all around!

Whenever we were in there, Mac and I tried to come up with some of our own little ad slogans for Nozzle Nolen. We had some doozies over the years that we felt were certainly urinal-worthy:

With Nozzle Nolen, getting rid of bugs is a whiz

Don't let bugs bug you, call Nozzle Nolen to bring out their hose

When you see a bug, don't say eek—just take a leak

I even came up with a little saying for my fellow Jewish fans attending a game:

When it comes to taking out bugs,
you get a lot of mazel with Nozzle

I was working on coming up with another slogan as we headed to our seats in the grandstands, but was distracted as the field came into view. There was nothing like taking in a professional baseball field. Somehow seeing the perfectly trimmed diamond infield and plentiful green outfield, with a backdrop of billboards from local businesses and the gleaming lit-up scoreboard with the starting line-ups and players' statistics, was mesmerizing. It created a whole enchanting world of its own.

After taking in that special moment, we both scanned the field to see if any players were signing. Sure enough, Mac immediately spotted one of those high-numbered guys on the Expos signing near the team's bullpen, and with his bright white, never-used baseball and black Sharpie in hand sprang into action and made a beeline for the player, with me tagging along behind, trying to keep up. At that point, timing was key as the challenge was to try to get there before the player stopped signing. Mac made it in time and ended up getting the guy's signature, even though we weren't sure who he was. And then Mac got a bunch more, all of whom were sporting the higher numbers.

Meanwhile, the clouds were completely taking over the sky, and it was getting darker. The thunder was sounding closer and closer. And then, just as the home-team Cardinals took the field, just before the singing of the national anthem, a streak of lightning bolted across the sky. As fast as the players ran out to the field, that's how fast they ran back into the dugout, reacting to the lightening and crack of the thunder as though it was the crack of a bat hitting a ball. Then, just as soon as all the players had returned to the dugout, the grounds crew took their cue and quickly rolled out the tarp. They got out there just in time for the heavens to open up with a thick, rapidly increasing downpour amidst more lightning and thunder. Mac and I abruptly got up from our seats and ran down the stairs to the concession area for cover.

I was beginning to think maybe it was a blessing in disguise that my father wasn't with us. It would have been tough enough for him to negotiate the stands and the crowd on a nice day, but to have to contend with this kind of weather on top of everything would have definitely been too much.

Starting to get soaked, we made our way down to the main walkway of the stadium and squeezed ourselves in between others under the overhead of the first concession stand we came to. While there, we figured we might as well have lunch. Usually, as though it was a tradition, we waited until at least the second or third inning, after the game was well underway, to eat. But we were going to have to wait it out anyway and we were right there, so without moving we placed our order, a slice of pizza and an order of fries for Mac, his standard fare at the ballpark, and a bratwurst for me.

While we ate, Mac wanted to see the baseball that I had stuffed in my pocket, along with the Sharpie, to have a look at how many graphs he got so far and from whom. He had amassed a total of six signatures, but we were only able to recognize a few. We would have to get a program and cross-reference the team rosters, based upon the players' numbers, to try to decipher the other signatures. Also, we were going to need another Sharpie, as ours was no longer in my pocket. It must have popped out when we catapulted from our seats at the start of the downpour.

Before we had finished eating, the rain began to let up a little bit and then it stopped altogether, so it looked like there might be baseball after all. It had only rained for a short time, and the sun was suddenly beginning to peak out through the clouds again. Although it still didn't look all that great out and you could tell there was still something in the air. Nasty-looking clouds were still looming in the distance, and I had overheard some folks saying another wave of rain was on its way.

But indeed there was an announcement that the game would resume in 20 minutes. The grounds crew was rolling the tarp back up and people were beginning to file back toward their seats.

All the while, Mac was eyeing the souvenir shop. As to be expected during a rain delay, the store looked like it was wall-to-wall people inside, with a line wrapped around the outside perimeter and fans waiting for others to leave before they could go in. During rain delays, a store like this was a magnet. Nevertheless, we needed a program and another Sharpie, and Mac, of course, wanted to get something else, so we got in the outside line that actually ended up moving faster than we thought and we were in the store in no time.

The store offered a hodgepodge of all kinds of stuff, most with either a Cardinals or Expos logo on it. There was a ton of different types of baseball gear, including a wide assortment of baseball hats, all different styles and colors; shirts with various names of each team's star players on the back – including Edmonds, Rolen, Puljois, and Morris for the Cardinals and Guerrero, Cordero, Vidro, and Vazquez for the Expos; sweatshirts, lightweight jackets, running shorts, and socks. Then there was a whole slew of other logo-marked baseball paraphernalia, such as balls, bats, helmets, etc., as well as all the tchotchkes – Cardinals' and Expos' keychains, magnets, coffee mugs, tumblers, pencils, pens, you name it.

As to be expected, Mac insisted on getting an 18-inch miniature wooden bat, of which he already owned so many. He had a collection of at least 10 or so of these miniature bats at home, which he would frequently like to switch off and use down in our basement to hit the ball against the wall. Every time he visited a new ballpark, he was intent on getting one of these mini-bats with the respective logo of the home team. This time he got a red one with the Cardinals logo on it. Fortunately, they were out of the Montreal Expos bat; otherwise I would have probably been pressured into buying that one for him as well to add to his collection.

Sharpies were about the only writing instruments they didn't sell, so when we got up to the checkout counter we opted for a regular pen instead. Staying with the bat theme, we ended up getting a pen in the shape of a bat. It was your typical ballpoint pen, except on the outside there was a plastic shell of a red bat with the Cardinals logo on it, a much smaller version of the mini-bat we were buying. We also of course picked up a program.

The rain didn't hold off for very long. For when we came out of the store, it was already starting to drizzle and we could just tell we were probably going to be in for it again. It certainly didn't look very promising. Although we hadn't heard any official announcement yet, at this point with the skies continuing to look ominous and the rain starting to fall again, it seemed inevitable that the game was going to be called.

While part of me wanted to stay and wait it out with the outside chance they were going to get the game in, my paternal instinct was kicking in and getting the better of me, as I felt that it was probably a good idea for us to pack it in for the day and make a break for the car before we got thoroughly drenched. I knew Mac wasn't going to be happy with the decision to leave, but I figured he would be a lot more unhappy if we stayed and it turned out to be a complete washout.

The walk back to the car was long, which my companion constantly reminded me of during our trek. As it always does, it seemed much longer going back than coming into the park, particularly when you're walking in the rain. We were almost back at the car when we heard a public address announcement coming from the stadium, which I couldn't quite make out but presumed must have been a confirmation that the game for today was officially cancelled. Suddenly Mac got excited and claimed that the game was on. No doubt his hearing was better than mine, but I figured he was just hearing what he wanted to hear. Meanwhile, some guys near us were high-fiving and getting ready to head back into the stadium, further bearing out Mac's proclamation that the game was on. You had to wonder why they weren't calling the game. After all, it was only a spring training exhibition game. What was it about this game that those in charge felt compelled to get it in?

Knowing that Mac had his heart set on seeing the game, yet still questioning that the game was going to actually happen, I agreed to do an about-face and we headed back toward the stadium. Sure enough, it turned out that Mac had heard right. Apparently, the off, on-again, seemingly off-again game was back on again and it was "Play ball!"

As we made our way back to our seats, we noticed there was someone who was signing. But there were so many people around him, you couldn't see who it was. Someone shouted out that it was Girardi. Joe Girardi was the starting catcher for the St. Louis Cardinals. This was an opportunity you didn't want to pass up. He was one of those veteran players who had certainly made his mark on the field, coming off of an illustrious 15-year career in which he earned three World Series rings with the Yankees in '96 ,'98, and '99. As someone whose playing career was probably drawing to a close, this could perhaps be his last year as a player. So, we got in line.

While we waited, Mac got into the ready position as he took out the baseball from the souvenir shop bag, as well as the St. Louis Cardinals bat pen we had just bought. When it was his turn, he handed them over to the veteran catcher in awe.

"Is this a pen?" Girardi quipped. It was amazing the conversation Mac elicited from star players, without even saying anything. First it was from Fergie Jenkins with the "lipstick ball," and now it was Joe Girardi with the bat pen. I thought maybe it was because it wasn't a normal pen that Girardi must have been impressed that this little bat could actually be a pen. But nope, that wasn't what provoked his question. Truth is, it wasn't a pen anymore, as apparently the pen part had slipped out of the bat part, and it was now just an empty plastic bat shell with a hole in the bottom! Sure enough, the pen part was still in the souvenir bag. So much for bat pens! Everybody in line was laughing, and even Girardi was cracking a smile. Thoroughly embarrassed, in a panic we turned to our fellow fans for assistance while we laughed along with them. Luckily the party in back of us quickly came to our rescue and lent us a marker.

Upon return to our seats they were still soaking wet, so it was back to the men's room and the world of Nozzle Nolen to get some paper towels to bring back with us to wipe them down. As we each pulled down paper towel after paper towel from the dispenser, another one of my favorite Nozzle Nolen signs caught my eye.

As usually is the case with paper towels, we didn't get nearly enough, especially since we had forgotten that we had three chairs to wipe down – Mac'a, mine, and at Mac's insistence the empty chair next to him on the other side where Pops was sitting in absentia. So our seats were still a little wet, and consequently so were our pants as we settled in for the first pitch.

Finally, it was time to play ball. It was still hard to believe that the game was actually going to be played. Although the crowd had certainly thinned out as a result of the rain delay, I was surprised to see the number of fans that had hung in there. The stadium must have still been half full. It remained pretty dreary. A light drizzle came and went, as did the innings, as we watched both teams put up some runs on the scoreboard and trade leads every other inning or so. The Expos came up with a run in the top of the first, then the Cards came back with two in the bottom of the second, then the Expos with two in the top of the fourth, and so on.

Throughout the whole game I kept checking the scoreboard, especially between innings. It wasn't until the middle of the sixth inning, with the score tied 4-4, when I looked back at the scoreboard and I finally saw what I was waiting for. I thought I could make out a faint acknowledging roar from the crowd as the scoreboard flashed…

Congratulations to Al Levin
Celebrating his 95th Birthday

Dad's Birthday Message on the Roger Dean Stadium Scoreboard

Taken by surprise, Mac stood up with me and we both gave a hearty applause. Realizing that I was the one who must have set this up, Mac gave me one of those acknowledging looks that a father thrives on, that made me think he must have been rather impressed that his old man arranged this. I just wished my old man was there to witness this. I was always amazed at how my dad was able to pull strings and make things happen, and I guess deep down beyond the essence of my tribute to him I wanted to show him my stuff and have him impressed with something I was able to pull off. Sons never stop trying.

When we got back to my parents' condo later that afternoon, Mac couldn't wait to tell Pop-Pops all about the game… about how it looked like it was going to be rained out several times, only to end up being played; about all the details of the game with an inning-by-inning account and who ended up winning, which was the Cardinals 5-4; how he got a new bat, which he showed off to him; how, bringing out his newly autographed ball as evidence, he got a total of seven autographs, including that of Joe Girardi; and what happened with our bat pen when he got Girardi's signature. But most of all how Pop-Pops had his name on the scoreboard and how everybody really cheered for him. Of course, we might have built up the cheering a little bit, but that's how we remembered it. Besides that's what you do when you come back from baseball games.

Chapter 26

DIVINE INTERVENTION

THE ROCKIES-DIAMONDBACKS game was still on as I turned off of I-81 and entered into the parking lot of the Wilkes-Barre Hilton Garden Inn about 11:00 pm. I went inside and got a dolly to bring back out to the car. While it was tempting to just leave the Torah in the car overnight, there was no way I was going to do that. It was coming in with me up to the room. And so, I unstrapped all its seat belts, all the while trying to memorize how it was strapped in to begin with, so I could remember how to recreate the configuration of the belts in the morning when I brought it back, and very carefully transferred the Torah out of the car and laid it out lengthwise onto the dolly, with its overlaying sheet completely concealing its identity. There was then just enough room for me to stand my suitcase up at the end of the dolly. I also grabbed the tin of cookies and placed it on top of the suitcase, just in case I wanted a snack for later.

As I wheeled the dolly into the hotel and stopped to check in, I could see the apprehension in the eyes of the clerk behind the desk. She might have been thinking I was trying to smuggle something in. In an attempt to avoid any questioning, I told her that this was a very valuable piece of art, which in a way it was. I figured that brief description would be much more relatable to her versus going into a whole explanation of what a Torah is, which I couldn't expect her to know anything about or, let alone, had even ever heard of. She nodded, acknowledging my explanation but in a non-convincing way, still probably suspecting that there was something I was hiding. I wouldn't blame her for being curious—it wasn't too much of a stretch to think at first glance that I was carting in a small person's body.

But as soon as I said something, I realized I probably shouldn't have said that, or anything for that matter, especially using the words "valuable piece of art." What was I thinking? I mean, here I was in an unfamiliar place, amongst people I didn't know, and not sure how trustworthy this clerk behind the desk checking me in could really be. For all I knew, she could be an inside partner and accessory to a theft ring. She was certainly in an opportune position to know the ins and outs of the guests staying at the hotel, and if they had some valuable possessions with them. She could easily tip off some of her cohorts that so-and-so in room such-and-such was a prime target. And furthermore, she had the wherewithal to give them a room key to gain access to the goods. Perhaps I was letting my thoughts run wild, but I couldn't help but think that maybe the "Great Torah Caper" was about to take place at the Hilton Garden Inn in Wilkes-Barre.

When I got in my room, conscious of and careful not to let the Torah touch the floor in any way in keeping with the principles of *The Code of Jewish Law*, I took it off the dolly but kept it wrapped in the linen sheets and propped it up on the traditional-style gray cloth winged chair next to the bed. I then returned the dolly to the lobby, giving a friendly nod and smile to the woman behind the front desk. Still somewhat suspicious of intruders, when I came back to the room I dead-bolted the door as I settled in for the night and even dragged a small desk against the door, just in case.

I turned on the TV to catch the last couple of innings of the Rockies-Diamondbacks game, as it was still going on. With the Torah alongside propped up on the chair, it was as though the two of us were watching the game together. I was wondering if this was a first. It was certainly different from watching with the guys. But then in a way, I guess I was watching with other guys, namely Abraham, Isaac, Jacob, and company. I thought of it as a bonding experience with them, taking in a ball game together.

I wondered if they had a sense for the game. Some say Abner Doubleday invented the game of baseball in the summer of 1839 in Cooperstown, New York. There is even a commemorative stadium in Cooperstown named after him to show for it. But many historians challenge that as just a popular myth, claiming there are traces of the game going back to ancient Egypt, as far back as at least 1500 BC. And one had to wonder if perhaps people were playing baseball, or at least some form of it, even before that. No doubt the game has transcended from generation to generation, for I couldn't imagine there ever being a world without baseball.

For all we know, the game may have even gone as far back as our forefathers. They could have been out there playing, using a big, caveman-like club for a bat, and a stone for a ball, or perhaps they crafted a ball from scratch, out of some tightly packed straw that they kept winding 'round and 'round. Maybe they even had a team back then. They probably called themselves the Israelites or something like that. And, who knows, maybe they were even in a league with various other tribes.

I could just imagine the Israelites' starting line-up. It would likely have been a team made up of our forefathers and their sons, a total family undertaking. Leading off and playing shortstop would be Isaac. Ishmael, although chronologically being Abraham's first son whom he begot with Hagar (who was his wife Sarah's handmaid and who, because Sarah couldn't conceive at the time, was put in to pinch-hit for her so that Abraham could be sure to have an heir), was really considered more of a second son compared to his younger brother Isaac, whom Abraham and Sarah subsequently ended up conceiving together. Accordingly, as sort of a second son, Ishmael would be batting second and playing second base. Abraham would be the player manager batting third and catching, as he would be calling all the pitches behind the plate. Whether or not they would have been sophisticated enough to have the full repertoire of different types of pitches that we have today, I'm sure they would have had a few options up their sleeve in addition to a straight fastball. Esau, Jacob's twin brother, being the big, strong, burly guy that he was, who might have had a nickname such as "The Big Bopper," would be batting cleanup and playing first base. The three brothers, Joseph, Judah, and Rubin, sons of Jacob, would be the three outfielders and bat next in the order; Benjamin, Jacob's youngest son, would bat eighth and play third. And finally Jacob, known for his trickery and no doubt his crafty pitches, would be out on the mound and bat ninth.

1	**Isaac**
2	**Ishmael**
3	**Abraham**
4	**Esau**
5	**Joseph**
6	**Judah**
7	**Rubin**
8	**Benjamin**
9	**Jacob**

Israelites' Starting Line-up

Later on, I could see Ishmael and Esau branching off to form their own respective teams, with Ishmael starting up the Ishmaelites, and Esau going with the appropriately named Hittites for his team, after having married into the rival Hittite clan. With a name like that, the Big Bopper's team would no doubt have led the league in hitting.

The Rockies ended up winning the game 5-1. They had taken the first game of the National League Championship Series, making it their fourth playoff win in a row. They had had a magical season that year, as their stretch run was among the greatest ever in the history of Major League Baseball, winning 14 out of their final 15 games to end their season. This included a wild extra inning, 9-8 tie-breaker, play-in game win over the San Diego Padres to get into the playoffs, when they came back with three runs in the bottom of the 13th after the Padres had scored 2 runs in the top of that inning.

At the time, baseball pundits were saying that there was some divine intervention going on with the Rockies. To quote their general manager at the time, Dan O'Dowd, "You look at some of the moves we made and didn't make. You look at some of those games we're winning. Those aren't just a coincidence. God had definitely had a hand in this." And the way they were going, indeed one had to wonder if this team was going through some type of spiritual experience and destined to win the whole thing.

It was going to be a long day on the road tomorrow. After the game concluded, I figured I had better pack it in for the night. But before I did, I dove into the tin of cookies and had a few for a midnight snack.

I had already checked in with Gail several times during the day to give her some updates. But knowing that it was an hour earlier in Chicago and thinking that she might still be up, I gave her a quick call for one final check-in and to say good night. I started the conversation telling her that I had just polished off some of her delectable cookies, telling her that it was a fitting way to cap off my good day. Although I was much too tired to really talk that long, I gave her a quick rundown of the trip thus far and let her know that everything was going well. And that the Torah and I were now safe and sound in our room at the hotel in Wilkes-Barre and ready to call it a night. I told her I'd check in with her again tomorrow.

I then set the alarm for 7:00 am, hit the lights, and looked forward to what hopefully would be a comfortable, peaceful night sleep, feeling particularly safe with all my ancestors watching over me, as I drifted off.

Chapter 27

STOPPING FOR DIRECTIONS

IT TURNED OUT **I** DID A LOT of tossing and turning that night. Even though I took some comfort in knowing that the spirits of my forefathers were close by and would hopefully have my back, it seemed as though I kept waking up and checking on the Torah to make sure it was still there. I must have woken up at least five times. Despite locking the dead-bolt on the door and setting up a barricade, I guess I was still a little paranoid that someone would break into the room to steal my prize possession. But, when the alarm went off, I was rarin' to go. I had to stay on schedule so I could be at the Pittsburgh Airport by 4:30 pm, when I was supposed to pick up Mark to accompany me on the rest of my journey home.

Wheeling the Torah through the lobby on the way out of the hotel, with the large white sheet draped over it, I could feel all these suspicious stares following me, from the staff behind the registration desk to the hotel guests milling around. They must have all wondered what was under there. They had to suspect something, perhaps that I was sneaking out a dead body. Despite the silent skepticism, somebody was nice enough to get up from their seat and hold the door open for me as I headed out.

I tried to remember the exact way I belted in the Torah when I first put it in the car, but I could not. Even though I tried to memorize the configuration the night before, I couldn't seem to duplicate it. But after trying this way and that, and pulling and tugging to test its stability, I was satisfied the belts were as secure as before and I started up the Torah Blazer to continue my journey.

As planned, I got back on I-81 and headed south for about 20 miles, where I connected with I-80 and headed west toward Bloomsburg. It looked like it was going to be a nice day, no threat of a torrential downpour like the night before—a good day for traveling.

On I-80, not too far after the Bloomsburg exit, a sign for Williamsport, Home of the Little League World Series and Museum, caught my eye. The Little League World Series was an event that Mac and I had become accustomed to watching on TV together every year. My favorite part was at the beginning of the game, when each participating 12-year-old player introduced himself and mentioned who his favorite Major League baseball player was. This year, the team out of Warner Robins, Georgia, had won it, as they defeated Tokyo in the championship game. It marked the second year in a row that a team from Georgia had won.

Being the baseball fan that I am, I was tempted to stop and check it out, but I wasn't really sure exactly how far away it was and given that I was somewhat up against the clock, I figured I had better stick to the plan. Besides, this was something that I wanted to do together with Mac. We had always talked about going there together and it wouldn't be the same without him. So I just continued on I-80 west, making my way across central Pennsylvania.

There were two ways I could have gone. That may sound like the Robert Frost poem "The Road Not Taken," in which Frost talks about having to make the choice of two roads that diverged into a yellow wood. Both ways seemed as though they would take about the same amount of time. One was more of a straight shot on the expressway, where I would stay on I-80, and then when I got to western Pennsylvania, I would go south a little ways on US Route 28 to hook up with I-376 and then on to the airport. The other route, consisting of more secondary roads, had me exiting I-80 earlier on, to go south onto US Route 220 that would turn into I-99; and then hook up with US Route 22, just south of Altoona, taking that west and merging onto I-376 toward the airport.

I opted to go with the latter route, partly because it was 15 miles shorter and slightly more direct, but more so because it included going on Route 22, which was one of the roads Dad and I used to take when we made the rounds to his stores together, specifically when we would take that long, one-day round-trip drive between Reading and Johnstown. I felt it would be only fitting to take some of the same roads he and I did before and retrace those memorable father-and-son car rides we had together. If only he could be with me this time around. If only I could have just one more ride with him. But I figured going on Route 22 would at least be a way to feel his presence and have him there along with me. Plus taking that highway would be an appropriate way to honor him, for if it wasn't for him, there would be no Torah in the back seat, and there would be no journey.

Also, as alluded to in Frost's poem, I wanted to take the road that I assumed was less traveled. This route included going on two-lane highways, like Route 22, for a longer period of time, which seemed more fitting for a journey such as this. This whole Torah road trip seemed more like the kind of expedition one would take across America's grassroots highways, rather than on interstate expressways. Like the type of journey that was featured on the TV show "On the Road with Charles Kuralt" that I used to watch when I was a kid, where the popular, roaming American journalist would travel on backroads and through the rural towns of America to uncover interesting feature stories about the places and people along the way. It certainly seemed more in keeping with the journeys and adventures of our forefathers. Plus, having been on the expressways for pretty much the whole time to this point, these backroad highways would certainly provide a welcome change of landscape that I figured would be more scenic and pleasurable.

I took Exit 161 off of I-80 to get onto US Route 220 South near Bellefonte, which was supposed to turn into I-99. All told, I was on I-80 for a little over 100 miles. When I got off the exit ramp, it was evident I was smack in the middle of rural Pennsylvania, just endless farm fields. No signs of commercialization, not even a gas station in sight, although there was a sign with an arrow on it advertising one a couple miles away. I wasn't even entirely sure if I was on the right road, if indeed I was actually on Route 220; or if not, how to get on it. When I found myself approaching a local firehouse, which seemed to be the only building around, I turned in to get some directions. That's what my dad would have done for sure. A chip off the old block. He would have been so proud of me.

I presumed that this fire station must be there to serve the town of Bellefonte, or maybe it was just one of the town's branches as it only housed one truck. An old truck at that, like one of those bare bones, boxy fire trucks used back in the day, not that much bigger than a glorified pickup truck, with one ladder on one side and just two large pipe-like hoses on the other.

At first, when I walked in, I didn't think anybody was there manning the station, but after yelling out a couple of hellos, an old-timer with a white beard wearing overalls appeared from the back with a rather puzzled look on his face as though he wasn't used to seeing folks here and gave me one of those standard colloquialisms, "What can I do for ya?"

"I guess I need some directions," I answered. "I'm headed to Pittsburgh and was just wondering if I was going the right way… is this Route 220?"

"Pittsburgh huh… everybody seems to want to go to Pittsburgh today. Not too long ago, I had another guy in here, an older gentleman, who was asking me the same thing. What's going on there today? You're quite a ways from there, young man. Take you a good three hours or so to get there. And yup, this is Route 220. I'll tell you what I told him. Just follow this same road you're on, up a mile or so and it becomes the interstate. It's this same road, you'll see the sign for it. You can't miss it. You'll be going south on I-99. You'll be on it for around 50 miles or so. Then just take the exit for Route 22 going west toward Ebensburg."

Sounded easy enough, I thought to myself as I thanked him, exited the station, and started making my way back toward the Torah Blazer ready to get back into the saddle. Maybe it was the whole overly quiet rural setting and that feeling like I was out in the middle of nowhere that created an air of desolate eeriness that seemed to prevail over the area. It was the type of place where you felt out of place and didn't want to hang around too long. The type of place where, maybe because you were a stranger, someone was watching you.

I was just about at my vehicle when all of a sudden I thought I heard some kind of a muffled whistle or a similar-type sound. At first I couldn't quite make it out. It was almost like that of a bird, like a whippoorwill or something… "Whill, Whill…Whill, Whill." But it sounded kind of familiar, enough so that caused me to stop in my tracks for a second. Then a few seconds later, there it was again… "Whill, Whill…Whill, Whill." This time it was little less faint and more discernable.

No… it couldn't be! I figured I must have imagined it, that perhaps my mind was just playing tricks on me. A call I hadn't heard for a while, a call that I had missed so much, and that I had been so longing to hear. Then I heard it again… "Whill, Whill…Whill, Whill." This time even louder.

As I turned around, I saw a fellow approaching me from a distance, starting to come into view. He was still a little too far away to completely make him out, but I could see he was wearing a solid white sports shirt, red pants, a kelly-green cardigan sweater and a visor-type hat. He looked like he had just gotten off the golf course. He was carrying a white cardboard sign with the words "Pittsburgh Airport" written on it. As he got closer and came into focus, my eyes seemed to bulge out and my mouth opened in shock on what I gathered could only be an illusion, as I was greeted with a "Hiya, Tiger!"

"What the...?"

He hadn't aged at all. It was as though time had stood still for him. He looked exactly the same as I last remembered him, high forehead with short, grayish-black hair slicked back and glasses with slight jowl-type wrinkles on each side of his face, yet still maintaining that much younger, age-defying look about him.

If there was ever an occasion for a kiss or at least a hug with my old man, this was it. But instead, maybe it was just a matter of habit, we just stuck out our hands at about the same time, and I found myself shaking hands with him. There was nothing like a firm handshake.

I still couldn't believe it. Was this really him? Was this really happening? Was I going meshugenah? How could this be? What was he doing here and how did he get here? Hello, good ole Mr. Brown from Mooreland Hill School... if only he was around to witness this phenomenon.

My first thought was perhaps he had come back to say goodbye. I mean, with him being in that comatose state just before passing, we didn't get the chance to impart any meaningful goodbyes to each other. Even if he knew I was there with him at the end, it wasn't the same as a formal or even informal farewell. We never had that last exchange of parting words, that last father-and-son talk, that last bonding opportunity, that last chance to say "I love you."

Or had he forgotten to tell me something? Something he meant to tell me, and he was now coming back to make sure to get the message across and seek closure. To share with me some magical fatherly advice, perhaps a treasure chest of worthy tidbits and insights from his experiences and learnings, that perhaps was going to help me put it all into perspective. Or was he here for just one more ride together, to keep me company on my adventure? Maybe all of the above.

Naturally, I was lost for words. "Dad...What...How...Wow...Are you really here?" were the only initial morsels of conversation I could blurt out. There was so much to say, so many questions to ask, I didn't know where to begin. But instead, I found myself reverting to logistics. "The

Pittsburgh Airport, huh? It's funny… that's where I'm headed." I thought it was more than a coincidence that, like me, he was going to the Pittsburgh Airport. Although on second thought, I guess an airport would typically be the type of place I would be taking him to, as I had done so many times before. And so here I was about to take him to the airport yet again.

Still in a state of shock and not really believing what was happening, I just stood there and stared at him for a while. He stared back at me and didn't say anything either. Then, lost in my surreal world and losing track of time, all of a sudden in fear that this opportunity might slip away from me as though it might not be real, I found myself blurting out the words, "So, you coming?" as if I had to ask and he needed a formal invitation.

He gave me an affirmative nod, discarded the sign in a nearby dumpster, and started walking toward the passenger side of the Blazer, with me following behind.

Assuming that he didn't know about it, although somehow I suspected he might have, I gave him a heads-up that I had a Torah in the back seat, the Torah he had donated to Temple B'nai Israel in honor of Yale. I explained that I had just picked it up from the temple yesterday and was driving it out to my temple outside of Chicago. And that I was planning to pick up a friend at the Pittsburgh Airport, to keep me company on the drive. I told him I would tell him all about it when we were on the road.

Still trailing a little bit in back of him, I watched him take a brief glimpse of the Torah in the back seat as though he was looking for a quick validation, and then with a little kick in his step, he opened the door and easily hopped up into the front passenger seat and closed the door. No sweat! Apparently, he didn't need a footstool anymore.

Once I saw that he was safely in, I double-backed behind the car to the driver's seat, jumped in, and was ready to go. I took one more stare at him, still questioning whether this was really happening. Then, as I started the engine, I found myself bellowing out a rather emphatic, "And away we go!"

Chapter 28

ON FAMILIAR ROADS

"So how you going to go?" Dad asked.

If there was any doubt that this was actually him, that question pretty much confirmed it right then and there. Same guy, alright!

"I got it all mapped out, Dad."

"You sure?"

"Got it, thanks," I almost snapped back in somewhat of a defensive tone but was able to catch myself. It doesn't take long to go back to your old ways. Sensing where this conversation was going, that he'd probably suggest that I stop at a gas station for directions, I continued on.

"And I confirmed it back there at the firehouse. We're taking this road up a little ways to when it turns into I-99, and then we take I-99 South for 50 miles or so and then get on US 22 going west. You know, Route 22 is the road we used to take to your Johnstown store, remember?"

The mention of the Johnstown store brought a smile to his face, as he seemed to perk up a little bit. "Oh yeah, that's right, heh… heh! Remember those days, those trips we used to take out there?"

"How can I forget! But yeah, we'll take Route 22 for about 85 miles. Then we hook up with I-376 for about 30 miles on into the

224

airport." He shook his head with an approving nod, as he seemed pretty impressed with my command of the logistics.

As the road turned into the interstate, I hit the gas. We were trucking along! Here we were, father and son, heading down the open road on yet another adventure. It was like old times, just he and I, taking it all in. Except this time, I was doing the driving.

"Chocolate chip cookie?" I asked him as I reached for the tin in the back and extended it to him. "Gail baked them."

"Sure, thank you!" He always said thank you for stuff like that.

"There's some bottled water back there too if you want."

"Wow, these are good!"

"Yup, she's quite good in the kitchen. They're made with a lot of love."

"Hey, that must be Penn State over there," I blurted out as we passed what looked like part of a large campus on the left side of the road. I had never been there before and other than my good friend Bob Karp, I didn't really know anybody who went there.

"They still have a good football team?" my dad asked. Under its legendary coach Joe Paterno, Penn State had had a long-standing reputation for being a powerhouse Big Ten team.

"Yup, they're always competitive." It was cool how we were starting to talk about sports, but he quickly changed the topic.

"So, anyway, how is everybody?"

I wondered how much he knew about all of us in the family. Maybe he already knew everything that had been going on and was just asking as a course of conversation, or he just wanted to hear it from me. Just the same, I played along.

"How's mother?" He never referred to her as mom, always mother.

"She's doing ok, except of course she really misses you. We all do." I proceeded to tell him just how much she truly missed him. To her, my father was her everything. Maybe it was a generational thing back then, but he was the center of her universe. Without him, it was really hard for her to move on.

Without my father there to take care of all the administrative details, she had immersed herself in managing the day-to-day finances.

I told him she was on top of them like no one you've ever seen. At an early age, having seen her once well-to-do family financially stricken by the Great Depression, she was a stickler when it came to managing her money. And while my father had done a great job of providing for his family and had left my mother with a fairly comfortable nest egg, she always remained in fear that another depression was around the corner and that she might not have enough funds to sustain her existence. It was always a cloud over her head. Consequently, she watched over her finances like a hawk, depriving herself of living life to its fullest in fear that her money would run out.

"And how about Deborah and Gianni?" My mother and father always tended to call my sister Deborah, as they were old school. I guess they were so rooted in and attached to her original name that they never could seem to get on the Lexye nickname bandwagon.

"I think they're good. Haven't seen them in a while as I haven't been down to Florida lately, but I think their business is doing pretty well."

My sister's primary business was incentive travel. Client companies hired her company, Professional Touch, to put together trips for their annual sales meetings or as a perk for their top management or their high-performing sales staff. As a consummate event planner, Lexye offered a total turnkey operation soup to nuts, from choosing the destination with the client, making all the arrangements including planning a detailed itinerary of all the trip's activities, developing a theme, putting together all related promotional materials, and even going on the actual trip with her clients to oversee things and ensure that everything went as planned. As the name of her company implied, she was a master of her craft and became quite successful. Given her organizational, social, leadership, and theatrical skills, she played a major role in bringing these trips to life and giving them some extra pizazz that based on client accolades made for an unforgettable experience.

Lexye's trips spanned the globe. She put together these corporate groups to just about everywhere, leaving me a bit envious. I went on a couple of group trips with her, to the Bahamas and Rio de Janeiro, but for the most part she was another one in our family, in addition to my father, who I had to live vicariously through.

Lexye's husband, Gianni, who my sister first met on one of her incentive trips to Italy where he was the general manager of the hotel her group was staying at, was in the travel business as well. In addition to helping Lexye plan trips, he had his own consulting gig as a representative for travel agencies in Italy, and helped Americans plan and book their leisure trips to his native country.

Plus, Gianni was a great cook. He did most of the household cooking. Whenever we went to their house for dinner, we would have an Italian feast that always included roasted peppers and one of his famous pasta dishes.

"And you know Lex… she's always involved in a lot of stuff." Travel wasn't the only career path she followed. She was always exploring potential business opportunities. She was my father's daughter alright, with his same entrepreneurial blood flowing through her veins, always on the lookout for the next big opportunity.

"So bring me up to date on the kids."

"Well, your granddaughter Danni just turned 15, cute as ever. This past summer she was a counselor at Camp Agawak, the overnight camp up in Wisconsin where she's been going for a while. And last month she started her sophomore year of high school. She did great her freshman year and was on the honor roll. She even received a letter of commendation from her social studies teacher, and what the teacher said about her really stood out."

I had practically memorized the teacher's comments word-for-word and was starting to beam as only a proud father can, as I repeated these words to him. "She said Danni is a great person. She is so kindhearted and always committed to helping others. How heart-warming is that, huh?

"Also, she's on the school's badminton team and she's pretty darn good. You know, when you think of badminton, you think of a leisurely backyard kind of sport, kind of slow and easy-going. But these games are all indoors, and surprisingly it tends to be a really fast game and quite competitive.

"She had her bat mitzvah two years ago. Sure wish you could have been there. We held it in the banquet room of a golf club called the The Arboretum near our house. Her theme was 'The Dannis'… a takeoff on the Grammys. We had the whole room decked out to the nines, with a red carpet rolled out leading up to the stage. Our DJ was all spiffed up in a tuxedo as the emcee.

Danni celebrating during her Bat Mitzvah

"And she's such a great sister. To this day, she still sits down with Mac to play baseball cards with him."

This triggered a natural progression to have him ask about her sibling. "And how about the Big Macher?"

"He's a Big Macher alright. Can you believe it… Mac is 11! That's the number he wore on his baseball jersey this year. It's funny, I figure he's got to be the only baseball player in history to have a number on his jersey that represents both his age and his last name. 'Levin', get it?

"The number must have been good luck, as his Bronco House League team, the Kansas City Jayhawks, ended up winning the championship this year… "Rock Chalk Jayhawk!' His House League teams had come close before, but this was their year. I basked in the glory, not only as his father but also as one of the coaches on the team.

"Plus, he's played Travel Baseball now for the last four years. I don't know if you remember, but he played up a year and started playing Travel when he was only 8." As I said this, I realized that Mac had first started playing Travel in the spring of 2004, six months before Dad passed.

"I wish you could have seen him pitch." I wondered to myself if he had. Perhaps he had been out there sometimes sitting in the grandstands watching his grandson in action. "He's got great stuff out there on the mound. One thing is for sure… he sure loves baseball. Now he's already gearing up for tryouts for Travel for next spring. His tryouts start tomorrow, actually."

Of course, being the baseball aficionado that I was, I loved that Mac also loved baseball. I guess all those baseballs on the wallpaper in his room showing four different kinds of pitchers' grips—the fastball, the curve, the slider, and the split-finger, of which I always referred to as the "pitches of life"—apparently must have somehow seeped in all these years, perhaps through osmosis, while he was sleeping.

"He's now a big sixth-grader and has just started middle school. Believe it or not, his bar mitzvah is only a year and a half away. We've already reserved the date, which at our temple, you need to do two years in advance. It's going to be March 21, 2009, so save the date. And the plan is to have him read from your Torah there in the back seat. It's good timing!"

His eyes seemed to light up with this news. I think he liked that I called it his Torah. I also imagine that he must have liked that his grandson was going to read from it at his bar mitzvah.

"And how's Gaily?" He sometimes called her that.

"She's terrific! She's some kind of gal, that's for sure. Like you with mom, I guess I'm a pretty lucky guy. We couldn't have picked any better ones, huh? All the qualities in a woman you could ask for, and more. Kind, thoughtful of others, genuine, loving wife, super mom… can multi-task with the best of them, smart, talented in everything, and is a great cook to boot. And we married much younger ones at that."

Like my father, I had been accused of "robbing the cradle." While not quite to the same extent as the 16-year difference between my father and mother, there was an 11-year difference between me and Gail. To put it in perspective, when I became a bar mitzvah, Gail was only 2 years old.

"Worth waiting for, that's for sure," I said with conviction, alluding to the fact that like him, I had waited a long time to tie the knot, until six months shy of my 40's to get married. I ended up beating him to the aisle by only a year and a half.

"She's still working, but is continuing to cut down more and more, in order to be there for the kids. She's always there when they come home from school and is there for all their school activities. It's nice. Plus, she just joined a woman's golf league." I figured he would be impressed with that. "She plays every week at a nearby course. Heck, she plays more than I do now."

"And how about you, Tiger?" I loved that he still called me "Tiger."

The words "how about you" echoed a little bit in my mind. I had always wondered if in the hereafter my father would be able to continue to track my career, and if so, what his thoughts would be in terms of how I had turned out. If not, here was my chance to tell him.

"Moi… you mean the prodigal son?" That's what he would call me sometimes, especially when I would return home from being away for a while.

"Yeah, what's going on with you? How's business?"

"All good, I guess. I have to say our business is doing pretty well. It looks like we're going to have one of our best years. It's been a good business. You know… you were right! You always felt that I should go into business with Gail."

I was referring to the fact that, seeing Gail do what she did, he had always felt this would be a good career path for me to take on as well, instead of staying in the corporate world. I had spent most of my career in marketing brand management at a couple of large consumer packaged goods companies. First at General Mills in Minneapolis, where I started out working on Trix cereal, which was a blast, reliving the "Silly rabbit, Trix are for kids" slogan I had grown up with; then moving onto Gold Metal flour, coinciding with the brand's centennial anniversary; and lastly onto Chef Saluto frozen pizza, a regional brand out of Michigan that, at the time, General Mills had recently purchased.

Then I made a jump to Sara Lee outside of Chicago to help introduce its new line of frozen croissants, which took the world by storm as the company couldn't make enough of them to keep up with demand and was faced with the challenge of needing to expand capacity. Originally, there were three flavors: regular, cheese, and whole wheat. But we had to temporarily discontinue both the cheese and whole wheat, in order to free up production capacity to make the top-selling regular flavor.

In 1984, Sara Lee's parent company Consolidated Foods took on the Sara Lee name for itself, in an effort to leverage the widespread awareness and quality recognition associated with the strong Sara Lee brand name. Like the slogan said, "Nobody doesn't like Sara Lee." Consequently, to differentiate our subsidiary name, our company became known as the "Kitchens of Sara Lee."

To make things even more confusing, shortly after the name change, the newly crowned Kitchens of Sara Lee purchased Sara Lee Ice Cream from our sister subsidiary company Popsicle, which had previously licensed the Sara Lee name through its parent Consolidated Foods and had been marketing ice cream under that mark. The super-premium ice creams like Haagen Dazs and Frusen Glädjé had become very popular; and accordingly, given its equity in the dessert business, Kitchens of Sara Lee wanted to re-establish control of the Sara Lee mark and leverage the hot trending ice cream category.

So after working a while on croissants, I was transferred over to be the brand manager of our newly inherited ice cream product, the type of dessert that was near and dear to both my father and me. Little did I know, during all those nights when we had ice cream together, that someday I would be working on this delectable treat. It was a fun business to work on, but not without its challenges. It turned out that Sara Lee's eyes were bigger than its stomach, as the company ended up walking away from its new venture after only nine months. I was afraid that management would think I drove it into the ground. But there were a number of key factors involved that contributed to its demise, one of the most pressing was that ice cream had to be shipped at a temperature 10 degrees colder than all of the company's other frozen dessert products. This required different and more expensive shipping equipment and storage, such that the company couldn't achieve the economies of operation that top management had hoped for and was counting on.

Feeling as though my ice cream responsibilities had been giveth and then quickly taketh away, I was then moved onto managing all of Sara Lee's other desserts, including pound cake, all its various cheesecakes, and its dessert cakes, the latter of which were favorites of mine when growing up. Unfortunately, it was during my tenure and watch over these products that eating habits were trending away from the sugar-laden, perceived bad-for-you stuff to the not-so-bad-for-you stuff, causing Sara Lee's dessert business to experience a significant decline. Its dessert cake category was particularly hard hit with sales going down by 25% versus the previous year. Having seen the heydays of croissants, I was now experiencing the other side of the curve, that of a sharply declining business. The upshot of this was that as the manager in charge, I was being pressured by top management to discontinue Sara Lee's German Chocolate Cake, its delicious cake with toasted coconut frosting. How ironic that the demise of this German chocolate cake was happening upon my watch, as it was probably my very favorite of all of Sara Lee's dessert cakes. It was one of the cakes, along with the banana cake, for which I had the fond memory of licking the frosting off the piece of parchment paper that would be lying on top of the cake when you first opened its foil package. I tried to reason with upper management that this was one of the staples of the line, that our customers, particularly me, would really miss it, and that its sales would come back; but it was to no avail. I had to deep-six it, something for which to this day I still haven't been able to forgive myself.

As a brand manager, it seemed as though I was killing Sara Lee's products left and right. I was beginning to get a complex. I was seeing myself as the "hit man" for destroying so many consumer favorites. I figured from a career standpoint that couldn't be good. But fortunately, the company continued to hang in there with me, as after my dessert course, it was onto the breakfast category as I was promoted to group brand manager in charge of all Sara Lee's frozen breakfast products. I figured it was the least management could have done for me after discontinuing some of my most favorite desserts when growing up. And so it was back to croissants, back to where I started, but also I had responsibility for muffins, cinnamon rolls, individual Danish, round Danish and our newly introduced bagels. Later on, when I first met Gail at a murder mystery party hosted by one of our research vendors, she dubbed me the "Bagel Boy," one of the nicknames she continues to call me.

Then, after 10 years of classic consumer packaged goods brand management experience under my belt and with a little bit of my father's entrepreneurial blood boiling inside me, I moved west to San Diego to seek fame and fortune as I took on a high-risk, high-reward position as head of marketing for a biotech company. Specifically, I came in to work on a little badge that one would wear on their skin or clothing that measured the ultraviolet rays of the sun by changing color and indicating when it was time to seek shade or reapply sunscreen. This being in the early '90s, the lifestyle pendulum was swinging toward minimizing your exposure to UV light and protecting your skin, versus going out and maximizing your sun exposure to get a good tan. So the product was very much on trend, but it turned out the risk was higher than the reward as the company ended up having some quality control and financing issues with the product. Consequently, the product never saw the light of day. True to form, I guess you could say I had killed yet another product.

And so it was back into corporate, back to the East Coast to work at a promotion agency in New Jersey, where I headed up a bunch of accounts including Dr. Scholl's, Reynolds Aluminum, Citbank, Mobil Oil, and Amtrak. The latter, of course, was one of my favorites to work on, given my love for trains.

All this time, Dad had always been a strong proponent of me going off on my own to join Gail in her business, RapSessions, to get out of the pressures of corporate life. And to be able to be your own boss and have more control of your own destiny, just like he had done in his career. It seemed whenever we talked about my job or career, he would always bring up the notion of looking into doing what Gail was doing.

And so I did. I had now been working with my wife for 11 years. Despite my initial resistance of giving up the more seemingly safe and secure corporate life, I had jumped into the world of qualitative market research in 1996. Gail and I were partners, working with consumer product and service companies on enhancing their marketing efforts by obtaining consumer feedback and insights on new product ideas and advertising campaigns.

It was kind of funny how I got into it. An opportunity just happened to come knocking at my door. One of Gail's clients, Kellogg's, had called her about a Rice Krispies project, but she had a conflict and couldn't make the client's desired timing. So being in a bind, she served me up to pinch-hit for her. Even though I didn't have any experience whatsoever in the field, somehow, by touting my consumer packaged goods brand management background and stretching the envelope a little in terms of my marketing research experience, she was able to sell me in. So I bravely flew from New Jersey to Chicago to give it a shot. And with a little "snap, crackle, and pop," I had embarked upon a new career and never looked back.

I really liked everything about the job. I liked conversing with consumers about different products and services. I liked the strategic side of making recommendations to companies based on what those consumers shared in focus groups, for which of course my brand management experience came in handy. I liked the freedom and flexibility the position allowed, that I could pretty much make my own schedule. And I liked that I was working on a variety of products and types of projects, from exploring new flavors of Pop-Tarts to evaluating potential new TV advertising for Miller Lite.

As Dad and I were talking, I was hoping that I had impressed him. While I hadn't built up a company like he had, all in all I had amassed a pretty good career. I had worked at some Fortune 500 companies; had led some big-name brands; had seen some of the fruits of my efforts flourish in the marketplace despite some having bit the dust; and thus had pretty much climbed the ladder of success, at least a couple of rungs. And I did what he suggested to take the plunge and do my own thing along with Gail, which seemed to be working out pretty well. I was just hoping that at the end of the day, I had lived up to his expectations. That I had aptly represented and carried on the Levin name. That he was proud of me. I guess I was still intent on showing him my stuff. Us sons never stop trying.

"It's a great field, alright," I explained to him. "Really like what I do. Although you know it's kind of tough to get new clients. It's hard to break in with companies. As a potential new vendor, you're lucky these days if you even get an opportunity to sit down for an introductory capability meeting. It's like what we just went through with this one prospective client. Finally, finally, after several months of follow-up calls and emails, we were able to get a capabilities presentation set up with Jewel, you know, one of the major grocery chains in Chicago. It's coming up in a couple of weeks."

"Got a clean shirt?" Whenever I had an interview or important meeting coming up, he would always ask me if I had a clean shirt to wear. I figured it must have been left over from his dry-cleaning days.

With kind of a half-smile, I gave him a reassuring nod. I loved that he would always ask me this. It was one of his trademarks. The other words he would leave me with for these big meeting type situations were "Go get 'em, Tiger!"!

"Grocery stores, huh? Heh...heh, did I ever tell you about the time I was in the grocery store business?"

Of course, I knew the whole story. Heck, I could have told it myself. It was another one of my favorites. But I let on that I wasn't sure, as I wanted to hear it again. Besides it seemed I was doing all the talking. I wanted to hear him talk.

It was when I first got down to Florida with Leo Blumenthal. We were looking for an opportunity to work on something. A cousin of our family friend Judy Burstein, whom she had introduced to me before I left, was down there as a real estate salesman. So we made contact with him, and he said there were a couple of fellows, one named Hymie and I don't recall the name of the other guy, who had a little grocery store in Hialeah. He told us that they were constantly fighting and wanted to sell it. So we went out there and it was wilderness, it was all wilderness. The store was really little, not even half the size of today's mini-marts. And there were no electric lights or running water. Instead just a gasoline lamp and a well. But in the back was a bedroom, a bathroom, and a small kitchen.

We ended up making a deal with them to buy the place for $2,500. I used some money that I had saved up in the bank at home. We each came up with a down payment and gave them $1,500 and owed them the $1,000 balance.

As it happens, a month or two after we were there, Hymie, one of the original partners of the store whom I had become kind of friendly with, came over and spent the night with us. Maybe he was homesick for his old place. Anyway, he and I got into a card game, and I won $1,000 from him. So we didn't owe any more money for the store.

But let me tell you, being there was quite an experience, because money was very, very loose down there. We used to work on what we called, what-you-macall-it, 8%. Except 8% had a different definition for us. Everything that came into the store, we multiplied it by 8 and that was the selling price. So if an item cost us $.10, we'd sell it for $.80. We called it 8%, but it was really 800%", heh-heh. We were doing very, very well, we were making a lot of money.

Every night there were a few of the hillbillies from the area that used to come into the kitchen in the back of the store. And we used to sell them bottled home brew that cost us only about $.06 a bottle but we sold it for $3.50 a bottle.

So if we sold a total of $2500 of goods per week, we were clearing over $2,000 a week.

But of course, heh...heh, as fast as we were making it, we were going to the racetrack, the dog track, and jai alai games and blowing it.

Our best customers were only 300 yards away from us, the 16 to 18 houses of ill repute, heh...heh. That's where all our business came from. The madams used to come into the store and grab stuff and pay us. It didn't come from general store traffic—most of it came from them. Anyway, over time there was a little more action, a few more people coming into the area and all. I also imagined that the business must have been spreading through word-of-mouth at the 16 to 18 brothels.

So Hymie, who I was still on friendly terms with even after I beat him in cards for the money, came out and decided to buy a piece of land, just next door, maybe 10 feet away from us. He built a place just like ours, built up on cement blocks on each corner of the building with no foundation, and was running a restaurant there.

Anyway, one day Hymie got mad at us, as he found out that we were selling home brew out of the back of our store. I guess he was trying to sell it too, but all the guys kept coming to us for it. So he informs the sheriff down there that we're selling home brew, which technically was illegal as Florida was a dry state at the time.

The sheriff, who was one of our customers at night occasionally, dropped by to inform us that he was going to stop by at four o'clock the next day to raid us and so to use our own judgment accordingly.

And so, about three o'clock the next day, I said to Leo… 'Go outside and get into some kind of argument with Hymie. Do whatever you have to do keep him occupied.' I don't know what Leo said to him, but sure enough he got Hymie irritated and they started to get into it. Meanwhile, while they were arguing, I got one of those large burlap bags we had on hand and put about 30 bottles of our home brew inside the bag, I carried the sack over next door without Hymie seeing me and put it under his restaurant.

And so, sure enough, four o'clock comes and the sheriff comes over and Hymie is out there with a smile on his face, thinking that the sheriff is going to knock us off. Well, the sheriff goes through our place and can't find anything. So he comes out and says to Hymie… "Well as long as I'm here, I might as well go through your place too." So he goes over to Hymie's and finds the sack of home brew under his building.

Hymie got so damn mad because he knew exactly what happened. the sheriff didn't arrest him, but heh… heh, it was really funny.

We had just passed the town of Tyrone, making our way toward Route 22. There was so much to talk about, yet somehow, we fell into a period of silence as though we were searching for words. Not that we needed to say anything. Just to be in the car with him, to hang together, was good enough for me. It didn't really matter what we talked about or whether we even talked.

I guess I was kind of struggling with how I was going to bring up the whole subject of the hereafter. There was so much to ask him. The obvious questions of what happens to you when you die? How does it all play out? Where do you go? Is there a heaven? What has he been doing for the last three years? Had he gotten a chance to get out on the course yet, which of course I assumed he had, judging by his outfit. If so, I wondered if he had used his ole Tomahawk that I had left for him in the casket. Had he been able to find some good Chinese? I wanted to hear all about it, but where do I start? The mere fact that he was here with me was a good sign, and surely a testament that there must be some type of life after death.

Supposedly, in the Jewish religion there's a school of thought that indeed there is an afterlife, a life beyond called *Olam Ha-Ba*, meaning the "World to Come." That this afterlife can possibly manifest itself in several forms, from the spiritual form to reincarnation through many lifetimes, or resurrection with the coming of the *Messiah*. And as part of *Olam Ha-Ba*, your right of passage is determined by your performance in life based on your actions and merits. That's what seals your fate. Righteousness and devotion to others can certainly help your cause.

The fact that Dad passed away during the Days of Awe, the 10 days between Rosh Hashanah and Yom Kippur, was further testament to that. It's supposed to represent a special window in time. Some say that if one dies during that time, you are what's called a *tzaddik*, a person of great righteousness. Supposedly, this righteousness is rewarded.

Based on his "Al-truistic" life and the type of man he was, I had to figure that my father had earned a ticket to heaven if he wasn't there already. He had to be destined for a fruitful afterlife and be a bearer of all good things to come… an opportunity to play golf, play gin, and drink gin every day if he wanted. After all, he had lived up to his biblical name Abraham in every way. He was the epitome of someone who was kind, honest, righteous, thoughtful, considerate, generous, and everything good. And while maybe I wished he'd have been around a little more and I had gotten to spend a little more time with him, he was always a great father. There was a reason I called him "Al Pal."

The very fact that he was the consummate wingman for his buddy Yale, and that he had purchased and donated a Torah in Yale's honor had to count for something special. Just based on this mitzvah, that he had donated the precious gift of a Torah to our hometown temple back in Connecticut, he no doubt had sealed his name in the book, his fate in the *Olam Ha-Ba*, and gained entry into Gan Eden (the Garden of Eden).

And I figured maybe, just maybe, he had even achieved such an impressive record over his lifetime that he was ordained to be an angel or messenger of God. Perhaps that was it, as an angel of God called *malakh* (or alternatively *shaliyakh*) in Hebrew, he was here as my guardian angel to watch over me during my trip to help make sure the Torah got to its new home safe and sound. As the original donor of the Torah, it would be only fitting that he would be the guy to accompany me on my journey. Or who knows, maybe like Clarence who helped George Bailey in the movie *It's a Wonderful Life*, he was here to perform this mitzvah in order to earn his wings and become an angel.

He suddenly broke the silence. "So what's with the Torah in the back?" If he knew about the Torah he certainly didn't let on.

"Oh yeah, right, the Torah." I was so preoccupied with the thought of the hereafter that I had forgotten about the here and now and our prized possession in the back seat.

"Well, like I was saying before, the Torah back there that you donated in Yale's honor to our temple in New Britain is headed to a new home. After 46 years there, it's going to be in a new ark. You know what they say within the temple brotherhood… "When one ark closes, another opens.'"

Again, I didn't know what he knew about the Torah, so I started out from the beginning and didn't leave out any details. I made sure to touch upon all the different shipping and transporting options I considered in moving the Torah from its former home in Connecticut to its new home in Illinois, as I figured he would be especially interested in the logistics of it all. When talking about this, I took the opportunity to ask him about his experience with the Torah.

"By the way, when you originally donated the Torah, how did you end up shipping it?"

"Oh, let me see now. They put it in a crate and shipped it by boat from Israel to New York, and then I think they kept it in the crate and shipped it by truck right to New Britain. But it took a long time. If I remember correctly, it took well over a month to get it."

"That long, huh? It must have seemed almost as long as the Israelites' journey out of Egypt to the Promised Land!"

"Not quite, but yeah it was pretty long. It looks like the exit is coming up... you better get over."

"Oh, right!" I got so wrapped up in telling him about the Torah that I almost missed Exit 28, the exit for Route 22. Luckily I had my front seat companion to remind me. He still demonstrated his keen sense for being right on top of things.

And so, there we were, back on good ole Route 22, that same road we used to take to go to his Johnstown store. It was comforting to know that we had been on this road together before.

Once on Route 22, I continued to tell him about the Torah, while every so often we would encounter one of the those Amish horse-drawn buggies clip-clopping its way down the side of the road. I talked about the previous day's handoff at the temple, and how afterwards, we went for a celebratory meal at Great Taste, one of his favorites, to give the Torah a proper send off and as a way to pay tribute to him. I said that the food there was still as good as I remembered and mentioned that I'm sure the owners would want to send their regards. I also brought up my drive to Wilkes-Barre, starting out on I-84 through the torrid, pouring rain, past his hometown stomping ground of Waterbury, and then into New York and Pennsylvania.

"That was quite a storm I had to drive through. It was a humdinger. You couldn't see in front of you. Cars and trucks were pulling over left and right to wait it out."

"Hope you pulled over," he asked.

"Well yeah, actually I ended up stopping at a McDonald's just outside of Waterbury to charge up my phone and wait for the storm to pass."

"Heh, heh, if you think that was bad, you can't imagine what it was like when we were hit with that terrible hurricane down in Florida back in 1926. They say it was one of the worst storms of all time."

"Well also you just had that hurricane in '04, when you went to Lexye's to stay."

"That was bad, but it was nothing like the one in '26."

Of course, I had heard this story before as well, many times, but I wasn't about to interrupt him. It was a classic.

It happened during a long Jewish High Holiday weekend. I owned a dry-cleaning business at the time, the one I traded the grocery store for, and I remember I had to work late that Friday night. I was in a show, in the chorus of a local show heh…heh, a place called Jimmy Hodges Nightclub. It was local people in the show and i was in the chorus.

I had a date with this girl from Miami who came out to Hialeah because her uncle was the director of the show. So after the club closed up for the night, I took the girl out, had a bite to eat, and dropped her off at her uncle's house. It was a small house. All the houses were small, built up on cement. Very few solid buildings there.

I went back to the small hotel where I was living and went to sleep. It was around 11:00. I woke up in the morning at 7:00, and I heard all kinds of noises and screams, and everything else. I looked out the window, but I couldn't see anything. I was on the first floor. So I got dressed and walked out. And I found out there was a hurricane that had come through during the night, and lasted from about midnight to 5:00 in the morning. Believe it or not, I slept through the whole thing.

I was outside, and across the street from this hotel there was a place called Tent City. It was a bunch of platforms built up and tents over it. There were about 50 of these tents, with families living there. Well, after the storm, there was nothing there, just a bunch of debris around the whole thing.

Incidentally, the girl I went out with the night before got killed. I couldn't believe it. Unfortunately, her uncle's house that she was staying in got turned over and she died. Luckily, I guess, for the uncle, he never made it back to the house that night.

I went down to my place of business, the dry-cleaning store, which was a store in a row of one-story shops, like a strip mall. The door used to slide up against the wall, with no windows. The place was about 15-18 feet wide, and 40-50 feet deep. We did pressing in the back. Well, the whole place was, what-you-macall-it, topsy-turvy, with clothes strewn all over the place and the roof leaking… it was a mess.

My car started. I had a little Ford at the time in Florida. That's where I learned how to drive. So I went up to Indian Village and picked up the two fellows that worked for me and brought them back to the store. We started to straighten out the place. But then around 11:00 am, the wind began to blow again severely. The two fellows said "We're getting outta here."

I didn't know what to do with myself. I got into my car to drive somewhere and try to get out of the storm, but now my car wouldn't start up. By this time, the wind was blowing pretty good. I walked down the street, where there was a small building where a Jewish couple had a poolroom. All the jockeys from the racetrack used to come down and play there. It was a pretty solid brick building, so I went there thinking it was going to be secure. There were about 50-60 people in there. Well, after about a half-hour, the roof began to disintegrate, it was so windy. So I decided to get out of there.

I made my way down Bougainvillea Avenue and saw a car stranded with a flat tire. The guy inside waved me in with him. We sat there from 1:00 pm to about 4:30 pm during the storm. We saw portions of houses flying through the area, everything you can imagine. It was something. We were lucky.

A fellow came along and saw us and asked for our help, telling us that a friend of his was hit by a beam or something back at their rooming house and was afraid that his friend had broken his back and needed help to get him to the hospital. The guy asking for help had an old Hudson, in which the back of the seat folded down into the front. I kneeled in the back and put a mattress down, and we managed to get the injured guy into the car. On the way to Jackson Memorial Hospital, which was only about six miles away, we had to go over trees and around everything. It took us about two hours to go those six miles. Unfortunately, shortly after we got there, the fellow passed away.

This was Saturday evening now. I got back to town and went to my hotel.

Word got around that the sheriff, you know, my friend the sheriff who had been a grocery customer of mine and had given me the heads-up that he was going to raid my grocery store for moonshine, wanted all the merchants in town to come down to the police station because looting had already begun. He wanted to deputize us all. He gave each of us a pistol, and swore us all in. He said… "If you see any looters, stop 'em; and if they don't stop, shoot, and shoot to kill."

So being the courageous guy I was, I went back to the hotel and got into bed and stayed there, heh..heh! Unfortunately, the uncle of the girl that I had gone out with, the director of the show I was in, ended up getting killed. He was deputized, and went out on the streets that night and somebody shot him and killed him."

It was chilling to think that the uncle of that girl my dad had taken out the night before was shot and killed, just by going out and volunteering as a deputy. And that the girl herself, after my dad had dropped her off from the date at her uncle's home, had also perished.

It was something alright. And for a while, nobody from my family knew what was really going on down there or if I was ok. It wasn't until a few days after that I got my car working and went down to the police station to check in with my friend the sheriff, who in addition to being one of my dry-cleaning customers, I had a little something on the side with. As one day he had asked me if I ever played cards. I told him I've played cards all my life. I said, "Why?" He said, "You want to run a game for me?" I said, "What kind of game?" and he said, "A Poker game, we'll split whatever it is."

So I used to run the game at the hotel where I had rented the room. These guys would come and gamble, and all I did was deal the cards and draw out 50 cents if the pot was under $20 and $1.00 if the pot was over $20. I used to draw out like $70-$80 a night and split it with the chief.

He told me there were so many dead people from the hurricane. They were bringing them in left and right. Then the sheriff said to me, "You go out to the camp don't you?" meaning for my dry-cleaning business. When he said "camp" he was referring to the site where a construction company was building a railroad down to the Keys. They had a road built up over the swamps but no railroad running there yet.

He then said, "Do you think you can get out to the camp?"

Well, there was this fellow there at the station with a little suitcase with the payroll for all the workers. They all were out at the camp – all the workers who were building the railroad. Every Friday, this guy used to come from Miami with their payroll, but because of the storm he wasn't able to get out there. So the sheriff says to me, do you think you can take this guy out there?

I said, "Well, I'll try."

The water was way up – it was rough – it was about four miles out of Hialeah. But we made it.

When I got out there, I saw the general manager, who I knew from being around the community. He told me all the wiring was out, all the communications were out for 200 miles. He told me he was sending someone up to Tampa to send out telegrams and asked if I wanted him to send a telegram out to my family? I told him that would be great. So, I sent a telegram to Lou at the Tom McAn Store back in Waterbury, assuring him I had gotten out ok.

When Lou got up Monday morning, it was in all the newspapers that this whole part of Southern Florida had been wiped away. But when he got to the store and saw the telegram, it assured him I was ok.

Before I knew it, we had already gone about 75 miles together, as we had just passed a sign that said Ebensburg. Time was going by fast.

Chapter 29

IN SEARCH OF LOBSTER CANTONESE

"**You getting hungry?**" I asked. "I know I am since I only had a cookie for breakfast."

"Yeah, I could eat a little something."

"I wonder if we could get some Chinese around here?" I said without a lot of hope and conviction. Even though I had it last night, the occasion definitely called for it. We had to go for Chinese if we could. But out here, right in the heart of rural western Pennsylvania, I figured that could be a tall order.

"Well, why don't we stop and ask someone."

Kind of upset with myself that I didn't come up with that suggestion first, knowing that he would, I kind of begrudgingly mumbled, "Ok, I'll stop at the next gas station."

"How you doing for gas?

"You mean me or the car? I still got over a half a tank."

"Heh…heh, well you might as well fill it up." That was another thing about him, he always liked having a full tank.

I ended up pulling into a Sunoco station off of Route 22, somewhere near Ebensburg. After I hooked up the fuel pump to the Blazer, I went into the station and asked the guy behind the counter if he happened to know if there was a good Chinese restaurant around. I had to chuckle to myself that I was using the word "good," as though I was expecting there would be a plethora of Chinese restaurants around to choose from and that he was going to give me his best recommendation.

"Yeah, there's one about 10 miles from here just off 22 in Johnstown. I think it's called China House or something like that. You take the PA-271 exit for William Penn Avenue and go right, and it should be a couple of miles down on the left."

As sort of a thank-you for this information, I bought a couple of packs of gum. Not to press my luck, but as he rung me up, I decided to take things to the next level… "Do you know if they have Lobster Cantonese?"

"Lobster what now?"

"Cantonese."

He looked at me with a rather empty expression. "That I couldn't tell you."

I had a little skip in my step as I made my way back to the car to deliver the good news.

"Guess what… believe or not, there is a Chinese place around here. And guess where it is?" Before I gave him a chance to answer, I blurted out, "'Johnstown… of all places. It's calling us!"

Steel mills, most of which looked like they were abandoned, came into view as we began to make our way into Johnstown. It was your archetypal blue-collar town, with vestiges of industry practically everywhere you looked. Like the Connecticut cities of New Britain and Waterbury, it looked like another one of those towns where its once bustling industries had gone by the wayside.

Dad piped up, "Hey, if I'm not mistaken, I think that's where the store was," as he pointed out the window to what now looked like a run-down shopping mall consisting of a Giant Eagle grocery store, a Rite-Aid, and a bunch of small shops.

"Want to stop?" I asked as we started to pass it by.

"No, that's ok, but I'm pretty sure that was where it was."

As soon as we took the right onto William Penn Avenue, which looked to be a main thoroughfare in the town, I said "Ok, keep your eye out for this place."

Right on cue, as I suspected he would, Dad chimed in, "Here, there's a guy there on the sidewalk, why don't we pull over and ask him."

Even though I figured we were going the right way, I pulled over to appease him and we asked the guy. And sure enough, we got confirmation that the restaurant was just ahead less than a mile up.

The guy at the gas station was spot on: the name of the place was China House. As we pulled up, I asked my passenger, "Look familiar? Remember ever being here?"

The China House Restaurant in Johnstown, PA

Given his love for Chinese, I thought perhaps he had been here before during one of his many store check trips to Johnstown. Of course, I realized that was a long time ago, at least 40 years, so who knows if the place even existed then. Although judging by the outdated looks of the place, it very well could have.

"I don't think so, can't say I remember this place."

I had to admit the restaurant kind of looked a little dicey from the outside. It was very small, the storefront couldn't have been much more than 25 feet across. It had a very generic-looking, nondescript white sign with its name "China House" very plainly written in red, flanked by some Chinese characters on each side, with the descriptive line "Chinese Food Eat In & Take Out" right underneath along with their telephone number. The words "Eat In & Take Out" struck me as kind of contradictory, as it seemed a customer would either do one or the other. The ampersand should have been an "or." The only other signage was a couple of little neon fixtures in the windows, one on each side of the storefront, indicating whether the restaurant was open, both of which were illuminated and buzzing. The sound reminded me a little bit of the neon sign at the plumbing supply company across from the Berlin Station, where I would wait for my Dad's train to come in from New York.

"Uh, I don't know about this place... what do you think?" I said with some trepidation.

"Well, we're here. What the hell?"

I was able to park right in front, so that we could easily keep our eyes on the Blazer while eating.

Even though it was daytime, true to tradition for a Chinese restaurant, it was pretty dark inside. And there was an aquarium near the entryway. The size and feel of the restaurant kind of reminded me of this little Chinese restaurant right off the Berlin Turnpike near our house in New Britain that we used to frequent when I was growing up. This was long before the days of Great Taste. I think the place was called Toy Sun, or something like that. I can just picture its logo, a large, silver, Christmas-tree-like signboard in the front. It was a family-run place, as the husband and wife were the only ones

I ever saw working there. The place didn't look like much from the outside or the inside, but the food was pretty good, especially the egg rolls. Might have been among the best I've ever had. Whenever we went there, we always bought some extra egg rolls to take home.

Anyway, I remember this one time our family had just finished dinner there. It was getting kind of late, and all the other customers had left. So, my father called over our waiter/restaurant owner to bring us the check, and the egg rolls we had already ordered to take home. The guy smiled and nodded, implying that he'd be right back with it. But it turned out we had to wait awhile… we waited and waited. The egg rolls and check never came, as neither the husband nor wife was nowhere to be found. After at least 20 minutes of waiting around and looking at each other as to what was going on, my father says to me why don't you go into the kitchen to see what's going on with these guys. I had never gone into the kitchen of a Chinese restaurant before and wasn't sure I wanted to. But someone had to go in there to see what was up. So I go in there, only to find the proprietor, his wife, and their kids all seated on a couch watching TV. Apparently, they had forgotten all about us! The proprietor nodded apologetically, and ended up giving us our take-home egg rolls for free.

There was very little seating in the China House, only a handful of tables. But getting a table wasn't an issue, as we were the only patrons in the place. It made me think of the last time we had lunch out together at that Thai place in Florida, Orchids of Siam, during the summer about a year before he passed away. Like then, I had a pressing question for him this time as well, maybe even more pressing than inquiring about his virility.

An older, bald man with thick, black-framed thick glasses, who I assumed, as in the case of Toy Sun back in the day was the owner/host/waiter/and maybe the cook as well, greeted us at the door with a nod and escorted us over to one of the empty tables, passing out menus to us as we sat down. As I've always found in other Chinese restaurants, the hosts and servers aren't much on words, but they're big on nods.

The menu featured pretty much all the same type of dishes you typically find in Chinese restaurants, but we didn't see Lobster Cantonese listed. Yet, we noticed there were a bunch of other lobster dishes, such as Lobster Chow Mein, Lobster Lo Mein, Lobster Egg Foo Young and Lobster Fried Rice, so we figured maybe they could make it up special for us. I mean, supposedly they had lobster and probably had most if not all of the other basic ingredients in the dish like ground pork, black beans, egg, ginger, garlic, and soy sauce. And it wasn't like the place was very busy to not have time to make up something special for us.

At first when I asked, the fellow shook his head no. But upon further prodding and telling him what the other ingredients were in the dish in case he didn't know, he gave us some quick affirmative nods, although it was hard to tell if he really knew what we were asking for.

In addition to the Lobster Cantonese, or what we hoped would be something that resembled it, we ordered some egg rolls, had to have some egg rolls of course, some barbecue spareribs, General Tso's chicken, and white rice, plus a couple of Diet Cokes.

While we waited for our food, I was chomping at the bit to lay my big question on him as my curiosity was starting to get the best of me. But I thought I'd ease into things.

"So how does it feel to be back here in Johnstown? Back then, I bet you never thought that in 40 years you'd be back here having some Chinese together with your son, did ya?"

"Heh…heh, not exactly. But it sure brings back the memories, making the rounds to all the stores here in Pennsylvania. We sure used to move a lot of merchandise in those stores in those days."

"Yeah, I imagine discount houses must have thrived in these blue-collar towns like Johnstown"

I was just about to transition to my big question, but the food started coming, which temporarily put the kibosh on our conversation. With nobody else in the restaurant, we started getting things right away. First, the egg rolls and spareribs came, which must have already been made and were ready to serve. They were pretty good, better than expected.

Shortly thereafter came the rest of the dishes. The Lobster Cantonese actually looked pretty authentic. Quite a bit of lobster, and it seemed like it included most if not all of the other ingredients. But the true test would be the taste, the evaluation of which I deferred to the connoisseur.

"So, what do you think?"

After taking a couple of bites, he nodded "Yeah, not bad. You know this is pretty good, actually really good!" The more he ate, the more excited he seemed to get about the taste. "I got to say, this might be the best Lobster Cantonese I've ever had."

After that kind of endorsement, of course I had to taste it. And he was right, it was awesome, and I'm not even a Lobster Cantonese aficionado. Indeed, the lobster seemed very fresh, as though it was just flown in from Maine. The lobster meat was tender and incredibly succulent, rich, and flavorful. Primo stuff. And the vegetables were fresh and crisp.

It was hard to believe it was so good. I mean, who would have thought that here in Johnstown, Pennsylvania, a town in the heart of steel country, one would expect to find some gourmet Chinese; but sure enough the China House wasn't to be outdone. I guess sometimes the best things come when you least expect it.

The gratifying smile on my dad's face signaled to me that it would be a good time to pop the big question. "So let me ask you… what happens to you, when uh…. you know…you uh…pass? Where do you go?"

There was silence. He didn't say anything. It was as though he didn't hear me, almost as though I was talking through him. Maybe it was just that he was so consumed with his Lobster Cantonese. Understandably so.

I repeated myself.

"What?" He responded as though he was hard of hearing.

I gave it another try, repeating myself yet again.

Again, no response, as it was becoming obvious that he was avoiding the question. Then, with somewhat of a grimace, he kind of shook his head and said, "Heh…heh, wish I could tell you. You see, I was only able to come back here one more time, to be here with you, under the condition that I don't let on anything about what happens afterwards."

I knew it! Evidently, he had worked out some kind of deal for himself. Figures, leave it to him to make a deal.

"Can you at least give me a hint?"

"Afraid not, Tiger."

I was tempted to continue with a barrage of questions to try to get at some answers, but in deference to him I backed off. Here he was, in true Abraham fashion, just trying to be a man of his word, so who was I to try to make him cave? I shouldn't expect anything less from him.

After all, I thought to myself, I shouldn't look a gift horse in the mouth. I mean it would be nice to know something, anything really, about the hereafter and how things might play out down the road. But what really mattered was that he was with me here and now. I should just go with it and relish this special gift that had come my way; not get too hung up on or question too much about what was going to be, but make the most of whatever precious time I had with him. I should just be thankful for this one more ride with him.

So I bit my tongue, and instead just ate and wallowed in the serendipity of just being with him. We finished everything. Us Levin boys could still pack it away.

In an attempt to appeal to him in his native unspoken language, I gave our server a nod to bring the check. He nodded back and brought it right away, handing it over on a little tray, along with some fortune cookies of course.

Technically, it was my dad's turn to pick up the check, since I picked it up the last time we went out together, at the Thai restaurant in Palm Beach back in the summer of 2003. But being a good sport, I insisted on picking it up. I figured it was the least a son could do for a father who had made a special trip back from the hereafter to see him. I couldn't let him pay for it. Besides, I didn't know for sure if he was carrying any money or a credit card, although one would think he would be on an expense account.

I beat him to the punch. "I call… so what does your fortune say?"

"Heh…heh… **'New and rewarding opportunities will come your way.'**"

Ah-ah! So it looked like, if my guardian angel hadn't earned his wings yet, he was going to get them after all.

"How about yours?"

I was afraid mine was going to be kind of lame, something like, **"That wasn't really lobster."** But instead, I got a pretty good one.

I read it out loud, **"Every memory is a blessing!"**

Dad smiled back and said, "I like that one! You ought to hold onto that one."

Which indeed I did, as I slipped it into my wallet for safekeeping, right next to my **"Wherever you go, go with all your heart"** fortune that I had stuffed in my wallet back at Great Taste. I had a tendency to keep and collect all the good fortunes I had received over the years from Chinese restaurants and put them on my bulletin board at the office, if for nothing else than to showcase these quips and remind me of them. It was aptly named "The Wall of Good Fortune." Also, call me superstitious, but I thought if I kept these fortunes, they would have a better chance of coming true.

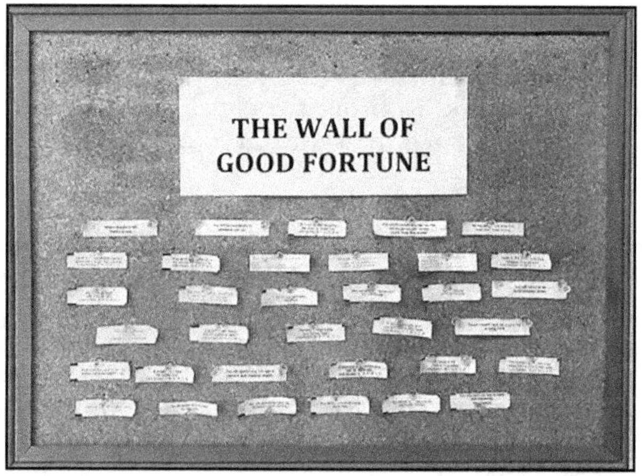

The Wall of Good Fortune hanging up in my office.

As we got up, we gave the proprietor one final nod, and we were off. Now if there was only a Baskin-Robbins or another ice cream joint around here to top things off.

Chapter 30

DROPPING OFF
AND PICKING UP

AS **WE PEELED OUT OF THE CHINA HOUSE** parking lot, one more time for good measure and old times' sake, I bellowed out another "And away we go!" and we were back on the road again.

My time with him was running out. Just a little over 80 miles to the airport. Only had a little over an hour or so left. He didn't give me his itinerary on where he was going or exactly what time he was leaving, but he said he wanted to get to the airport around 4:00. I figured his flight wasn't scheduled to leave until at least early evening, but I'm sure true to form he wanted to be sure to get there well in advance of his scheduled departure.

"Do you really have to go back?" I asked him, already knowing the answer.

"Afraid so, Tiger."

"Can you at least stay just a little bit longer? Maybe grab a quick G&T near the airport."

"Heh…heh, wish I could."

Sure enough, just down the road, before we got back on Route 22, we came upon a Baskin-Robbins, which of course was calling our names. We drove through the drive-up window, each of us opting for coconut in a sugar cone—like father, like son.

As we turned back onto Route 22, I turned to baseball. "I gotta tell you, those Red Sox of yours are looking pretty good!"

It wasn't that he was really that much of a Red Sox fan, although more so Red Sox than Yankees. When you're from Connecticut, especially when you live in New Britain, which is just about equidistant between Boston and New York, your allegiance could justifiably go either way. However, seldom did one support both teams, primarily because they were in the same division; and therefore, by definition, whichever of these two teams you rooted for, you had to hate the other one. This was especially true in the case of the Red Sox and Yankees, one of, if not the most competitive, fiercest rivalries that exist in baseball to this day. But Dad didn't hate the Yankees; rather I think he liked them too. It's just that he leaned a little more toward the Sox, which I suspect probably traced back to his days of living in Boston early in his career when working for the Allen Cut-Rate stores. I figured it might also have had to do with his connection to the world of socks, having been in the men's and boys' clothing business and in particular a sales rep for Mobil Socks. After all, he was known as "The Socks Guy" after he formally retired.

Of course, growing up in Connecticut and being a Braves fan, I was an anomaly. I suppose if Dad would have been a die-hard fan of the Red Sox or the Yankees for that matter, I might have found myself instead being a fan of his favorite team as sons often seem to follow the team that their fathers root for.

But regardless of his favorite team or how much of a devoted fan he was, it was easy to talk baseball with him. That's one of the things about baseball, it's a game that can be shared by fathers and sons, sometimes like an epoxy glue that they can always count on to bond them together. Even during communication breakdowns or times when they are struggling for words, or God forbid find themselves at an impasse, there's always baseball to come to the rescue and provide some common ground.

In case he wasn't up-to-date with the latest news in sports, I filled him in on the Red Sox and the whole playoff picture. I told him about how they had come off of a 96-win season, and had just shut out the Los Angeles Angels in three games in their first round of the playoffs and were now playing the Cleveland Indians in the second round. And in the National League, I took him through the uncanny winning streak and success of the Colorado Rockies.

"So you think the Sox are going to go all the way?" he asked.

"Maybe, but I don't know. After all, it took them 86 years to break their curse and win it in '04. So it's hard to figure they're going to do it again three years later. But they're sure knocking on the door."

The curse of course I was speaking of, known as the Curse of the Great Bambino, dated back to 1918 when Dad was only 10 years old and when the Red Sox had just won the World Series for the fourth time in the past 15 years, shortly after which, lo and behold, they sold the mighty Babe to the Yankees. Not only did this unfavorable, unforgiving move disappoint Red Sox fans and exacerbate the rivalry between the Red Sox and Yankees, but legend has it that the Red Sox were cursed to never win again.

"So they won it that year, huh?"

It suddenly occurred to me that he might not have known that the Red Sox had indeed won the World Series title back in 2004, having just passed away a month before.

"They sure did. They shut out the Angels in the ALDS; then edged out the Yankees four games to three in the ALCS, coming back from a 3-0 game deficit; and then to top it all off swept the Cards in the World Series."

While we were on the subject of baseball, I continued on. "You know, I wish we could have gone to more games together. I used to love going to the ballpark with you! It was one of my favorite things to do."

I remembered we had taken in a few games at Yankee stadium, including an All-Star game when I was 8; and at Fenway in Boston; and we had gone to several games at Shea Stadium to see my Braves play the Mets. But that was about it. Of course we could have gone to at least one more game at Shea, if only good ole Oscar Steege at

Mooreland Hill hadn't kind of put the kibosh on it that time my mother asked for his permission.

Dad popped up, "Yeah, I know. Looking back, I wish we had done a lot more things together."

"Actually, we did a bunch of stuff together. You took me on all those business trips, those ones through Pennsylvania just like what we're doing now; we hit the links together a lot, including all those father-and-son tournaments at Cliffside; and we went on those fishing trips to Maine together. A lot of good stuff."

I continued on, "Remember those father-and-son fishing trips? We went up there a couple of times... who was it with, Sig and Scotty Gourson, and another time I think with Jesse Eichenbaum and his dad. You and I would be in the boat together, along with our guide, on those mammoth Maine lakes, one of them was like, what was it, Sebago Lake? I would be fervently casting away toward the shoreline trying to entice a small mouth bass, while you would be reading the newspaper and trolling with a golf ball on the end of your line. And it would be you who would usually catch all the fish, those big salmon. And remember, we would meet up with the other guys and their guides for lunch on a little island in the lake, where the guides would cook up the fish we had caught that morning and sizzle up some steaks that they had brought with them in the event we didn't catch anything even though we always did. And they would make potatoes and onions over the fire in those black cast iron skillets. Man, those were good.

"Or how about the time, you, Mom, and I... I think I was pretty young then, maybe 7 or 8, went up to Vermont, and we went trout fishing with a guide in some brook or a small river. The guide had taken all of us out there from the hotel in his pick-up truck. He was a fairly young guy, and if I remember correctly it seemed like he had kind of a crush on Mom. Anyway, not sure of all the details but I think I slipped in the water and fell down, and ended up cutting my hand on a rock, and it kept bleeding. All I remember is that you ended up driving me to the hospital in the guide's pick-up truck to get my hand checked out, leaving the guide there at the fishing site with Mom to wait for us until we got back, which as a guarded son, I was little concerned about. But it was you who had to take me as we really couldn't have Mom drive the truck, which was a stick shift. Remember driving that truck, the gearshift had this big red dice on the end of it and you were constantly trying to get the thing into gear. It was quite an adventure."

"Oh yeah, heh…heh, that was something wasn't it? I hadn't driven a stick in a long time, not since my days in the army down there in Alabama at Fort McClellan. I guess we did have some pretty good times together, huh? But I just wish there could have been more of them. I was always travelling or at the club. It would have been nice to have gone to some more games of yours."

"I don't know," I retorted. "Based on that time when I was playing football at Mooreland and I looked back to see how close the defender was and ended up getting tackled, maybe it's a good thing that you weren't able to make it to that many games. But seriously, you were always there for me."

But deep down I guess I wish there had been more Major League games we had gone to together, and more of my games he came to watch, and more trips, and more adventures, just more time together. But what really mattered was that he was always there for me when it counted. He was always there to hit pop-ups to me when he could, talk to me, give me directions, give me his advice, tell me to keep my chin up and stay in there pitching, root for me, have my back, and be my guardian angel. He was there with me then and he was here with me now.

I thought to myself, according to the Torah there in the back seat, that's the sign of a good father. Isn't that what the Torah teaches us fathers, that we should always try to be there for our children?

I think that's what God might have been imparting to Abraham up there on the mountaintop with Isaac. As it is written…

**And it came to pass that God said unto him:
"Abraham;" and Abraham said "Here am I."
And he said "Take now thy son, thine only son,
whom thou lovest, even Isaac, and get thee into the land
of Moriah; and offer him there for a burnt-offering upon
one of the mountains which will tell thee of."**

(Genesis 22:1-2)

The test wasn't so much as to whether or not Abraham would sacrifice his son, for I'm convinced that God never intended to have Abraham do such a heinous act nor would he ever have let that happen. But rather, the test was about whether Abraham would come through and be there for his son. I think it might have been God's way of impressing upon him just how precious the father-and-son relationship is and whether he was worthy of upholding it. For I imagine there's nothing like a major sacrifice or the fear of losing your child that makes you as a father realize how much you love your child.

Not that Abraham and Isaac's little outing up there on the mountaintop would necessarily qualify as spending some quality father-son time together, but Abraham came through when it counted and their relationship endured. Just as Abraham had used the same words to answer God's call, Abraham answered the call of his son...

**Then Isaac said to his father "My father."
And Abraham said "Here am I, my son."**
(Genesis 22:7)

With those fatherly and comforting words, Abraham was able to meet the challenge and pass the test with flying colors, showing that he was worthy of earning the respect of God and proving that he was indeed fit to be the father of Isaac and the father of all nations, paving the way for fathers of all future generations to come.

It made me question myself, whether I was a good father, if indeed I was there for Danni and Mac. Sure, with my flexible schedule, I was lucky enough to be there at most of their sports activities and pretty much all of their major events and moments in the sun, even the small ones. Wouldn't have missed them. And that's part of it. But being there to me means always being there to encourage and cheer them on, to instill confidence, to share in their achievements and their obstacles, to catch them if they fall, and to listen and respect them. I was hoping I would always be there for them. As a father, that's first and foremost what I strive for.

And like father, like son, transcending generations, Isaac returned the favor and did his part to be there for his sons and keep the father-son relationship intact, as it came to pass that Isaac himself became a father to twin boys Esau and Jacob. As he aged, Isaac called his slightly elder son Esau, being the firstborn, to come to him, as he turned the tables a little bit from a page out of his own playbook and said unto him…

> **"My son."**
> **To which Esau replied, "Here am I."**
> **And Issac said, "Behold now, I am old,**
> **I know not the day of my death.**
> **Now therefore take, I pray thee,**
> **thy weapons, thy quiver, and thy bow,**
> **and go out to the field, and take me venison;**
> **and make me savory food, such as I love,**
> **and bring it to me, that I may eat;**
> **that my soul may bless thee before I die."**
> **(Genesis 27:1-4)**

Isaac's wife, Rebekah, overheard him speak to Esau. She favored the more docile twin Jacob over the more unruly, contentious Esau and recognizing the leadership qualities in her favorite son much more so than in Esau, encouraged Jacob to pose as his brother. After all, Jacob must have felt somewhat justified, that indeed he had his father's blessing coming to him. For Jacob, no doubt there was a feeling or sense of entitlement, as Esau had willingly given up his firstborn birthright to Jacob in exchange for some lentil stew.

And so, with savory food in hand prepared by his mother and a lot of chutzpah, the crafty Jacob disguised himself with Esau's garments, and even added some goatskin to his hands and arms to further resemble his more hairy brother, and came to Isaac whose eyes were dim with failing eyesight and said…

> **"My father." And Isaac said**
> **"Here am I, who art thou, my son?"**
> **And Jacob said unto his father,**
> **"I am Esau, thy first-born;**
> **I have done according as thou bequest me.**
> **Arise, pray thee, sit and eat of my venison,**
> **that thy soul may bless me."**
> **(Genesis 27:18-19)**

Sure enough, Jacob was able to pull it off, as it was him not Esau who Isaac ended up blessing.

> **"Come near me, and kiss me, my son."**
> **And he came near, and kissed him.**
> **And he smelled the smell of his raiment,**
> **and blessed him, and said: "See, the smell of my son**
> **is as the smell of a field which Hashem hath blessed."**
> **(Genesis 27:26-27)**

And it came to pass, after Jacob had left Isaac's side, Esau came back from his hunting expedition and indeed had brought back with him some savory food for his father, only to find that his father had blessed Jacob instead of him. Having been passed up, Esau was vehemently disappointed and lashed out at his father and brother. He became so bitter toward Jacob that he proclaimed he would seek his brother out and kill him. And while Esau was upset with Isaac and even though he missed out on the original blessing that was intended for him, he still asked him for his fatherly blessing…

And Esau said unto his father:
"Hast thou but one blessing, my father?
Bless me, even me also, O my father."
And Esau lifted up his voice and wept.
(Genesis 27:38)

Compared to Jacob, who was more like a model son, Esau left a lot to be desired. He was much more volatile and carefree, as evidenced by his behavior of trading his birthright to his twin brother Jacob in exchange for a plate of food, thus technically giving up his firstborn rights. What's more, much to Isaac's chagrin, Esau took two wives from the opposing Hittite tribe and lived among them.

But still, despite Esau's shortcomings and the fact that Isaac had already given his initial blessing to Jacob, Isaac came through for Esau and blessed him. According to one of the interpretations (midrash) from the Talmud, perhaps what this shows is that Isaac's love for his sons was unconditional. Isaac was still there for Esau and accepted him, just as he did Jacob. That's what dads are supposed to do.

"Want to stop by and say hello to Arnold?" I asked as we were approaching Pennsylvania Route 981, the exit for Latrobe, the home of Arnold Palmer. "Maybe he'll go out for a quick nine with us. You might have to give him a couple of strokes, but how about it? I mean, you're already dressed for it."

"Heh…heh."

Passing by Latrobe, we exited off of Route 22 and jumped onto the expressway, I-376, which would take us right into the airport. The minutes were ticking away, but I figured there had to be enough time to get one more story in. Maybe a story about a father and son.

"So Dad, what was that story you told me about, involving a business associate of yours and his son. You know, the guy who used to sell you ties and belts?"

"Oh you're talking about Seymour Greenberg and what happened at Treasure Town."

"Yeah, what happened there again?"

Remember Treasure Town, the big discount department store chain? They had a lot of stores in the Northeast. It was one of the accounts I serviced for Mobil Socks after I retired. It was a pretty big account for me. Anyway, as the account guy, I used to go into their stores from time to time to check out their socks section what have you, you know, kind of like you used to do up in Boston when you were up at what-you-macall-it. What was the name of it… Babson, right?

So one day I was in one of their stores, and I ran into their CEO Mr. Bernstein, Charles Bernstein, who just so happened to be in the store that day. So I went up and introduced myself to him. Being in the same business, I had heard a lot about him and I guess he had heard about me. So there was kind of a common bond there. And right off the bat we kind of hit it off. We would see each other occasionally at his stores, or sometimes go out to lunch together, and we became pretty friendly.

Well, another supplier of Treasure Town happened to be an outfit called S. Greenberg and Company, which sold them ties and belts, along with other men's and boys' accessories. They were out of Fall River, Massachusetts, where a lot of textile manufacturers were located.

When he mentioned Fall River, my eyes lit up as I immediately thought of Al Mac's Diner, Fall River's pride and joy, its picture of which was hanging on Mac's bedroom wall.

S. Greenberg and Company also had been our major supplier of ties, belts, wallets, and handkerchiefs when I had my discount stores. Geez, we bought a lot of stuff from them. So I had known Seymour for quite some time and over the years I got quite friendly with him. We would play golf together on occasion.

But you know, it's funny, even though his formal name was Seymour, a lot of people called him Hank. I later found out it was because he used to play baseball when he was younger and evidently he inherited the nickname from the great ball player Hank Greenberg.

I thought to myself, like everybody in my immediate family, here was yet another example of a guy who went by another first name.

You can only imagine, with all of its stores, Treasure Town was a huge account of theirs, much bigger than my company Regal had ever been. At the time, Treasure Town must have been well over a $1 million dollar account for them, which, heh…heh, was a pretty sizeable account in those days.

Anyway, one day when Charlie was walking through one of his stores, he passes by the necktie section and notices some of the designs on the ties are kind of wild-looking and I guess a little risqué. I don't know, there must have been some pictures of semi-nude women incorporated in the designs or something like that. But whatever, Charlie thought they were kind of off-color and a little sketchy I guess.

So when Charlie gets back to his office that day he immediately calls over to his accessories vendor to talk to Seymour, with whom he had at least an acquaintance-type

relationship given that S. Greenberg and Company
was one of Treasure Town's major suppliers and all. But
Seymour happened to be out that day and for the rest of
the week on vacation, so instead Charlie is transferred
into his son who is taking his father's calls in his absence.
Having recently graduated from an Ivy League school, his
son had decided to go into the family business, but at the
time was fairly new to the company. I don't think he had
been there very long. And so, Charlie starts in to tell him
about the ties and that he feels they are out of character
for his stores, but the kid kind of brashly cuts him off
and says to him that these types of ties happen to be very
popular these days. The kid goes on to tell Charlie that
as Treasure Town's vendor, his company closely follows
the trends in the marketplace and knows what's in and
what's going to sell. Apparently, instead of acknowledging
Charlie's discomfort and concern, the Ivy League know-it-
all kind of brushes him off.

When Charlie hangs up, he's pretty upset and goes to his
head buyer and tells him that he wants all of those ties out of
his stores immediately and, furthermore, to drop S. Greenberg
and Company and line up a new vendor for their accessories.

Well so the next week, Seymour comes back from
his vacation only to find out that all of a sudden he's lost
the Treasure Town account. He asks his son what the
hell happened, but the son who must have figured that
his conversation with Mr. Bernstein was what must have
triggered everything, wasn't about to reveal anything.
Seymour tries to call Charlie, but can't get through to him
and Charlie won't return his phone calls.

A couple of weeks later, I'm having lunch with
Seymour in New York, and he says to me, "Al, I can't
understand what happened with Treasure Town. I mean
they were such a big account of ours and I thought we

were doing a good job of servicing them, so for the life of me I can't understand how all of a sudden they just dropped us. You're friendly with Mr. Bernstein, aren't you? Did he ever say anything to you about it?"

Of course Charlie had told me all of this after the fact, so I knew what happened. But still, when Seymour asked me, I just didn't have the heart to tell him. I'm sure it would have crushed him. So instead, I just shook my head that I had no idea and tried to give him some positive support and that maybe in time he could get the business back.

Naturally, Seymour asked me if I could find something out and ask Mr. Bernstein the next time I see him, but as time went on I just tried to skirt his request. To this day, I don't know if Seymour ever found out what happened.

I wondered to myself if Seymour ever did find out, would he have forgiven his son? Even after such a gut-wrenching experience, would he have been there for his son? Like Isaac, would he have accepted his son's shortcomings and unconditionally shown his love for him?

Soon we were coming up on the airport. I didn't want the ride to end. The thought suddenly crossed my mind to try to get lost, which I figured for me shouldn't be a problem. I was used to it. Maybe just before the airport, I could accidentally on purpose take the wrong turn or something. And of course, that would mean stopping for directions a couple of times, thus further prolonging our trip together. But instead, I stayed the course. I guess I didn't want to bring on any more angst for myself that I was already anticipating I was going to experience during our last few minutes together.

We pulled into the airport just before 4:00. As I got to the curb at the US Air terminal, it felt a little bit like old times... just like all of those times I dropped him off at Bradley Field for one of his business trips. Lost in thought, I looked him in the eyes and paused a little bit, searching for the right words. Alas, here I was, being given another chance to say goodbye to him. Originally denied that valued time to exchange with him some last words just before he passed, I had yet another opportunity to step up and take a crack at it. Maybe come up with something profound this time around.

But still I was struggling to come up with something that would be fitting for this precious occasion. Somehow, I couldn't find the words. All I could come up with was, "So I guess this is it, huh? I can't thank you enough for the company… it's been unreal! Hope you enjoyed the ride as much as I did. I'll remember this forever. Maybe I'll see you on the other side, huh?"

I was hoping to catch him off guard or in a weak moment, and that he would say something about the other side. Instead, he just gave me a half smile and a noncommittal nod. Still, I took it as a good sign.

"And I'll continue to miss you. But just so you know… you're with me all the time!"

I gave him one final stare down, still not believing this whole thing really happened and as proof hoping to imprint this whole experience in my psyche. Then I fumbled around in thought a little bit and almost went in for a kiss, but instead just stuck out my hand as did he. There was nothing like a firm handshake. It was our thing.

He responded, "I'm going to miss you too, Tiger. And by the way, I think it's great what you're doing with the Torah. It sounds like it's going to have a nice new home. It means a lot to me. I'm proud of you!"

I let that word "proud" sink in and resonate for a few quick moments.

Then, as he opened the door, he left me with some of his, and also my, favorite phrases of encouragement… "Stay in there pitching," and then a "Go get 'em, Tiger!"

I gave him a good-bye nod and told him that I loved him, as he exited the Blazer and gave one final glimpse back at the Torah, as though he wanted to make sure it was safe and secure in the backseat and that it was in good shape for the rest of the trip. He then gave me a quick glance back and waved, and then started to make his way to the terminal door.

My eyes continued to follow him, silently calling out to him and wondering if he was going to take a peek back, hoping he would turn around and then come back. Sure enough, just before he entered the terminal, my imaginary man, my utility man, turned and gave me one final reassuring look back and then proceeded through the translucent sliding doors, through which I imagined he would ascend up into the sky on his way back to what I could only hope would be the land of milk and honey. And then poof—just like that, he was gone.

I still had about half hour before Mark's flight was scheduled to arrive. So I doubled back and did a half loop around the airport again, and turned into a temporary parking area that I presumed was the cell phone lot. While I waited, I had enough time to re-listen to the tapes of some of the same stories Dad had just shared with me during our ride together. I wanted to hear them again.

Chapter 31
HOLY TOLEDO

Upon getting out of the airport and onto I-376 West, with my new driving companion by my side, we immediately jumped off at the first exit where there was a gas station. Even though I figured we would still have to stop for gas one more time before we got home, my dad had ingrained in me to top off the tank if you have the chance. No doubt that's what he would have done. So we filled up on gas as well as grabbed some bottled water and ice tea, and we were ready to go.

Mark offered to take the wheel. He mentioned to me that he loved to drive and that he would be happy to give me a break. Plus, I think he was anxious to see how the Torah Blazer handled on the open road. While I didn't want to burden him at all, having already put in a good day's worth of driving, I took him up on his offer and we made the switch at the gas station.

Our route was simple enough, just take I-376 West for about 30 miles, then hook up with I-76 West for another 30 miles or so, merge into I-80/I-90 West, and then onto I-94 West. A total of 479 miles, all interstate highways.

We began talking mostly about our girls, Danni and Jamie, reminiscing about our "Me and My Daddy" days. Back then, we had done a lot of fun stuff together with the girls, from bowling to going to sporting events including a Chicago Wolves hockey game and a Cubs game, to doing arts & crafts projects, visiting a nursing home, taking a tour of a matzoh factory, and even going on a few overnighters together in Wisconsin. It all added up to great memories for us to relive together.

I was afraid I wasn't being a very good conversationalist, as my mind kept wandering off and thinking about my previous passenger. But still we managed to keep the conversation going with all kinds of sports talk.

After three hours or so, around 7:30, with a little more than 200 miles under our belts, almost to our halfway point, I suggested we stop for dinner. I figured Mark must be getting hungry. I was beginning to get a little hungry myself, as my big Chinese lunch was starting to wear off. That's the thing about Chinese, it doesn't really stay with you that long.

After we got home, of course, I was intending on taking Mark and his wife out to a nice restaurant to thank him for accompanying me on my journey. But for now, we would have to make do with whatever respectable eatery we could find on the road. So, we started to keep an eye out for a place to eat. We were coming up on Toledo, Ohio, where we figured there was bound to be a bunch of restaurants to choose from, so we took the first Toledo exit we came to.

This would mark my first time in Toledo. I wasn't really all that familiar with the city. I knew it was considered the Glass Capital of the World and aptly called The Glass City, with a lot of glass manufacturers having settled there over the years. I also knew that it was the home for its beloved Mud Hens, the Triple A Minor League affiliate for the Detroit Tigers. And I knew that Toledo was the hometown for Corporal Klinger in the long-standing TV show *M*A*S*H* and that he was a big fan of the Mud Hens. But beyond that I didn't know much about the city.

Apparently, when the city was first discovered by pioneers in 1833 along the shores of the Maumee River in Northwest Ohio, Toledo was originally dubbed Frogtown as it was nothing but an expansive muddy, frog-laden marshland known as the Great Black Swamp. Frogs, frogs, everywhere frogs, a microcosm of Egypt when it was smitten with frogs as one of God's plagues administered upon the Pharaoh and the land of Egypt to let the Jewish people go. As it is written…

> **"And if thou refuse to let them go, behold,**
> **I will smite all thy borders with frogs.**
> **And the river shall swarm with frogs,**
> **which shall go up and come into thy house,**
> **and into thy bed-chamber, and upon thy bed,**
> **and into the house of thy servants,**
> **and upon thy people, and into thine ovens,**
> **and into thy kneading-troughs."**
> **(Exodus 7:27-28)**

In addition to frogs, the wetland was home for a species of birds with short wings and long legs called Mud Hens. Hence the name of their Minor League baseball team.

Another interesting tidbit about this fourth largest city in Ohio, behind Columbus, Cleveland, and Cincinnati, is that the derivation of the name Toledo comes from the Latin word *toletum* or "city of generations," as well as the Hebrew word *toledot* also meaning "generations." In fact, the sixth *parashah* or section of Genesis (25:19-28:9), is called Toledot with the translation being "Generations," which is the same section that includes the story about Abraham, his son Isaac, and Isaac's sons Esau and Jacob.

Indeed, one might think it was Isaac who coined the phrase "Holy Toledo", which could have been what he cried out in surprise when he found out, upon the return of Esau from his hunting expedition in the field, that it was Jacob not Esau that he had previously blessed. But as it happens, the phrase has a different origin. Rather, it supposedly originated during the 1920s and 1930s when Toledo became a sanctuary for gangsters. At the time, the Toledo police made a pact with local gangsters that they would leave them alone if in turn the gangsters would halt their reign of terror on the city. And so, by being granted sanctuary, the gangsters referred to the city as "Holy Toledo." But today, the term would be taking on another dimension and a whole new meaning, for Toledo would receive a fresh dose of holiness with the presence of the Torah.

We ended up pulling into an Olive Garden, which was right off the exit. It was a well-known chain that we had each been to before and figured we couldn't go wrong. Its claim to fame was that it offered as much salad and breadsticks as you wanted. And I thought to myself, its advertising slogan kind of tied into Toledo's whole generation theme… ***When you're here, you're family.***

After taking a couple of laps around the parking lot, we grabbed a space near one of the restaurant's windows. Luckily, we were able to get a seat near the window where we had parked.

As we were walking into the restaurant, I joked with Mark that given the circumstances, just for today we might want to call this the "Olive Garden of Eden." That led the marketing guy in me to come up with a concept for a new line extension restaurant that I thought Olive Garden's parent company Darden might want to consider. That being a sister chain called the "Garden of Eden" that would leverage off of Olive Garden's equity. I envisioned it would have a Mediterranean cuisine with an all-natural bent to it, offering up healthier, farm-to-table type foods made from simple, organic ingredients from the good earth. In addition to its unprocessed-type dishes featuring meat from grass-fed cows, free-range chicken, fresh garden vegetables and the like, it would offer up an assortment of better-for-you desserts using apples of course as the base. Everything apples—apple crisp, baked apples, applesauce with cinnamon sprinkled on top, apple cobbler, apple betty, and apple slices and honey, which would always be on special during the Jewish New Year. But, at the same time of course, with all those all-natural, healthier apple dessert offerings on the menu, there would have to be something that was a little more inviting, a little more tempting, reminiscent of the real Garden of Eden. Something that would be off the menu so to speak, a little bit more decadent such as a big piece of calorie-laden traditional apple pie or perhaps even apple pie a la mode. They could call it "The Forbidden Dessert."

At dinner, our conversation turned back to the world of sports, mostly basketball, with me every so often taking a quick glimpse out the window to make sure nothing was amiss with the Torah Blazer. Mark was more of a basketball guy. While in college at the University of Illinois, he broadcasted basketball games for the Fighting Illini. The start of the college basketball season would soon be upon us, and we talked about what teams would be the favorites come the Final Four Tournament in March.

We ended up eating kind of fast, as we were in and out of there in under an hour. Then, after we quickly stopped for gas again at a nearby station to top off the tank, we bid adieu to The Glass City and were on the road again.

Chapter 32

TAKING IT TO
THE HOUSE

WE WERE ON THE HOME STRETCH. A little over 250 miles to go, only about three and half hours or so more. It was pretty much the same road from here, continuing on I-80/I-90 West through Ohio, where it was called the Ohio Turnpike, and then through Indiana where it would become the Indiana Toll Road, on through the city of Chicago, and then hooking up with I-94 north to our home in Deerfield.

Mark was back in the driver's seat, as he seemed to want to continue to take the wheel. I could tell he liked driving the Torah Blazer. Having convinced me it was his preference to drive and that it wouldn't be too taxing on him, I settled in as the passenger again, although I still kind of felt a little guilty that he was doing all the driving.

Apropos to our sports discussion during dinner, I asked Mark if it would be ok if I turned on the radio to listen to some playoff baseball. We started listening to the first game of the Red Sox-Indians Championship series, which was well underway. It turned out it wasn't much of a game as the Red Sox were trouncing the Indians, so we switched over to the Rockies-Diamondbacks once that game started, which being the late game out in Arizona wasn't until 10:00 pm Eastern time. That was a much closer game, so we stuck with that one for the rest of the way.

277

Thanks to Mark's company and with the game being on the radio in the background, the drive went by quickly and before we knew it, we found ourselves leaving Indiana, the Hoosier state, and approaching the Chicago Skyway, an eight-mile or so elevated roadway that is part of I-90 in between Gary, Indiana, and the south side of Chicago connecting the Indiana Toll Road and the Dan Ryan Expressway. I had been on it many a times. It's basically a long, extended bridge stretching over the Calumet River and a sea of industry, but one that was built really high up. It's appropriately named, since when you're on it, you feel like you are way up high in the sky. It was kind of cool to be up there, but at the same time a little bit eerie, especially at night, suspended in total darkness, overlooking the sea of lights from the various steel mills and other factories down there that seemed so distant.

Whenever you made your way across this mystical stretch of road, you got the feeling that you were bumping up against heaven. I suppose it could have also been called the Heavenly Expressway, as this had to be the closest someone in a car could ever get to heaven. As my mind turned back to my father, I was wondering if perhaps he was up here somewhere. It was comforting to think that he was out there.

It was close to midnight when we pulled into Deerfield and I dropped Mark off at his house, which was right around the corner from mine. I couldn't thank him enough for meeting me in Pittsburgh and accompanying me on the rest of my journey, especially since he had done all the driving. I told him that Gail and I would be setting up a dinner date with them soon.

When I got home, Gail and Danni were still up, waiting for me. Mac had already gone to bed to try to get some sleep for his travel baseball tryouts the next day. After some quick hugs hello, I went back outside and unstrapped the Torah from the seatbelts, and brought it through the garage and into the house, onto the counter of the laundry room for the time being.

I proceeded to give my girls a complete playback of the trip. About the only thing I left out, of course, was my "adventure" with you know who, a cherished experience I was tempted to share but was still inclined to keep to myself. I mean, who would have believed me? They would have thought I had gone *meshugenah*.

While I was tired from the long drive, I was still pretty wired. So after the girls called it a night, I grabbed a glass of milk and the two leftover cookies from the tin and flipped on the TV, only to find the Rockies and Diamondbacks still going at it. It was a real nail-biter and ended up going into extra innings. Finally, in the top of the 11th inning, the Rockies scored a run and held on to win 3-2. It was their fifth win in a row in the playoffs. As it turned out, their magical run would continue for two more games, as they ended up sweeping the Diamondbacks the first four games and taking the National League Championship Series to give them a ticket to the World Series. It was their second sweep in the playoffs. They had now won 21 of their last 22 games, a mystical streak that's pretty much unheard of in the annals of baseball. But while the year of the playoff sweeps continued in the World Series, in a twist of fate it was the Red Sox that ended up sweeping the Rockies. Yep, it turned out that indeed the Red Sox ended up winning it all again.

Before I went to bed, I wanted to chill out a little bit more and reflect on the incredible journey that I had just taken. It had been a magical ride. It certainly qualified right up there as one of the most exhilarating and rewarding experiences I've ever had, one that I will always cherish. It had proven to be a spiritual journey in more ways than one. Spiritual in the religious sense, in that while I still considered myself to be a seasonal guy when it comes to practicing my faith, this experience opened the door for me to get closer to my Jewish roots and the teachings of the Torah and no doubt enhanced my appreciation for my Jewish heritage. It certainly got me up to snuff on *The Jewish Code of Laws*, of which I had no idea there were so many, let alone that there was even such a thing as a *Code of Jewish Laws*. So I'd like to think that this whole experience has made me more religious, however one defines that. Well, at least I felt more religious. But beyond religion, the journey was, of course, spiritual in another sense, for it had rekindled and brought to life my connection and love for my father, an everlasting spirt that lives deep inside of me and always will.

The next morning, Gail followed me to the rental car lot at O'Hare to drop off the Torah Blazer. The car had served both me and the Torah well. It had been our ark on wheels and had proven to be totally reliable, as it delivered us safely through the torrential rain, over potholes, and around all other elements into the Promised Land. It would forever be remembered and go down in the annals of the great Levin classics, along with the likes of The Gray Ghost, my Foxy Lady, the Biffer, LeVan, and Bully.

Typically, you won't find too many laundry rooms that have a Torah perched in them. Based on *The Jewish Code of Laws*, the protocol would have been to place the Torah in some type of cabinet that would have served as its temporary ark. But unfortunately we didn't have a cabinet that was big enough to house it. So, for the time being we thought the laundry room would be a logical temporary sanctuary for it. After all, every time we would be in the laundry room or pass through it going out to the garage, we would indeed be standing up for it. Plus, as Gail and Danni had pointed out to me upon first seeing it, the Torah's outer silver shell was somewhat tarnished and needed some serious cleaning and detailing. As to be expected, it had taken a beating over the years, and no doubt the journey across half the country over the last couple of days, even though it was thoroughly wrapped, had probably added to its wear and tear.

Gail and our good friend Susan Reingold took on the arduous task of cleaning and polishing up the Torah. The two were devoted in their efforts, attending to every nook and cranny of the silver casing.

Originally, the plan was to keep the Torah at the house for the weekend, and then bring it to Temple Beth-El the first thing on Monday morning. But after two days of continuous rigorous rubbing and scrubbing, Gail and Susan still had a ways to go. It had turned out to be a much bigger job than anticipated. So on Monday I called the rabbi to let him know we were still in the throes of polishing it up and wanted to keep it for a couple of more days so we could bring out its true shine. Also, I had to admit it was comforting to have a Torah in our house, as perhaps I subconsciously wanted to prolong its stay. I thought of it as providing a protective halo over our home. And I was hoping just by its mere presence in our house, the Torah would continue to bring good luck and good fortune to us Levins. Certainly, it couldn't hurt.

Per *The Code of Jewish Law* (which says it is forbidden to have intercourse in a room where a Torah is found), I resigned myself to the fact that Gail and I wouldn't be able to have sex in the laundry room. Not that we ever have, although come to think of it that does sound fun. But this was pretty much out of the question, even though one would think that a laundry room would be somewhat permissible and blessed from a religious standpoint, as having coitus in there would no doubt qualify as clean sex. Nevertheless, while the laundry room was off limits, I wondered if it might still be ok to do it in the bedroom. Yet, maybe it was a feeling of Jewish guilt, but somehow I still had second thoughts about it even if we were in another room, as I was afraid we might be pressing our luck a little bit.

Gail and Susan had done such a great job on the cleaning and silver polishing, and by the end of Tuesday the Torah was shining bright and looking like its old majestic self, back the way I remembered it originally looked in the ark of Temple B'nai Israel when I was growing up.

That evening, after all the finishing touches, we moved it from the laundry room to the middle of our dining room table, where it became the centerpiece of the room. This was where we would always have our holiday dinners on Rosh Hashanah and Passover. So in the absence of a cabinet, we thought this would be the best place to put it for its last night in the house. As such, the Torah, in its glistening splendor, seemed to light up our house with a special aura and provide some additional warmth and glow, and if for just that night it seemed that our home had turned into a temple.

Chapter 33

THE DEDICATION

The date had been marked on the calendar for a while. As part of its regular Friday night Sabbath service, Temple Beth-El was planning a formal dedication of the new Torah on May 2, 2008, when it was to be officially placed in its special customized ark in the vestibule of the temple. Up until this time, while its ark was being built, the new Torah was temporarily placed in the main sanctuary ark along with the temple's collection of other Torahs.

My mother and sister had flown in from Florida for this momentous event. And representing the next generation to come, Danni and Mac were present for the ceremony as well, sitting alongside Gail. Plus, just about everybody else who was somehow involved in this spiritual Torah transfer and making this night happen was there. My fellow Temple B'nai Israel classmates and good friends Norman and Laura Kaplan, who had met me at the temple in New Britain to help me wrap the Torah and prepare it for its journey and who later gave me a proper sendoff in the consummate Jewish tradition by sharing a celebratory Chinese dinner, were nice enough to fly in from Connecticut for the occasion. In addition, my fellow road warrior Mark Gluskin and his wife, Diane, were there. And Susan Reingold, who along with Gail had worked so diligently on making the Torah shine to its fullest, attended with her husband, Arthur. Other friends showed up as well. And then there were the regulars, those who typically attended Shabbat services every week. All in all, a pretty good crowd for a Friday night.

I only wish that Estelle Bernstein, who first got the ball rolling toward finding this new home for our beloved Torah, could have been there along with her husband, Abe. I wish I could have shown them the Torah's beautiful new home. But they were certainly there in spirit.

The sanctuary was especially beautiful that night, with a plethora of gorgeous flowers adorning the pulpit, courtesy of the Levin family. The service started out like any other for a Friday night, with the opening hymn sung by the cantor welcoming the congregation, followed by the ceremony of lighting of candles signifying the beginning of the Sabbath. Then everyone stood up for the *Bar'chu,* the formal call to worship summoning the congregation. The congregation remained standing for the *Shema,* considered the key affirmation and basic principle of the Jewish faith, declaring God as the absolute, singular sovereignty. The first sentence of the *Shema, She-ma Yisrael, Adonai, eloheinu, Adonai echad,* is right out of the Torah itself, *Hear, O Israel, the Lord is our God, the Lord is One* (Deuteronomy 6:4).

Traditionally the Torah isn't read at Sabbath evening services. But in Reform congregations, where Friday night has become the major communal gathering for Shabbat, many congregations incorporate a brief Torah reading into the service. Plus, given that this night was also a special occasion, a Torah reading was included in the service. When there is a reading on a Friday night as part of the Sabbath service, only a small portion from the week's full *parashah* of the Torah is read at that time, and then it is read in its entirety during the next day's Saturday Shabbat morning service.

As a lead-in to the Torah reading for the evening, the rabbi called me up to the *bimah* to take the Torah out of the ark and place it upright onto a flat-top wooden pedestal that had been specifically set up on the pulpit just for this occasion. The pedestal was right next to the main pulpit, on which the more commonly used Ashkenazi Torah is normally placed and read from. But unlike the Ashkenazi Torah that is always placed on top of a slightly slanted pulpit, the Sephardic Torah is vertically placed on a perfectly flat surface and read in the upright, vertical position. Interestingly, the reading positions of the Torah associated with each Jewish sect follow the same respective positions of the placement of their *mezuzot* (small fixtures placed at the doorposts of Jewish homes as a reminder of God's presence). That is, at an Ashkenazi home, the *mezuzah* is placed in a slanted position outside the door, whereas at a Sephardic home the *mezuzah* is placed in a vertical, completely upright position.

At this time, while it was being showcased on the pedestal, the rabbi took the opportunity to unveil and introduce this new Torah to the congregation and inform them that a formal dedication for it was planned for tonight as part of the service. But first he would read from the Torah in its vertical position the selected passage for the evening from the respective week's *parashah* called *Emor*, which would mark the first time this Sephardic Torah would be read from in its new Temple Beth-El home. Prior to beginning his Torah reading, the rabbi called my mother up to the *bimah* as well, to join me for the one and only *aliyah* that night, which is the blessing for the reading of the Torah. Then, with the Sephardic Torah being absent of any scroll handles, the rabbi used a scarf-like cloth to move across the top of the parchment to find his place and begin his Torah reading. Upon the conclusion of the reading, the Torah's outer silver shell was closed. But instead of being returned to the main ark, the Torah was temporarily left standing upright on the pedestal for the congregation to continue to admire.

Then it was time for our speeches. The rabbi introduced both me and my sister as we began to share a little background on my father, the Torah, and the story of how the Torah came to Beth-El.

I led off with the story, tracing back to 1939 when, in the wee hours of a fall morning in downtown New Britain, Connecticut, this rather well-dressed man named Yale Sabel stumbled up to the store window that my father was putting the finishing trim on for the store's grand opening at 9:00 the next morning, and in somewhat of an inebriated state proclaimed he wanted to be the store's first customer. And how Yale indeed not only became the store's first customer, but also became my father's best friend. Yet, sadly, Yale ended up dying at an early age, which prompted my father to commission the creation of a beautiful silver-encased Sephardic Torah from Israel and donate it in his friend's honor to our local temple, Temple B'nai Israel, in New Britain, in the early 1960s. And how when I was growing up and attending services at our temple, I would sit there in the congregation and marvel at this magnificent Torah shining out from the center of the open ark and feel a sense of pride in knowing that my father and my family were linked to this Torah. And that I myself had the privilege of reading from it during my own bar mitzvah. I then talked about the closing of Temple B'nai Israel due to its dwindling congregation, and, hence, the connections and arrangements that were made to bring the Torah to Temple Beth-El. And then of course I touched upon my special, spiritual journey driving it from Connecticut back to Chicago, giving a call-out to all those present who had participated in this journey and thanking them for helping to make this transfer happen.

My sister then took the podium. In her expressive, most eloquent way, she talked about roots and the importance of her Jewish heritage while growing up and the bond us Jews all share together that has grown out of the teachings of the Torah. Her beautiful, inspiring words continued as she talked about our dad and the type of man he was…

My father was a man who trusted every man. He was a man of integrity, a man of honor, a man whose handshake was his word. He was a man who never had a disparaging comment about his fellow man. He was a man of heart, warmth, kindness, humility, and whimsy. He was a man of great generosity to his family, and a man who shared a great love with his wife. He was

a man beloved by all who knew him. My father was Abraham.

In terms of alluding to my recent road trip, I got a kick out of how she referenced my journey as putting a new spin on the term "wandering Jew." She ended her speech, leaving the Levin family with an inspirational, call-to-action message:

> **May this Torah continue to be a guiding light for my family, my brother, his wife, Gail, and their children; and may you, Danni and Mac, remember these words of your father and aunt tonight, and may they give you comfort and exhilaration as you recount this celebration to your children and theirs in the generations to come.**

Upon the conclusion of the service, the rabbi invited the congregation to all stand up and accompany him and my family to the newly built ark out in the shul's vestibule for the dedication ceremony and the placement of the Torah into its new permanent home. With that, he called me back up to the pulpit to pick up the Torah from the pedestal; and with the Torah in my arms and with the rabbi and my immediate family by my side, I carried the Torah and made my way out to the vestibule, with the rest of the congregation following along behind, making for a rather long processional. Once we arrived at our destination, with everyone crowded around us, the rabbi opened the newly built ark, my cue to go ahead and delicately place the Torah in its new home.

Once the Torah was secure in its new ark, the rabbi then began the formal dedication ceremony with these thoughtful words…

> **The Torah represents many things:**
> **Our relationship with God,**
> **Our chain of memory,**

The survival of our people.

It represents:
A way of life,
Ancient wisdom,
Eternal values.

It is the story of our people:
The trials of Abraham,
The faith of Joseph,
The courage of Moses.

It is a book of love and law,
Containing the heritage of our people,
Cherished and told by every generation.

This Torah we dedicate tonight represents all these ideals and more:

It tells the story of the bond that connected two men, who treated each other as brothers. It tells the story of one American community, which successfully nurtured generations of Jewish souls, and sent them off across America, where they continue to raise children of their own.

And it tells the story of a family who cherish the memory of their husband, father, and grandfather; and hold dear the traditions of faith and friendship which he instilled in them.

Tonight, we dedicate this Torah, which has journeyed from Jerusalem, Israel, to New Britain, Connecticut, to Northbrook, Illinois, and we bless the family of Abraham Levin who has brought it to us to cherish; for all the enduring values it represents to our people; and to honor it for the memory of good and loving men whose names

are inscribed on it, and on this wall.

We are now linked to Temple B'nai Israel, to carry on their tradition through this Torah.

The rabbi then turned it over to me for a few closing comments:

Today, as the Torah is officially placed in its new home, our family wishes to dedicate this Torah to my father. Abraham Levin, who passed away in 2004 at the age of 96. My father was a wonderful and terrific man, who was always doing for others as exemplified by his benevolent act of donating this Torah to Temple B'nai Israel in his friend Yale Sabel's memory. It's great to be able to recognize and honor my father's name in connection with this Torah, in my mind one of the highest honors one could have.

It is our intention and hope that this Torah shall stand as a symbol of the continuity between families and generations. Our family is proud to honor the memory of husband, father, and grandfather Abraham Levin, and may his legacy, the legacy of his family, and legacy of all families shine through future generations, just as this Torah's outer shell will continue to shine through the upcoming years.

And with that the Torah was officially established in its new home, where it will hopefully reside for many, many years to come.

As a frame of reference to communicate the handing down of the Torah from generation to generation, the original little black and white photo of my father and the Torah from back in the early '60s, the one that I originally showed to the rabbi, was placed inside of the ark to the left of the Torah. It was really nice of the rabbi to let us put this picture in the ark right next to the Torah.

The Sephardic Torah in its new home, the specially designed ark at
Beth El Temple that was formerly a pay phone.

Flush to the wall on the right side of the ark was a little metal plaque that provided further explanation of the source of the Torah.

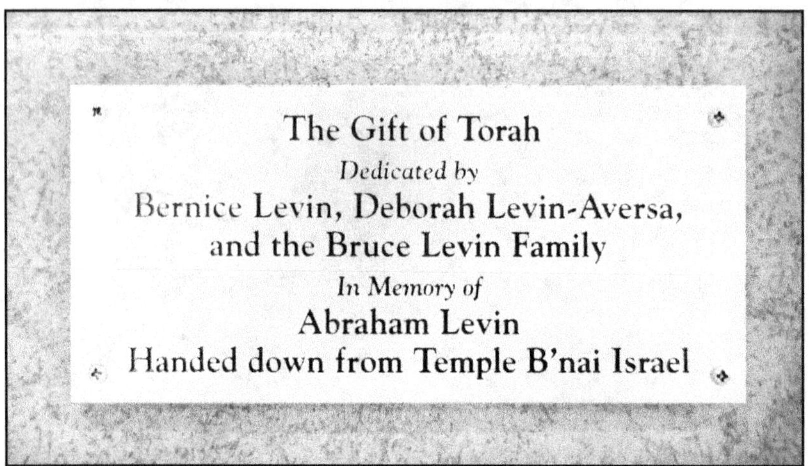

**Our Family's Dedication Plaque on the wall
just to the right of the Torah in its new Ark**

The dedication was a great segue to the *Oneg Shabbat* that was all set up in the room across the way, with a spread of beverages, fruit, cookies, and cakes. We kicked it off with the *Kiddush*, the blessing over the wine, and then the *Hamotzi*, the blessing over the bread, and it was time to celebrate.

Chapter 34
LEGENDS NEVER DIE

I BELIEVE THE 25TH DAY OF ADAR in the year 5769 of the Jewish calendar, or March 21, 2009, on the English calendar, might have marked the first time the Torah was taken out of its new ark. It was for Mac Levin's bar mitzvah. The day had finally come. Even though we weren't Sephardic, he was going to read from it for his Torah portion, just as I did for my bar mitzvah. Not to cross religions or anything, but I guess you could say he was going to be the first one, other than the rabbi of course as part of the Friday night dedication service, to christen the Torah in its new home.

Accordingly, just for this day of Mac's bar mitzvah, the Torah had been transferred from its home in the temple vestibule back to the ark in the main sanctuary. As the ark was opened and the congregation then stood up, two Torahs were taken out. There was the lighter Ashkenazi Torah for the bar mitzvah boy to hold and the heavier Sephardic one for his old man to embrace.

After the singing of the *Shema*, just like the father-and-son team at my own bar mitzvah, Mac and I began the processional proudly with our respective Torahs. As we made our way through the congregation, the congregants stepped out of their aisles, extending their prayer books or tallit to our Torahs and then bringing them back to their mouths to kiss, all the while giving us warm, congratulatory smiles and pats on the back for the bar mitzvah boy. Apparently, there were a few in the congregation who must have been of Sephardic descent, as they displayed a slightly different custom for showing their respect for the Torah. Instead of touching the Torah with their prayer books or shawls, they raised a finger toward the Torah and then kissed their finger.

When it was time for the Torah reading, the Sephardic Torah was placed upright on a makeshift flat-top pulpit in the middle of the *bimah*. Standing up and facing east with yad in hand pointing to his *parashah*, Mac proceeded to read from the beloved Torah that his grandfather had arranged to bring over from Israel almost 50 years ago and that his father had read from as well. Given the absence of scrolls with handles, the rabbi, who was standing alongside Mac, used a scarf-like cloth across the top to move the parchment.

Mac reading from Temple Beth-El's new Sephardic Torah at his Bar Mitzvah

Most Torah readings include only one *parashah* of the Torah. But Mac's Torah portion consisted of two *parashahs*, both of which were included in the book of Exodus – *Vayakhei* and *Pekudei*. He had two because based on the Jewish calendar that year there was a total of

54 *parashahs* in the Torah across its annual cycle starting and ending on Simchat Torah. Upon aligning it to our standard 52-week year, a couple of these Torah portions were combined into a single reading. And it just so happened that Mac's bar mitzvah date fell during one of these weeks when there were two Torah readings.

Vayakehi is all about the Israelites bringing gifts for the portable sanctuary or tabernacle (*Mishkan* in Hebrew), a Jewish worship site. Upon God's commandment, Moses had summoned them to build this tabernacle in the wilderness at the base of Mt. Sinai.

And God said… "Let them make Me a sanctuary, that I may dwell among them."
(Exodus 25:8)

In *Vayakehi*, while leaving it up to the Israelites themselves as to what they felt they wanted to give and how much, Moses tells the Israelites the kind of things that are needed for the sanctuary.

"Take from among you gifts to the Lord; everyone whose heart so moves him shall bring gifts for the Lord: gold, silver, and copper; blue, purple, and crimson yarns, fine linen, and goats' hair; tanned ram skins. dolphin skins, and acacia wood."
(Exodus 35:5-7)

The response from the Israelites was overwhelming, as they came bearing an abundance of gifts.

The children of Israel brought a free willing offering unto the Lord; every man and woman, whose heart made them willing to bring for all the work, which the Lord had commanded by the hand of Moses to be made.
(Exodus: 35:29)

One had to wonder whether the abundance of gifts was spurred on by the fact that the gift-giving was totally voluntary. That yes, there were some suggestions, but there was no specific type or number of gifts requested. And thus, the Israelites ended up donating probably much more than they would have if there was a specified requirement. Often one's heart pours out more when not asked.

The Israelites brought so many gifts that it turned out that there was more than what was needed. And enough was enough, as they were instructed by Moses not to bring any more.

> **Moses thereupon had this proclamation made throughout the camp: "Let no man or woman make further effort toward gifts for the sanctuary."**
> **So the people stopped bringing; their efforts had been more than enough for all the tasks to be done.**
> **(Exodus 36:6-7)**

Now that more than enough gifts had been brought, *parashah Pekudei* describes the actual setting up and completion of the tabernacle. And after all its finishing touches are made, the tabernacle is blessed by the Israelites.

> **Thus was finished all the work of the tabernacle of the tent of the Meeting; and the children of Israel did according to all that the Lord commanded Moses, so did they.**
> **(Exodus 39:32)**

After his *parashah* readings and his subsequent *haftarah* reading, which consisted of excerpts from the Book of Prophets, Kings 7:40-8:21, Mac addressed the congregation to summarize these Torah readings and share his interpretation of them.

To me, one of the most interesting ideas to teach about this portion is that the Israelites bring so many gifts that God decides that there is too much. The Israelites are so enthusiastic about this new tabernacle and wanted so much to donate and give of themselves, it teaches us to think about when we know we have enough stuff and when we have too much.

I recently had a personal experience when this advice would have been very helpful. I went to Puerto Rico during winter break, and one night we went to an Asian restaurant where I ordered lo mein noodles, vegetarian of course. I was so full that I didn't finish it. So, I got a box to take the leftovers back to our hotel. After dinner I had the box in my hands as my sister and I waited for my dad outside a Starbucks. This is when a homeless guy comes up to me and points to the box and then to his mouth. I was very startled by this situation, not having had much interaction with the homeless. So I said, "No, I'm very sorry." Then I realized I had more than enough food to eat, while this homeless guy had very little to eat. I was very upset with myself all that night, and I even wanted to go back and find him to give him the noodles. I definitely have enough stuff that I should start giving more than keeping or getting more.

Later in the service, the rabbi calls Mac up to the main pulpit. With the two of them standing side by side, I had a flashback of my one-on-one pulpit chat with my rabbi; except unlike me, Mac wasn't standing on a step stool or swaying back and forth and bobbing up and down like the bar mitzvah bobblehead his father was when he was a boy becoming a man. The rabbi proceeds to tell him…

Mac, you know when you read this particular Torah portion, there's a lot in this Torah portion that seems to be not very exciting. There seems to be a lot of stuff that seems to deal with the construction of this tabernacle, and I guess maybe if you're a builder it's very interesting. If not, it sort of feels, you know, a little bit of a letdown.

Actually, and Mac I think you hinted at in your speech, I think honestly it contains secrets to a happy life. I think one secret to being happy in life is having a heart that is open to giving to others. Whatever that timeline would be, you need a heart that is open to giving to others. How you achieve this, how you accomplish it, and again I think Mac you mentioned this in your speech a lot, I think the answer is to be content with what you have and be willing to share with others. Can you imagine, and I think it would be an event that would be unique in history, a congregation that's having a fund-raising appeal that says, "Stop, enough, we've got enough… don't give us any more money." We've got more than what we need. It never happens. But think about it… Moses says to the people, "Stop I have enough!" If only people were able to say, "You know what, actually I have enough! I don't need any more. I can be happy with what I have.

His words took me out to Stanley Golf Course, when I recalled how my dad had brought some of his own old clothes out to that older fellow who was stationed at the seventh tee selling golf balls. A good example, I thought, of a guy who had opened his heart to others.

The rabbi ended his talk with Mac with these words…

Your journey through life is just beginning today. And where it goes, we don't know. Our paths through life

take many turns and twists along the way, but remember wherever your journey takes you, you'll never travel alone because your families that love and care for you will always be there to love and care for you. God will always watch and protect you. And the Jewish people, who are so proud of you today, will always be here to stand by your side.

Bar mitzvah celebrations had sure come a long way—a far cry from my era, when it was pretty much a boilerplate type of affair with the Saturday morning service followed by a two-hour luncheon held at the temple and then that was it. Although in my case I was lucky, as my parents stretched out the celebration a little bit, with a catered backyard soireé for their friends and a handful of my good friends on that same night following my bar mitzvah service.

I don't think I ever remember coming into as much money at one time as I did that night. Upon greeting me with congratulations, guests would pat my shoulder or in the case of some of the women kiss my cheek, leaving a smear of lipstick on my face, while stuffing envelopes containing checks or U.S. Savings Bonds into the lapel pocket of my sport coat. Oh sure, I got a fountain pen here and there, which was still a mainstay bar mitzvah gift in those days, but cash was king—I was in the money!

Back then, my mother, with her goldfish bowl centerpieces and New York-imported frozen fruit desserts at my bar mitzvah's temple luncheon followed up by our at-home evening backyard gala, no doubt would have been considered a pioneer in the world of bar mitzvah celebrations. And I would like to think she did her part in paving the way for a new wave of bar mitzvahs to come. But no doubt about it, the bar mitzvah parties of yesteryear didn't have anywhere near the glitz and panache of what they are today.

Nowadays, it's often a whole weekend affair, not that different from a wedding. There can be a Friday night dinner for the out-of-towners, the Saturday morning service with a follow-up *Oneg Shabbat* luncheon, an all-out wing-ding of a party at night at some fancy venue that had to be reserved at least a year and a half in advance, and then capped off with a brunch on Sunday.

Unlike the basic bar mitzvahs in my day, these days just about every bar or bat mitzvah party has a theme attached to it that isn't revealed until the evening of the party. For this momentous event, some parents hire a whole team of consultants, including a party planner, a caterer, a stage designer, suppliers of promotional items, a videographer, and a photographer who are all brought in well in advance of the event to carry out the theme and bring it to life. And the party would be emceed by a DJ accompanied by his ensemble of dancers dressed in theme-appropriate attire and be well choreographed throughout the evening with tightly scheduled activities for both the kids and the adults. It's a party of a lifetime.

Naturally, there's often an underlying competition, a la "the Goldbergs versus the Silvermans" that goes on among every bar and bat mitzvah class as to who can come up with the most creative theme and activities, that is, who can outdo the other. I must admit the Levin family was probably as much swept up into this bar mitzvah extravaganza as anybody, especially given that Gail and I come from the world of marketing and promotions. Coming off our debut of "The Dannis" for Danni's bat mitzvah in 2005, we were challenged to keep our creative juices alive in coming up with something just as resourceful for Mac's big event.

Early on, we knew of course the overarching theme was going to revolve around baseball, so for the venue we were fortunate enough to be able to reserve what was at the time called US Cellular Field, the home of the Chicago White Sox. The party would be held in its Stadium Club, where season ticketholders and other privileged fans would typically come to have dinner or a drink before each home game. It was a very spacious area that featured a myriad of TV monitors all around the room. Plus, what was most appealing about it is that it overlooked the whole field. It was perfect for a baseball-themed party. However, one could only reserve this venue for an event during the off-season. Luckily, even though we had to commit well over a year in advance and the specific baseball sched-ule for that following year hadn't been determined, we were able to reserve the date of March 21 because the management of the venue knew our date would be at least one week before the baseball season would conceivably start. We had just made the cutoff.

Coincidentally enough, one year before Mac's bar mitzvah, during a spring break family trip to Arizona, I had a serendipitous opportunity to meet the head of field operations at US. Cellular Field, who just happened to be staying at our same hotel. I told him about the big upcoming baseball-themed event that we were planning at the White Sox stadium and asked him if there was any possibility of putting a bar mitzvah prop on the field for showcas-ing purposes. Even though he explained to me the field itself was considered sacrosanct and nobody was really supposed to be on it except ballplayers and the field crew, for the night of the party he was nice enough to make an exception. He let us put a 10-foot-high paperboard replica of Mac, in the wind-up position, on the pitcher's mound for our guests in the Stadium Club to look down on the field and see. He also granted us the opportunity for our immediate family to go into the White Sox dugout and actually step out onto the field for pictures that evening before the party, including taking a snapshot or two of the bar mitzvah boy himself on the mound, standing next to the 10-foot replica of himself.

With the overarching theme of baseball, we had a lot to work with. Putting our creative juices to the test, after a considerable amount of brainstorming, we came up with something we knew would be very recognizable to everybody and would be near and dear to our bar mitzvah boy's heart… simply "MLB," which was a double entendre of the initials for Major League Baseball and Mac Levin's Bar Mitzvah. Specifically, the theme was built around famous Jewish baseball players who had made it to the Majors, and in Mac's case, one who was destined to be.

We went all out with our efforts. We even had a product sponsor for the event, as we distributed its samples as part of the introductory festivities when folks first sat down for dinner. At each place setting was a chewing tobacco-type pouch with a cartoon baseball player on it, that to some might have looked familiar and initially mistaken for the popular bubble gum "Big League Chew". But upon closer look, the package had a little twist to it. The word "Chew" had been relabeled with the word "Jew"—rebranded as "Big League Jew."

**A little place setting gift for everybody when sitting down
for dinner at Mac's Bar Mitzvah party**

We also showed a commercial for the product, which included the tagline:

Big League Jew…
The Bubble Gum Jewish Baseball Players Love to Chew

Keeping with the baseball theme, we also put together and ran a public service announcement featuring Mac promoting the Coaches Curing Kids Cancer Foundation, based out of Atlanta, Georgia, which tied into one of the mitzvah projects he did in connection with his bar mitzvah. Mac spearheaded and organized this charity program within the Deerfield Youth Baseball Association (DYBA), the governing organization of his league. As a season-ending thank-you gift to DYBA coaches, instead of the customary token gestures of thanks like gift cards to local retailers such as Starbucks or Dick's Sporting Goods, parents of the participating players were encouraged to make a donation in the names of their respective coaches to the Coaches Curing Kids Cancer Foundation to help support pediatric cancer research. The program ended up being very successful, as the year of his bar mitzvah, the first year the program was initiated within DYBA, Mac's efforts helped to raise a total of $1,600 for this worthy cause. What's more, he helped to keep the program going within DYBA in subsequent years.

Meanwhile, at the centerpiece of each table was a large, oversized baseball card of a Jewish MLB player. History has it that to date there have been a total of almost 200 Jewish players who have suited up in the Majors. We showcased 24 of these Jewish stars of the game, one for each table. These included ones who were currently playing in the Bigs or ones who we considered to be among the most famous, as well as, of course, one prospective Major Leaguer. In addition to Mac, whose baseball card adorned the head table, among those players featured were Moe Berg, who aside from being a catcher for the both the Red Sox and the White Sox as well as a few other teams, was a spy for the U.S. government as featured in the book *The Catcher Was a Spy* by Nicholas Dawidoff; Ron "Boomer" Blomberg, who when playing for the Yankees in 1973 had the distinction of becoming among the first designated hitters in the Major Leagues and then after he retired fittingly enough wrote an autobiography titled *Designated Hebrew: The Ron Blomberg Story*; Rod Carew, All-Star and Hall of Famer who played for the Twins and the Angels, and while as a Panamanian never actually formally converted to Judaism, he married a Jewish woman, brought up his kids Jewish, was a member of a synagogue, and wore a chai necklace when he was out on the field, so close enough we considered him to be Jewish; two Greenbergs – Hank Greenberg, nicknamed Hammerin'

Hank, the same name that Hank Aaron would be called later on, or was sometimes called Hankus Pankus, who not only was an All-Star, MVP and Hall of Famer first baseman playing for the Tigers and the Pirates, but beyond his baseball prowess out on the field became famous for refusing to play a game on Yom Kippur despite being involved in a playoff race (as Detroit Free Press columnist and poet Edgar A Guest wrote in his poem titled "Came Yom Kippur"... "We shall miss him on the infield and shall miss him at the bat, but he's true to his religion and I honor him for that;" and hard-luck Adam Greenberg, whose claim to fame was the misfortune of being hit in the head by a pitch in his very first and only Major League at-bat, even before having ever taking the field, which resulted in a career-ending head injury; plus Sandy Koufax, maybe one of the most famous Jewish players of all time, who was a Cy Young winner and Hall of Famer and who pitched four no-hitters including a perfect game.

As an aside, taking a page out of Hank Greenberg's book, Sandy Koufax was also known for putting his faith above his career. His first nod toward religion came into play in April 1955, when he opted out of a scheduled start in observance of the first night of Passover. Then in 1959, and again in 1961 and 1963, Koufax decided to forgo his turns in the Dodgers' pitching rotation during the playoffs due to a conflict with Rosh Hashanah. But the true test occurred in 1965 when he was scheduled to start against the Minnesota Twins in the first game of the World Series, which that year happened to fall on the same day as Yom Kippur. Being a devout Jewish player, he elected to sit out that game in respect to the Day of Atonement, as fellow Dodger hurler and Hall of Famer Don Drysdale took the mound in his place. Evidently, the baseball gods didn't look to favorably upon this substitution, as Drysdale was batted around and the game turned out to be a Twins' killing with the Dodgers losing 8-2. It was reported that after the game, Drysdale went up to Dodger manager Walther Alston and asked him "I bet you wish I was Jewish today too, huh?"

Also featured was pitcher Al Levine. We wanted to be sure to include him in our short list of Jewish Major Leaguers to whom we wanted to pay tribute. He was born in Park Ridge, Illinois, which is very close to where I currently live, on May 22, 1968, three years later to the day I became a bar mitzvah. He was drafted by the White Sox in 1991 and made his MLB pitching debut with the Sox in 1996, the year Mac was born. Throughout his 15-year career, he was mostly a relief pitcher, pitching a total of 416 innings for a total of seven different teams: the White Sox, the Rangers, the Angels, the Rays, the Royals, the Tigers, and the Giants. And, of course, I remembered him as one of the Tiger pitchers on the mound back on that Friday night of September 17, 2004, the eve of the weekend my dad died, when Mac and I went to the Tigers-White Sox game and were sitting next to former Major Leaguer Steve Grilli. Levine's best years were in 2001 when he pitched for the Angels and recorded a 2.38 ERA in 64 games, and then in 2003 when he split time between the Rays and the Royals and put up a 2.54 ERA. Those were impressive numbers. But then what else would you expect from a guy with a name like that?

Another highlight of the bar mitzvah party was the video montage, which in addition to being shown on the TV monitors in the Stadium Club was showcased on the stadium Jumbotron that could be seen outside the club window. The short movie started out by showing a baseball field with a black & white background, with pictures of baseball cards of some of our featured famous Jewish baseball players streaming across the screen – Ryan Braun, Brad Ausmus, Shawn Green, Hank Greenberg, Steve Stone, Lou Boudreau, Sandy Koufax, then Al Levine, and ending with the baseball card of soon-to-be Major Leaguer Mac Levin, in sync to the introductory soundtrack used for all of the Milwaukee Brewer games broadcasted on the radio as narrated by their announcer Bob Uecker… "It was here that boys became men, that men became champions, and that champions became legends." We felt this intro was a fitting tribute to a guy about to enter into manhood and destined to be in the majors.

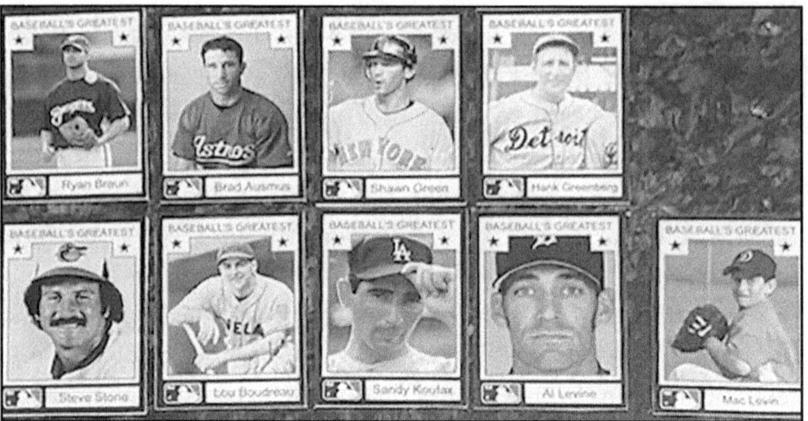

**Baseball Cards of some famous Jewish Major Leaguers
portrayed in Mac's Bar Mitzvah Montage**

The montage then went on to feature Mac dubbed into various scenes from famous baseball movies, taking on the persona of Wild Thing in the blockbuster *Major League*, the main character Smalls in *The Sandlot*, and as Roy Hobbs in *The Natural*. It was great to watch Mac alias Roy Hobbs hit it out of the park on the Jumbotron, as his home run lit up the stadium scoreboard with fireworks.

Mac and I together had watched practically every baseball movie ever produced, many of them multiple times. Who knows how many times we've seen *The Sandlot*, which rates right up there as one of our favorites. We both loved everything about the movie, but one of the best scenes has got to be when the ghost of Babe Ruth, alias The Great Bambino, The King of Crash, The Sultan of Swat, The Colossus of Clout, comes to visit Benny the Jet Rodriquez in his bedroom one night.

To provide a little background, as the story goes, the fleet-footed Benny had been struggling with how he was going to help his sandlot friend Smalls get his stepfather's prize possession back, the baseball with none other than The Great Bambino's autograph on it, which Smalls had lifted from his stepfather's den so that the guys would have a ball to play with. The boys were having a hard time getting the ball back, because Benny had hit it over a fence that had a big, ferocious beast of a dog named Hercules on the other side guarding it. Encouraging him to go for it, the Babe says to him… "Let me tell you something, kid. Everybody gets one chance to do something great; and that most people never take that chance, either because they're too scared or they don't recognize it when it spits on their shoes. This is your big chance, and you shouldn't let it go by."

But it's what the Babe says to him as he's just about to leave that really stands out. First, having noticed this one particular baseball card in the room, he picks it up and stares at it awhile, and then asks Benny "Henry Aaron, huh… I don't know why but can I have this?" Then as the Babe begins to walk out of the room, he turns around and says to Benny… "Remember kid, there's heroes and there's legends… heroes get remembered, but legends never die. Follow your heart, kid, and you can never go wrong."

Later, after the montage, about three quarters of the way into the party, we had a seventh-inning stretch, shown on the monitors in the room as well as the Jumbotron, with everybody at the party singing along to "Take Me Out to the Ballgame."

Then it was onto the Hora.

Chapter 35

L'DOR V'DOR
FROM GENERATION TO GENERATION

MY FATHER'S MOST RECENT CONTACT INFORMATION in Florida, his home phone number, 561-586-2225, and his address at The Barclay, 1546 S. Ocean Blvd. in Palm Beach, is still in my phone. It would have been nice if he had had a cell phone number and/or email address that would have moved with him to his new place. Fact is, he never used a cell phone or a computer. He was among that last generation not to have these points of contact.

But regardless, it's going on two decades since he passed, and I still haven't been able to delete this information. I know I never will. Part of it is my non-admission to or denial of the finality of it all. But part of it I suppose is I just want to feel that I can call him anytime, and hopefully hear his salutation, "Al Levin talking," on the other end. That he would just be a phone call away to be there for me... to give me some advice, to help smooth things out, to encourage me and tell me to keep my chin up and stay in there pitching, or just to schmooze with.

Not a day goes by that I don't think of him. I miss the pop-ups—boy, what I wouldn't give for just one more pop-up from my pops. I miss the father-and-son golf tournaments. I miss our lunches together. I miss the ice cream we always had after Chinese or Thai food, or in the evening for our midnight snack. I miss the drop-offs and pick-ups at train stations and airports. I miss our car rides together. I miss hearing his stories firsthand, although it's nice at least to have some on tape. And I even miss him stopping on the road for directions. Yet I know he's always there with me.

It was mid-September, and like every year about this time, although it varies slightly year to year based on the Jewish calendar, I was in temple attending the Friday night service in observance of my dad's yahrzeit, the anniversary of his death.

Before we left for the temple that evening, as is customary in the Jewish religion when there's a *yahrzeit* in the family, we light a small memorial candle at home, starting at sundown, to burn throughout the night and into the next day until sundown.

There's one more thing we always do at the Levin house in observance of Dad's *yahrzeit*. At Mac's insistence, we make sure to turn the lights on at Al Mac's. It was originally Mac's idea to flip the switch underneath the Al Mac's picture during Dad's *yahrzeit* as well as for Dad's birthday on the Ides of March. It was a fitting tribute to honor his Pop-Pops and former business partner.

Al Mac's is all lit up on Mac's Bedroom Wall during Dad's Yahrzeit

Every time I go to our temple, be it for a Friday night service or a bar or bat mitzvah, I always make it a point to visit the ark in the vestibule, going Torah-side as I call it. It's kind of like my own silent prayer that I consider to be part of the service, my way of paying respects to the Torah and my father and recapturing the memory of our journey together. And so, per my routine, a little more than halfway into the service, I popped out of the congregation to go Torah-side. It always seemed to be so quiet and peaceful out there by myself, with only the faint sound of the cantor's melodic voice in the background.

The Torah had now been in its new home for well over 10 years. But despite its natural wear and tear from aging and its occasional use for Sephardic occasions, it was still looking shiny and bright, still radiating its majestic glow. No doubt all that laborious scrubbing and polishing that Gail and Susan had put in at our house prior to me dropping the Torah off at our temple had gone a long way to help maintain its luster.

I turned my attention to the small-framed black and white photo of my father and the Torah that was standing up behind the glass just to the left of the Torah. This picture, along with the metal plaque next to the ark on the right hand side with the Hebrew words "ldor vdor" at the top, always left me with a valued sense of pride knowing that these little touches would continue to link our family to this beloved Torah and to Temple Beth-El throughout generations to come.

My father, who must have been in his early-to-mid 50s at the time this picture was taken, quite a bit younger than I am now, was all dressed up for the occasion with a clean shirt of course and a jacket and tie with a white handkerchief perfectly propped up in his breast pocket. Working in the world of men's apparel and having previously put in several stints in the dry-cleaning business, he always suited up pretty well. Looking at his jacket, it reminded me that the suit I was wearing was getting a little too big on me. Sure enough it was happening…as was the case with him, once a large, I was now becoming a medium! Then I noticed something about the picture I hadn't really noticed before. There seemed to be some light streaming into the picture, from what I can only assume was coming from the temple windows high up on top of the wall. It dawned on me that the picture must have been taken in the late afternoon when the sun was going down and the light from the west exposure was streaming in. I took it as a sign, signifying the light of a new generation to whom this Torah would now be passed down. It was time to head back to the service, as I didn't want to miss the Mourner's Kaddish.

Back in my seat, a warm chill came over me as the rabbi read the name of Abraham Levin among this week's list of those to be remembered. The words "We remember Al Levin" continued to reverberate in my mind. After everybody's name was read, the rabbi asked us to all please rise for the *Mourner's Kaddish*.

Following the service, per tradition, there was an *Oneg Shabbat*, during which I thanked the rabbi for reading my father's name and including him in the *Mourner's Kaddish*. I also wanted to catch up with him a little bit and inquire into whether there had recently been some Sephardic bar or bat mitzvahs for which the Torah had been used. He was always so congenial, always seemed to have time for you. But conscious that other congregants were waiting to talk with him, I didn't want to take up too much of his time, so after about 5 minutes of chatting I thanked him again and bid him good night.

As Gail and I left for the evening and passed by the ark in the vestibule, I glanced over to the Torah and to the picture of my father for one last look until next time, and as I did I gave him a little wink and whispered the words I always leave him with… "See ya at Ebbets!"

Like Father…

My father (on the left) donating the Torah to Temple B'nai Israel in
New Britain, Connecticut in the early 1960's

Like Son…

Over 40 years later, that's me (on the left) transferring the Torah
over to Temple Beth El in Northbrook, Illinois in 2007

ACKNOWLEDGEMENTS

There are a lot of folks to whom I'd like to tip my *kippah* and thank in helping to pave the road to compose this book.

First and foremost, there's my father Abraham, alias Mr. What-you-macall-it… Al, Al Pal, Al-truistic, Senex, The Socks Guy, Alouisius, or Al Levine the Putting Machine to thank, who's the real legend in this book. For being the type of dad he was… for taking the time to pop them up to me, to go on fishing trips with me to Maine despite not really considering himself to be a fisherman (even though he ended up catching most of the fish), for letting me tag along on business trips to his men's and boys' clothing stores, and for always being there for me when it counted. Also, for taking the time to relate and record some of the fascinating stories of his life that have become precious memoirs, which I have included in this book.

And speaking of those precious memoirs, I owe a tremendous amount of thanks to my sister Deborah Faith Levin, alias Lexye Aversa, who passionately devoted endless hours sitting down with Dad to capture these great stories on tape and then transcribing these recordings, making it possible to incorporate them verbatim in the book. Even though we had heard many of Dad's stories over the years, it took a number of structured interviews over several months to recount the most memorable ones and chronicle them into a cohesive storyline.

Plus, I'd like to thank Lexye and my mother, Bernice, alias Nikki, Schenck Levin for flying to Chicago from their respective homes in Florida to attend the dedication of the Torah at Temple Beth-El on May 2, 2008, when it was formally placed in its newly built, customized glass-enclosed ark in the vestibule of the temple where it currently resides. It meant so much to have them there for the dedication, as they made this momentous occasion even more special.

Also, I can't forget Estelle Bernstein, who should be credited with starting the ball rolling on the transfer of the Torah from my family's former temple, B'nai Israel in New Britain, Connecticut, to my current temple, Beth-El in Northbrook, Illinois. It was Estelle, one of the lasting Board Members of Temple B'nai Israel, who upon its imminent closing had remembered that my father had been instrumental in donating one of its Torahs, a beautiful Sephardic Torah that adorned its pulpit over the years, and accordingly had reached out to my mother to see if anybody in our family was affiliated with a temple that might be interested in taking in a new Torah. So, a lot of thanks go out to Estelle for making that initial call to my mom.

I also wish to thank Rabbi Sidney Helbraun, Temple Beth-El's rabbi, who, upon approaching him with the prospect of transferring the Torah to Beth-El was very welcoming and embraced the gift of this Torah with open arms and enthusiasm. And a special thanks to Rabbi Sid for suggesting the idea of building a special glass enclosed ark for it in the vestibule of the Temple where there used to be a telephone booth. What's more, a lot of thanks go out to him for being so supportive to take on the role of advisor of the religious-related content referenced in the book, as he was kind enough to review this book in draft form and provide his blessings and insights on the subject matter.

Thanks also go out to my childhood, longtime Connecticut friends Norman and Laura Kaplan, who met me at Temple B'nai Israel that closing day of October 12, 2007, when I picked up the

Torah. They helped me wrap the Torah in my father's *tallis* along with some linens, and then pack it up in the car in preparation for its long ride to its new home. And then to top it off, they accompanied me to dinner that night at the Great Taste Chinese restaurant in New Britain to celebrate the occasion and to give the Torah and me a proper Jewish sendoff. Plus, they were kind enough to make a special trip out to Chicago from their home in Connecticut to attend the dedication of the Torah. So, I thank them for being there for me at both temples.

And I'd like to give a hearty shout-out to my friend Mark Gluskin for providing me with some welcome company on part of my Torah road trip. He went out of his way following a scheduled business trip to Raleigh, North Carolina, to fly into Pittsburgh to meet and accompany me on the drive the rest of the way. Thanks to Mark for being my fellow road warrior… for spelling me at the wheel, for keeping me company and sharing some conversation, and for switching off watching the Torah in the car when we pulled up to a rest stop.

Furthermore, I wish to thank my wife, Gail, the woman who makes everything shine for me, and our good friend Susan Reingold for all their hard work in polishing up the outside silver casing of the Torah during the few days when we had it our house, before I brought it to its permanent home at Temple Beth-El. The two spent many hours applying elbow grease to every nook and cranny of the Torah and its adornments to make it shine to its fullest. In addition to polishing up the outside shell of the Torah, I'd like to thank Gail for taking a first crack at editing and polishing up the words in this book. Like everything else in my life, she brings out the best in me and makes everything a little bit brighter.

Finally, I'd like to recognize and thank my talented support team for their assistance and contributions along the way. They all helped to bring this book to life. First, there's my professional copy editor Marci Altman, who was very conscientious in her approach and did a great job in helping to prepare the script for publishing. Also, there's my proofreader, Melissa Karp, Ph.D. Candidate in Literature at Duke University, who provided a valuable second set of eyes in going through the book with a fine-tooth comb to finalize. In addition, there's my professional graphic designer Glen Edelstein of Hudson Valley Book Design, who created the front cover design as well as the layout for the interior of the book. Glen also did a terrific job in touching up some of the photographs for optimal print quality. Lastly, I'd like to thank my good friend Dr. Rich Noren for taking a number of the pictures in the book, including some of the ones showcasing the beloved Torah.

BIBLIOGRAPHY

1. Ganzfried, Rabbi Solomon. *The Code of Jewish Law*. Revised Edition. New York: Hebrew Publishing Company, 1961.

2. Karo, Rabbi Josef. *Shulchan Aruch Yoreh De'ah*. 16th century.

3. Rossel, Seymour, *The Torah: Portion-by-Portion*. Los Angeles: Torah Aura Productions, 2007.

4. *Tanakah, The Holy Scrxptures*. The New JPS Translation. Philadelphia: The Jewish Publication Society, 1985.

5. *The Holy Scriptures*. Philadelphia: The Jewish Publication Society of America, 1917.